Trial

A Memoir

By

Wendell A. Thomas

Publisher:

Wendell A. Thomas; 547 Judson Ave.; Evanston, IL 60202

ISBN: 9780999176429

Library of Congress Control Number: 2017910646

Recommended citation:

Thomas, Wendell A. 2017. Trial. Publisher: Wendell A. Thomas, Evanston, Illinois.

Cover art by W. Thomas

Acknowledgements

I want to thank my family for their continued love and support throughout the hailstorms and downpours that the ordeals and experiences of these last number of years have rendered.

Thank you Michael, Lene, Steve, Peter, Leila,

Cecilia, Josie, Chris, Cassie, Olin

and Dear Carolyn.

Thank you also to the many friends who listened and lent their support both regularly and periodically as I spewed forth the unfolding of my continual dilemmas.

1

Grounded

I enjoy reading from time to time, say, a novel that makes me feel a part of the story. That's what a good writer can do, and it's certainly not the norm. Caring about the characters and usually identifying with the protagonist is how one of these good books stays comfortably on my lap while my mind can wander anywhere the story leads.

When I was younger the *Lou Gehrig Story* had me imagining that I too was going to play first base for the New York Yankees, just like my hero. That changed quickly when I started little league here in Evanston and was made a catcher. Not only did I not play first base, I never even saw Lou Gehrig play as his playing days ended before I was born.

A lot of the history of Chicago slipped by me also because it too was before my time. There was the Great Chicago Fire in 1871 and the Haymarket Square Riot in 1886. There was also The Columbian Exposition of 1893 which is more familiar. That's when Chicago got the moniker "The Windy City," and it was also when sociopath H. H. Holmes committed the many murders written about in *Devil in the White City*. H. H. Holmes was a doctor, educated at the University of Michigan, and I was surprised that a professional person with so much education could be a sociopath. There was obviously no connection to his educational achievements and the functioning of his psyche.

These events, interesting as they might be, happened long before I was born and this memoir is about me and a small portion of my life. This memoir is not a tale from one hundred years ago in Chicago or in Prague. Yet, one hundred years later, Kafka's fictional work, *The Trial,* bears similarities to modern day Cook County, Illinois, and how the legal system works in behalf of a citizen who has done nothing wrong and is in violation of no law or laws that he is aware of or that authorities have made him aware. In the hundred years that have passed since the writing of Franz Kafka's, *The Trial,* there currently are interesting and quite paralleled situations in Cook County, Illinois with lawyers, court and the many systems connected to court.

Things certainly have changed from the days in Prague one hundred years ago when Kafka lived there. Prague is now part of the Czech Republic and Franz Kafka has died. Joseph K., Kafka's protagonist, lives on only in the pages of his novel. As the chapters and episodes of this current *Trial* unveil themselves it is a time to reflect on, *The Trial.* Here, one hundred years later in our republic, we have everything in place to protect the innocent and to prosecute the guilty and the systems are working to achieve those ends. Or aren't they?

2

Up to Speed

Evanston, Illinois, hugs the shore of Lake Michigan; it's the first suburb north of Chicago. It has been my home for most of my seventy-five, soon to be seventy-six years. Although I've been involved in my community when something piques my interest, I have never worked for the city or run for office.

I became a single parent to my three sons after divorce in 1973, when they were two, five, and seven years. We moved into the home we built on Judson Avenue in 1978. By the mid 1990's, my sons had all gone on to bigger and better things—pursuing their dreams . . . and realities—along with their own families.

When my sons were growing up, I was goal-oriented. My goal was singular: to give them as much latitude as I could to become whoever they would become.

I wanted to be a perfect parent, having come from a family that was somewhat, by which I mean greatly, dysfunctional, and not having experienced many of the practices and values that can be passed on to offspring by parents who know something about what they're doing. "Perfect parent" to me had a very simple definition. It was a parent who didn't fuck his kids up. I had a pretty simple definition for a pretty involved, and sometimes convoluted, process.

Because of my childhood, I only knew to act the opposite of what had been done in my family and to me. I never wanted to yell at my sons, or corner and berate them. I didn't want them to avoid being home at all costs. I never wanted to hit my sons with a closed fist or slap them with an open hand. I did not want them to walk on eggshells in their own home. I did not want them to lack trust in me. I did not want to know better for their lives than they did. It seems that I took a backdoor approach, that being the only door I saw, and somehow it worked.

My sons are each their own, different, yet the same. The common threads are woven into them like a tapestry: integrity, honesty, compassion, openness, social consciousness and involvement, and responsibility toward the world in which they live.

On my end, I will say that I worked as diligently as I could and paid dutiful attention to my perception of what mattered, which was the emotional stability of my sons. And while we don't become parents to get dividends, I've ended up in the enviable position, since my sons were in their twenties, of being able to look up to them and turn to them for advice and help.

In a nutshell (an apt metaphor, speaking of myself), I think you could say that I've had, in many ways, a very middle of the road life. I've not been a hero or a bum. I've cared about the things that most of us care about and have always done my best toward my family and friends. I love the outdoors, and I still love to play sports. I cook my own meals, ride my bicycle to get groceries, vote in elections, complain about various situations, and can't find anything wrong with any of my grandkids.

Once in a while, I might wonder why the hell a friend does this or that, the same as I might wonder about my own adult children. But, alas, I usually find that they know just what they're doing, and it's me who hasn't thought things through.

3

It Hits the Fan

So, I go to my internist for my annual physical...

Dr. Todd Newberger became my primary care physician in 1995, just as I was about to have my first hip replacement. He told me he'd want me in for a physical exam annually, not as a suggestion but as a requirement. Until then, every five years had been good enough for me. I thought, "What the hell, I can do what he says."

The day after my exam in July 2001, Dr. Newberger calls to say that he thinks the lab has made some errors with my blood tests and that he'd like me to come in to have them done again.

Two days later, he calls again and says that he thinks they still might have made errors and that I should redo the tests.

Fine. Now I'm wondering, "How many times is this lab gonna mix me up with somebody else?"

Little did I know that at that very moment, Dr. Newberger was in the process of prolonging my life.

After the third blood test in a week, he says, "There's something that's showing up a bit odd with these tests. You have an anemia of sorts. I'd like you to see Lynne Kaminer, a hematologist. She's excellent."

I imagine going to the Carlson Building in downtown Evanston where many doctors, dentists, and therapists have offices. Her office would be there, fourth or fifth floor, and I could see her reaching across her desk and handing me a container with pills. She'd say, "One a day for six weeks should do it. Come back and see me then."

When I call, Dr. Kaminer is booked solid for the next six weeks, and the first slot available is mid-September. No big deal. Not at all.

I have dinner with a friend around this same time, and he asks if it makes me nervous to be making an appointment with a hematologist. "No. I'm probably low on my iron or something like that," and we go on with our smoking and drinking and easy banter, while we keep working on the pizza. My friend, Mike Houlahan, was an English professor and had been a dear friend since early on in high school. And talk we did. The rhythm, the natural iambic pentameters, the lilt, and the perfectly chosen words, instantaneously and adroitly culled from his vast vocabulary, made Mike the best raconteur I've ever known.

The irony of dinner that night at the Candlelite Bar on Western Avenue in Chicago was that Mike had a concern for my health that was far deeper than my own. I was going to have a few things to deal with that I wasn't aware of that night, and the same was true for Mike. About six months after our Candlelite pizza, Mike and his wife, Colleen, had me over for dinner and our regular once-a-week night of television and conversation. Earlier in the day, they had been to the hospital for a check-up, and they had some bad news to share, worse than bad. It was the worst. Mike had esophageal cancer. He had it, undetected, that night at the Candlelite, when he was concerned about my upcoming appointment with the hematologist. That night we'd both been in the dark.

I was at the hospital daily when Mike was there, which was often, during his last few months. I was watching someone very dear to me slowly lose his grip on life. Mike exuded love of life and of people, parties, and sports. Our comraderie came with a deep and serious side that was sensitive, insightful, and emotional. There wasn't anything from his side or mine that was out of bounds for sharing, or, often in my case, emoting about.

The last words I spoke to Mike were words I had said many times, and his response was true to our relationship. As I was about to leave his bedside in what would be his last night, I said, "I love you Mike."

Mike looked at me, cocked his head slightly, and with his lovable half-smile, said, "I love you, Wen." Those were the last words I would hear him speak, the only person who called me "Wen."

That was early November 2003, and the family held a memorial service at the Alice Millar Chapel on the campus of Northwestern University. I was honored to be one of the speakers at the service. I spoke briefly and straight from my heart. Mike was loved by many and liked by many more. His wonderful marriage to Colleen was fully evident in the more than 1200 people there that day. The chapel was not large enough, and many stood at the rear and in the side aisles.

* * *

As a kid, I was always getting low on iron. It seemed I was forever taking tablespoons of molasses, two or three times a day. The brown bottle with the yellow label. "Use the soup spoon. No cheating," I was told.

When I was twenty years old and having problems with my tonsils, I went into the hospital to have them removed, but every day there was another reason why it wasn't done. The surgery room was booked. My doctor didn't feel well. I had to get over a slight infection. "You have a low grade fever." It was one thing after another. Back then, I didn't question anything a doctor said. Whatever they said was true and golden. Godlike.

I had all the signs of leukemia, but the doctors never told me. They continued drawing my blood daily, examining me, pressing on my stomach, and looking at my pale white skin. "See here," the visiting doctor from Mayo Clinic said, as he pressed

7

his fingers into my relaxed abdomen. "The enlarged spleen is quite evident." He clenched an unlit pipe between his teeth. It was back in a day when doctors testified to the benefits of Chesterfield cigarettes. The final and definitive exam was the bone marrow test. I sat in a chair while a stubby, sharp, hollow, and pointed tool was used to puncture my sternum and withdraw the marrow.

The tests came out negative. It all became clear why the doctors visiting Evanston Hospital from the Mayo Clinic had been coming to my room every day to examine me, talking back and forth in their medical lingo, while I waited to have my tonsils removed. After a week, one of them said, "Good news. You don't have leukemia after all." I quickly put my few things into my duffle bag and got the hell out out of there.

***

So, no, I wasn't worried about the pills I expected to get from the hematologist in mid-September 2001 at a doctor's office in downtown Evanston. The "office," though, turned out to be at Evanston Hospital. When I asked at the front desk where Dr. Lynne Kaminer's office was, I was directed through a maze of hallways and corridors.

What the hell?

It was the Kellogg Cancer Center.

What's going on? I didn't need to meet her here to get the pills.

There were half a dozen patients walking around with babushkas or baseball hats to cover their bald pates. (I found out later it was a way to try to stay warm.) Their skin was sallow and loose. Some had tubes coming out of their bodies, in various loops and twisted arcs one way and another, and some had oxygen tanks, the tubes running into their noses. They were all waiting in and around the lobby to see their oncologists.

"...we will have to do a bone marrow exam," she said.

A week later after the marrow withdrawal and the laboratory results, Dr. Kaminer looked at me and said, in her straightforward and respectful way, "You have multiple myeloma ... cancer ... terminal ... no cure ... we can ... maybe four years ..."

Her mouth kept moving . . .

Coffee. A smoke. Bic's in my pocket. Light-headed. What am I doing here? Everything's grey. No daylight. I don't like her. I just set my record yesterday. Roller blades. C'mon, 11.6 miles in 51 minutes and 32 seconds! What're you talkin' about? C'mon, I'm sixty-one years old. I'm active. Sports. Life. *Grey walls. Corridor noise. Blood pressure machine.* This is bullshit. I've got to get to the café. Back to work. I have to pay for parking. You're costin' me money. C'mon! I gotta go.

I focused on Dr. Kaminer.

I took a deep breath and cupped my hand behind my better ear. "I'm sorry," I said. "You said, 'terminal,' but I kind of missed the rest. Could you tell me again, please?"

4

Doing It

The long and the short, of course, is that I became a patient.

Little did I know on that day how attached I would become to Dr. Kaminer, or how attached I would remain. Little did I know that the process she would put me through would be a continuation, instead of a discontinuation, of my existence.

I remain deeply grateful for knowing both Doctors Lynne Kaminer and Todd Newberger, as they have literally been my links to life.

After discussing my situation with Doctor Kaminer she was agreeable to me doing an outpatient therapy. And what did that mean? Quite simply it meant that I would have a minor surgery to implant a double port into my chest cavity and run a small tube through the artery that runs up and over the clavical bone and ends where it is able to diffuse the fluid into the system. The purpose of the port was to give immediate access to my system for intravenous fluids, blood withdrawal for tests and direct input of the chemotherapy that I was to undergo. The reason for the double port was that there would be considerably more area to put more needles in with different kinds of medications or transfusions if in time it were deemed necessary.

As an outpatient, with the heavy medication that I would look forward to experiencing, it would be next to impossible to be getting the various medications through the veins in my arms and remain ambulatory. The port would help keep me out of the hospital for a time.

I dutifully followed the program for medication. During the pre-chemo prep period, I had four days each month when I would take steroids as prescribed, in addition to whatever other medications I was being given. Ten steroids a day to discombobulate the cancer and throw it into turmoil. I was wired. I talked with my friend Rick most days of the eight-month process. I'd walk back and forth on the deck while I was on the phone, my mind racing, telling my dearest friend about all my great plans: I was going to sell my house. I'd get an apartment on the lake and watch the waves roll in as I waited to die. Maybe I'd leave the area entirely, or even the country. I could do anything I wanted. How about dying on the sands of a desert in the Middle East? Dry up and blow away as dust. Never a trace.

Then I'd get the downers. Four days of being wired and then four days of slowing things down a bit. My oldest son Michael and his wife, Lene, along with their daughters Cecilia and Josie, had returned from living in Denmark and were staying at my home while they looked for a place of their own. In the evening, with the kids in bed, I remember sitting in the den with Michael and Lene, talking about one thing and another, with the television on. My speech was slurred. My thoughts occurred randomly and were randomly expressed. I can still see Lene looking at Michael and raising her eyebrows as she smiled at one of these comments, which would surface suddenly from the never-never land of my mind. There were nights, as I sat in my rocking chair and talked with Michael and Lene, when my chin would drop to my chest and I would fall asleep by 8:30 p.m. Other nights, I'd still be awake when they went to bed at 10:30. Then I'd snap awake with the remote still in my hand, the television still on, at 2:00 a.m. The downers were as effective as the uppers, and things sure were in a turmoil.

After the uppers and downers for four days each, I'd begin the chemo. Once again, it was a four-day package, ninety-six straight hours of chemo. From Monday through Thursday, I

11

would get my 1,100 milliliters of chemo, with a battery-powered pump sending it through my system. The last drops of chemo left the now-empty bag at twenty-four hours to the minute from the previous day. The nurse would hook me up with a fresh bag of 1,100 milliliters, along with a newly charged battery, and I'd be off and running for another twenty-four hours. In the four days of chemo, I would gain fourteen pounds. The following week, I would lose fourteen pounds.

It felt like a teeter-totter, or a seesaw, same result either way.

I had the liter-plus bag set into a backpack, which I reversed on my shoulders so that it hung on my chest where my port was. It allowed me to be ambulatory. I didn't have to sit at home and listen to the drone of the pump every fifteen seconds for twenty-four hours.

I would sometimes go to my family's café, The Unicorn, in downtown Evanston, to enjoy a cappuccino and visit with some of the regulars, as opposed to having to work there. That was a welcome switch.

These chemo infusions went on for about five months, and the whole process took about eight.

In April 2002, having previously harvested 10 million healthy adolescent red blood cells from my own system over four days, I had my stem cell transplant and crossed my fingers.

There were thirteen different medications that I took in the process of preparing for my transplant. For a period of time, I was taking seven different medications on the same day. Some I was taking once daily; some twice; some three times; and one four times. I couldn't keep track very well, so my son Peter made a chart for me to check off what I had taken and what still needed to be taken. I had uppers, downers, and sleep medication. My mind was often more afloat than even I am used to.

As I struggled, I wondered, "But what about somebody who can't remember to take even one pill?"

After my transplant and a "minor setback," I returned to the hospital to stay in isolation for eight days. From the therapy in general to the final two doses of exceedingly powerful chemo injections one or two days prior to the transplant, my whole system had been cleaned out and there was nothing left of my immune system. I was vulnerable to whatever germ might float past that I might breathe in. In my case, it was pneumonia.

Everyone who came into my room, nurses and doctors included, had to wear a mask to protect me from getting even more infections.

My neck, throat, and other body parts were racked with pain. The nurses in the isolation wing of the hospital hooked me up through the veins in my arms and through my double port to about six different bags that dripped solutions into my body.

One of the bags had morphine for the pain. Aah.

I was on morphine for most of my stay, and it played with my mind. I would see bugs on the wall in my peripheral vision. When I turned my head to look directly at them, they would disappear. My soon-to-be daughter-in-law, Leila, told me from behind her mask that she thought I was hallucinating. I explained to Leila why I was not really hallucinating.

The next day, as a doctor stood at the foot of my bed asking me some questions, I explained the situation with the bugs and how I realized they weren't real and thus I was not hallucinating. I saw the doctor turn toward Leila and silently mouth, "He's hallucinating." (Peter and Leila, to whom I am eternally grateful, spent many, many hours with me daily at the hospital.) I was also the lucky recipient of visits from elephants and school children, standing outside the door of my room. Interestingly, other multiple myeloma patients I've known had elephants visit them too, the exception being theirs were charging!

Morphine in substantial doses does more, obviously, than mask pain.

13

Through this, I continued to wonder about the people who couldn't remember to take their one pill a day. How will they end up? There has to be some kind of solution.

Four or five months later, in the fall of 2002, I was struck with a great idea.

5

Voilà

What if someone who struggled to remember to take their medication could receive a phone call every day, and the voice on the other end would tell them that it was time to take their medication? The person could call a special number and use an individual code to record their message. Alternatively, their son, daughter, or nurse could make the recording. The phone company could work all of the electrical connections and use the right equipment for recording and resending the messages. They could probably code in the calls to a computer which would somehow cause the number to be dialed and the message to be given at the correct time, seven days a week. The patients would get the phone call, take their medication, and be healthier and more functional.

Coincidentally, I knew two people who had associations with AT&T. One was a high school classmate who had retired. The other was close friend of my middle son, Steve. He was an executive with the Bell System. I called my former classmate, Geoff, a bright guy with a masters in mathematics from Northwestern University, who worked for Ma Bell in research and development out in New Jersey. I swore him to secrecy and told him my idea. He said that, yes, it was possible but that I should probably forget the idea of doing it on my own. He explained the basics of the equipment needed and said that the money involved would be well into the millions. That pretty well cut me out from the equipment aspect of the idea.

Next, I called Steve's friend, John, who was climbing the ladder of corporate success two rungs at a time with AT&T. He worked in marketing, and I thought this would be a real coup for AT&T to be able to present to the world. It was going to be revolutionary. I wanted to be cut into the deal somehow and trusted that John would help me figure out how to do that. "Fair is fair," I thought. The problem, as John explained it, was in marketing. He spoke with some other executives about the concept, and while they thought the idea had merit, they couldn't see getting involved.

AT&T was trying to reduce the number of programs and presentations it was making to the public. The company had been too aggressive with new stuff for so long that they had worn the welcome mat of consumer acceptance down to bare threads.

So much for that.

I sat on the idea for few years longer, concluding that to get a patent I would have to know all the intricate details and understand everything that would have to be done. I would have to know the names of all of the pieces of equipment and how they functioned, in minute detail.

I'd have to know the electrical piece of the equation, which was a laugh. I've pulled wires, connected outlets, and hooked up new breaker switches, but I can't say I really understand how it all works. I could not explain "grounding" or "the hot," or "loops," or where electricity really comes from in the first place. I know from experience that if you touch your screwdriver to the wrong wire at the wrong time, it can give you a jolt, with a loud "crack" and flash of light that can knock you off your ladder and cause some reservations about trying again.

It's interesting the respect one develops for wires and the magical current that runs through them, after brushing off one's clothes and giving thanks to still being alive with all appendages still in place.

16

6

Still Kickin' and Breathin'

So I was still alive. In 2005, I passed my sixty-fifth birthday, which was the time the doctors originally estimated I could expect to live.

Not only did I pass my sixty-fifth birthday, but that same year, I had my second hip replaced and became a sleep apnea patient. From my perspective, this looked like progress!

I didn't want to get my hopes up too high that the multiple myeloma had not caused deterioration of my bones. I was encouraged when Jim Kudrna, the surgeon who did my hip replacements, decided to give me the replacement for people who are active, and have strong bones. He said later he had expected to give me the replacement for people whose bones were not strong enough to withstand the pounding associated with heavy-duty activities and court sports. "Once in there," he told my son Peter, who stayed with me at the hospital during my surgery, "I found that your dad's bones were like iron."

When Peter told me this, I felt lucky that for whatever time I had left, I would at least be able to do my best at whatever sport I undertook. "I'm grateful," I said, and a happy tear ran down my cheek.

7
Sleep Apnea

Over the years, I had been informed by friends that I often held my breath when I slept, and sometimes jerked spasmodically before once again taking in air. It was frightening, I was told.

"You stopped breathing. I thought you might have died! Can you do something, please?"

In 2005, after reading about the downside of sleep apnea and having had a brother who died from a stroke, I decided I would take the sleep test.

With sleep apnea, the afflicted person doesn't know he has awakened. He doesn't open his eyes and mutter about waking up or not being able to sleep soundly. The brain awakens detached from awareness. The restful dream state is interrupted. At the end of the night, as morning arrives and the day begins, sleep apnea patients often feel tired and sluggish—maybe a bit thick or foggy in their thinking processes. But without an official sleep apnea diagnosis, it seems this is just the way life is.

I took the test, and the results showed I was a moderately rated sleep apnea statistic. I awakened 53 times in a given hour, and the longest I held my breath was one minute and nine seconds. The first night I used the sleep apnea mask and machine, I awoke the next morning and felt like a new person. I didn't know where my alertness and awareness had come from. It didn't seem possible. It was amazing, the first night in years that I could remember having dreamt.

The euphoria was short-lived. My face is not particularly symmetrical, and I found, as time went on, that I continually clamped my mask tighter, causing the skin below my nose to become tender.

The problem-solver in me began working on an idea to create a mask for sleep apnea patients that would be molded for the individual face and that could be made in less than half an hour. I was pleased with the results of models I made. I took my models, which I assumed everyone did when applying for a patent, and showed them to Paul Hletko, a patent attorney working at Cardinal Law Group in Evanston. Paul wrote and filed my application. I waited a couple of years and was awarded a patent in 2007.

At that time, there were two or three major manufacturers of nasal masks for sleep apnea patients. My take on it was that none of these companies needed to provide a better mask to consumers because they had total control of the marketplace. There was no competition. To utilize my idea, the manufacturers would have to adopt extensive training programs to teach their employees the procedures involved in making the personalized masks, and they would have to open locations for patients to visit. Implementing my idea would require a great deal of work and expenditure on their end.

To incorporate my idea might have benefitted sleep apnea patients, but why rock the boat? I can't say I would have approached it any differently, if I were in their position.

Although I was not able to capitalize on the idea, the experience did open my eyes to the world of patenting. I would later learn that that world was not as I imagined, and the process was certainly not what Thomas Edison had experienced.

8
On a Roll

Fast on the heels of the sleep apnea mask innovation came another fantastic idea. Where were these ideas coming from? Perhaps some secret recess of my brain that I didn't know I had?

This new idea was sure to be a hit, thought I. It would change the comfort zone when riding a bicycle from just "putting up with it," to a state of, "Oh! How I love riding my bike now!"

Again, the idea was so simple, it was amazing no one else had thought of it.

I often ride my bike around town to run errands. I sometimes pedal instead of driving when I go to visit friends. When I used to work in downtown Chicago and spring would arrive, I would often make the 24-mile round-trip commute by bicycle. In fact, at one point in 1962, a friend and I rode from Evanston out to Seattle, where the World's Fair was taking place. We camped out and worked odd jobs along the way to fund the adventure.

In 1988, on my own, when I was 48 years old, I rode up to Eau Claire, Wisconsin. I stayed a couple of weeks with friends and family before catching a plane to Edmonton, Canada. From there, I took the Canadian National Railway train across the rest of Canada to Vancouver. From Vancouver, I rode down to Bellevue, Washington, to visit my dear sister, Carolyn, and then on down to Healdsburg, California, to visit my friends Judy and Rick. Although I carried camping gear, I only slept out of doors a few times. I was reaching the age where a bed with a mattress was necessary to get a good sleep and be better prepared for the rigors of the next day.

So, I've probably ridden more than most other folks. Still, while riding a bicycle might be the most efficient mode of transportation on land using one's own energy, it is not always the most comfortable. That's what I found to be the case.

The bent-under handlebars on the style of bike I rode required me to bend forward and down. Much of my upper body weight was supported by my arms. The only way around this was to ride no-handed, in order to get in an upright position, or to buy a new bicycle with a different style handlebar.

The idea I came up with was to place an insert into each end of the handlebar, after removing the endcap or cutting off the end of the handlebar grips. The insert worked on the principle of compression. As the outside was screwed tighter, it drew the inside rubber cylinder closer and caused it to expand in circumference. In other words, it became bound to and immoveable from the interior of the handlebar. From the end of this compression unit dangled a tube, which had a comfortable soft rubber hand grip covering its surface. As the rider of the bicycle became tired of being in the hunched position, he or she could simply take hold of the hanging tubes and sit upright, as the tubes were able to move in a universal configuration. The tubes effectively added eight inches to the length of the handlebar.

With no patent available, pursuing the idea did not seem worthwhile. Even after my patent application was rejected, I used these rotating handlebar extenders for years. Peter, who was living in Chicago's Hyde Park, also used them, and he, in fact, received regular compliments. I no longer use them because Michael and Leno have since gifted me with a very heavy, slow, and comfortable bike, a product of Denmark. Actually, I get compliments more regularly on this bicycle than I ever received on the handlebar extenders.

21

9

The Pippengers Move In

In 2007, the neighborhood changed in the way that neighborhoods are always changing. Somebody decides to leave, and someone else decides to move in.

Doris and David Sanders had been my next door neighbors for twenty-five years. They had been great neighbors and had also become friends. We shared many a beer or wine and conversation, along with many meals. We discussed Doris's upbringing in Mississippi and her becoming a nurse; meeting David and falling in love; David's agile and creative mind, with his love of Doris and his architecture; and his devotion to ideals and politics always made for an interesting get-together. To put a head on it all, David brewed his own palate-pleasing beer.

But alas, the political situation in the U.S., with our new war in the Middle East and a President, in David's strong view, of dubious distinction, led them to seek out a new place on the planet. And the winner was ... Canada. The Sanderses left for Vancouver, where Doris had found a niche in the nursing field and where David could continue working online with his creative architectural projects.

In their place, a youngish family moved in to the house south of mine. When I moved into my home with my kids in February 1978, having been in the process of building the home since buying the vacant lot in 1974, I didn't view myself as "youngish," although at the time, I was close to the same age as the Pippengers were now. In 1978, I would have considered myself "label-free." If pressed, I guess I would have just identified myself as "Mr. T," which is what my sons' friends called me.

It seems part of human nature that we often quickly detect things about each other and then just as quickly push those things into the background as things not to be too concerned about. It's just little things that might be described as ever-so-slightly quirky. As time passes, though—particularly if things become somewhat awkward, questionable, or objectionable—we often look back and start to wonder why we never wondered in more depth what it was that first gave us pause. Such is life.

Doris and David had left for Vancouver. Michael and Lene had been given the real estate listing for their home. An open house was set up for a Sunday. It was during the winter months. A woman in her thirties was looking at the home and was very interested in it. It was Mrs. Pippenger. Hilleory. She is the wife of Phillip Pippenger, and they had three children at the time: Alexandra, Jeremy, and Elias. The Pippengers were living a couple of blocks north in a condominium. I think it was her second or third visit to the house when I noticed something that seemed odd to me. As she went in and out, inspecting and viewing the home, and as we said our "hellos," her husband just sat in their van, waiting. For forty-five minutes, he never left the car. On that day he never came in to look at the home that he was soon to buy.

Within a month, the Pippengers had purchased the house next door to me and had moved in.

It turned out that their eldest child, their daughter, Alexandra, was a classmate, playmate, and friend of Michael and Lene's youngest daughter, Josie. Michael and Lene and family had moved from my home five years earlier to a place half a block away on the same street, Judson Avenue. Oftentimes, Josie would pass by and wave as she went next door to the Pippengers', or as she and Alexandra would pass going the other way north to Josie's house.

10

Stop For a Minute!

Today's my birthday! Happy Birthday to me.

I just turned 76. I'll take it. I'm luckier than I ever could have imagined and grateful for every day of life. I was a 1940 baby.

As I reflect on the last few years, I'm amazed at what has transpired. Many is the time recently that I've become absorbed into a powerful Kafkaesque piece that seems impossible. I dream that I will awaken with my freedom restored, and life will resume its normal state.

Or maybe it's not Kafkaesque. Maybe it's more like a surreal Salvadore Dali landscape. Or is it more like M. C. Escher, with me stuck on the staircase as I simultaneously go up and down. No wait a minute! It's all upside down. Which way am I going?

It's time to get on with it. And time is what I still have…until the other time arrives.

11
Neighbors and a New "Best Friend"

I said the Pippengers moved in in 2007, and I'm pretty sure that's correct.

The first winter they were here, Phil Pippenger did some traveling. While Hilleory attended to her kids and their needs, I thought I could help out my new neighbors by shoveling the snow off their walk. Fortunately, it wasn't a winter with any huge snowfalls that I can recall. Since they had just come from a condominium, I don't think they had a snow shovel. Besides, exercise has always been an important part of my life.

In my neighborhood, I've tried to be available to help neighbors with problems that entailed some manual labor that might have been a little much for one person. A few of my neighbors have been widows, and it has not put me out to lend a hand for this or that project.

Back in the 1970s, when I was having my own home built, I was "stung" by the builder, who took off when the foundation had been poured and the shell was up. He had signed false waivers at the bank and taken money that was earmarked for labor costs. When I filed a lawsuit against him, I discovered that I was third in line to recover money from this man, who had vanished.

So I became my own laborer. I acquired a wealth of tools. I used to get home mid-afternoon and head to the house to work until dinner. I had always enjoyed working with my hands, so that part was great. The heartbreak was that I had bought the lot in the late fall of 1974 and expected to move in with my kids by Thanksgiving of 1975. We did not move in until February of

1978. It was a little off schedule, but what a great house it turned out to be for the four of us.

My bedroom was on the first floor, and my sons were all upstairs. Each was fully in charge of his own room and could clean or not. It was his space. It wasn't a matter of not caring about them. In fact, it was because I did care about them that they were in charge of their rooms. They grew up in charge of their own lives. They had as much freedom and independence as they could handle. When things got a little out of hand, which occasionally happened, I was there to help. Beyond their own rooms, what they did have to respect was the rest of the house. We had one overarching rule in the house with regard to living together: Clean up what you mess up and, otherwise, your job is school.

So in addition to shoveling for the Pippengers that first winter, I also righted Phil's big and powerful motorcycle, as it periodically toppled over. The Pippengers have a driveway next to my front walkway, which they have since had paved. Back then, the driveway was gravel and dirt, and that's where the motorcycle was parked, actually closer to my house. There was nowhere else to park it.

Sometimes, as the motorcycle sat on soft or wet dirt, it would topple. Motorcycles the size that Phil had don't look that heavy, until you try to lift it. To my own surprise, I was always able to right the bike until the next topple.

Not too long after moving in, the Pippengers built a large two-car garage in the rear of the house, at the alley.

In the meantime, I was heating my house with a wood-burning fireplace that gave off heat instead of depleting heat by sending it up the chimney. I was always on the lookout for trees being felled. I have a chainsaw, and I would cut sections to the lengths I needed. I bought a log-splitter to prepare my logs for use.

Phil bought a load of logs from one of my sources, and the man dropped off the pickup truck full of limbs at Phil's garage. I lent him my log-splitter, which he finished using a couple of months later. I retrieved it, as I had a new load of logs to split myself.

When Phil's father-in-law came up from Georgia, he always did work around the Pippenger property. I believe he worked in construction back home. On one of his projects, he laid some large brick pavers in their backyard to create a patio area. The earth was soggy, and all he wore on his feet were gym shoes. I lent him my pair of leather work boots.

I had joined the Lincoln Park Archery Club in Chicago a couple of years after my transplant. Every few weeks in the summer, the club held an archery shoot in Lincoln Park or down on the south side of Chicago at Washington Park. I saw Phil in his backyard shooting arrows at a target and invited him to go to a shoot. He went with me to Washington Park and...well, let's just say he had an off day, or he was nervous. He did hit the target on a few of his shots, but I don't recall him going to another shoot. In addition to his regular bow, he had two imposing looking crossbows he kept in his basement.

My daughter, Lene, is actually my daughter-in-law. She is originally from Denmark. With her family back there (her mother and father having both since died), I became what Lene and I refer to as her "American dad." It has been that way since 1990, when Michael and Lene arrived back in Evanston from the island of Kon Tiki in the Pacific, where they met. Lene became friends with Hilleory, and they spent some time together, socializing in a group of about a dozen women.

Even though I had spent some time with Phil and lent him tools, it was surprising to hear from Lene that Hilleory had been telling people, "Wendell is Phil's best friend."

I'd known Phil for a few months. He seemed like a pretty good neighbor, but it takes more than that for someone to become a friend. My newest friendship is a twenty-year relationship. My oldest and dearest friend has been that for sixty-five years. A friendship has a history. Phil and I were friendly, but that isn't really what a friendship is. He was just my new neighbor.

C'mon now, *"Best friend?"*

Something seemed slightly amiss, I would say.

12
Cecilia's Back

It was late one March school day, and I had been up to the fabric store in south Evanston on Main Street. Vogue Fabrics was, not too long ago, one of the largest retail fabric stores in the country. When I came out of Vogue, I could see students arriving at Main and Sherman Avenue as Nichols Middle School let out. My oldest granddaughter, Cecilia, a seventh grader at Nichols, walked to school. I thought I'd hang out in front of the store until she showed up, and sure enough, within a few minutes, she was there.

This was at a time in my life when I was always at work on one art project or another. Lately, I'd been into working with fabric and making masks. A friend of mine, Michelle Stone, is a professional artist. She introduced me to her father (another superb and creative artist) and he showed me a full-size rhinoceros, made by covering framing with various fabrics and fabric stiffener. The result was a permanent outdoor sculpture which sat or, rather, stood in his backyard in Chicago. Not having known of such a thing as fabric stiffener, I now discovered a wealth of things that I suddenly needed to create.

From 1985 until the late 1990s, I had a wooden hot tub that abutted the deck in the back of our house. The redwood weathered after about 12 years and some of it began to decay. The tops of the uprights became soft and began to disintegrate until, finally, there was no way to repair the tub. Eventually, I was left to drain and dismantle it, the origin of which had been to ease the pain in one of my failing hips. The wooden uprights, which were about six inches wide, were cut with a precise angle on either side of their lengths, so that when they were placed one next to the other, they stood upright in a circle. When banded together with large metal hoops, the tub became leak-proof. When I dismantled the tub, I was left with a pile of redwood for the fireplace and four wonderful hoops of half-inch steel rod. The hoops were substantial, as the tub had been about twenty-four feet in circumference.

At first, I put the hoops against the garage, thinking I would put them in the alley and one of our recycling scavengers would pick them up. But the more I contemplated the hoops, the more I realized that something better had to become of these beautiful objects, and I had an idea.

I went to Home Depot and bought an arc welder. I already had heavy power out to the garage from a previous project. I had had a semiautomatic lathe in the garage with which I had planned to make every kid in the country his own signed wooden baseball bat. The idea never caught on. Eventually, I was able to get rid of the lathe but kept the power. When I got rid of the lathe, I also gave the buyer about 1800 ash bat rounds (cylinders) that I had bought from the Louisville Slugger Company. When the lathe was working properly, it could cut a cylinder into a bat in about three minutes. My ambition was not small-scale. I was prepared to get a good start, having bought 2000 rounds. After selling bout 30 bats and discarding another 170 due to poor craftsmanship, I gave up.

One thing led to another with my arc welder. I made a rotating sphere with the hoops and mounted it on a twelve-foot pole embedded in concrete. It sits in the backyard and revolves as the wind catches its copper sails. It's decorated with some of my favorite things in life, like birds, flora, Buddha, an elephant, yin-yang, the sun, stars, clouds, waves, fish and butterflies—all cut from sheets of copper, and which now have a patina from weathering. Also in the backyard is Oscar, a giraffe that stands about eight feet tall, composed of a superstructure of welded steel rod strung with copper discs representing his spots. When Oscar bows "hello," he bends his long neck downward in salutation. Cecilia and Josie named him years ago.

On the street side of my home hangs a peace sign about three feet in diameter and strung with white and blue lights that are lit most nights from late fall until springtime.

In addition to welding sculptures and painting, I've carved wood and made other objects as an idea comes to mind. It's like a compulsion. Once the idea occurs, I have to act on it. I made a bust that weighs eighty or ninety pounds, chiseled from a 150-pound slab of limestone. Most of the art on my walls or situated around the house are things I have made. I find the creative process enjoyable.

**

I spy her coming. "Cecilia!"

"Hi Farfi," she says. "What are you doing here?"

"Waiting for you, if you don't mind. May I escort you home?" I say, in a mock formal tone.

She laughs and nods, and we begin the walk home. It's about a mile from her home to school and a little more than a half mile home from where we are. We chit-chat as the blocks pass, and if I know myself, I was probably holding forth about how things used to be in the neighborhood. I grew up one block from where I now live and went to the same schools as my mother, my brother and sister, my sons, and now Josie and Cecilia. Four generations of Lincoln Elementary School, Nichols Middle School, and Evanston Township High School. It's unusual and so is Evanston, or as the younger set now calls it, "E-Town."

Cecilia is wearing her backpack, and by the time we arrive at her house, she is pitched forward, struggling under the

31

weight of her books. I take hold and lift the pack off her back; it must weigh thirty pounds.

"Why don't you use a backpack with wheels?" I say.

"Because they don't fit into the lockers, and we aren't allowed to leave stuff in the halls," She informs me.

I didn't like to see Cecilia hunched over like that, and it started my wheels turning.

13

A New House Guest

Over the years, I've had a number of people stay at my home. Some have stayed for as little as a week, others for months, and recently, for years.

With the exception of a friend who lived in Mexico and came north to spend summers here, the people who have stayed have always been of the younger set. My family and friends tease me about running a "free lodging and anything else you might need" type of establishment. The truth is that as long as I have the space, and somebody is "between places in their life," why not help out? It hasn't hurt to lend a hand, particularly when the person is a friend of mine or the family, or an employee of our family cafe. As my family was teasing me one night, we compiled a list of the people who have stayed over the years, and it came to sixteen or seventeen names. A couple of times, the guests were couples who were in transition. Otherwise, it was usually a single soul who got entangled in one or another of life's perils and needed a little time and space to right themselves.

In March 2008, I was walking home, and when I got to the house just north of mine, there was a young woman lying on the parkway grass in the newly fallen snow, moving her arms and legs in the pattern of a snow angel. She saw me and laughed.

"Hi!" I said.

"Oh, hi there," she replied with a strong southern accent. "Would y'all mind taking my picture while I'm in the snow? It's the first snow I've ever been in, and I'd like to send the picture to my momma."

"Be happy to," I said, using her phone. That was the first I knew of a phone being able to take a photograph. There would be much that would unveil itself to me about this new world of communication, (or the lack of it).

"Are you new in the neighborhood?" I asked her.

"Yes I am. I'm a medical student, and I'm renting a room over there," she said, pointing across the street to Geri Shapiro's house.

When I realized which house she was talking about, I thought, *"Well, good luck with that."* Then I said, "My name is Wendell, and I live in that house right there," as I pointed.

"Well, I'm so pleased to meet you. My name is Lesley, and thank you so much for taking my picture. My momma's going to love this!"

About three days later, in the evening, as new neighbor Phil Pippenger sat in my living room hanging out, there was a knock on the front door, and I answered.

There stood Lesley, a pained look on her face.

"Lesley! Come in. How are you? What's up?"

She came in as far as needed to see the living room where Phil sat.

"Lesley, this is Phil Pippenger. He lives next door," I said, introducing Phil. Lesley took a couple of tentative steps into the living room.

She said, "Wendell, I've got a problem. Maybe you could help me. That woman I'm staying with has accused me of stealing her jewelry. She has a sister in New York who's a lawyer, and she's been calling me all the time on my phone, telling me that she's going to file charges. I haven't taken any jewelry!

"I haven't even been in her home. I live separately. I live downstairs in one room, and I only go in and out of my own door. And now they're going to call the police. I don't know what to do. I can't stay there."

34

I have known Geri Shapiro for years. I've known her ever since she failed to pay one of my sons for work he did in her yard when he was fourteen. I have known handymen, painters, carpenters, and general laborers around town who have asked me, "You live across the street from that woman Shapiro, don't you?" When I've acknowledged that I did, they've unloaded with stories about how she didn't pay for work they had done, reneged on deals she had made, or she offered a lamp, a vase, or a plate for payment, as she suddenly didn't have the money. The stories ended with, "I'd never work for her again."

I said to Lesley, "So, you're stuck, right?"

She said, "Yes I am, and I don't even know anyone up here."

I said, "I don't think you took her jewelry. How long is your lease or whatever you have with her?"

"Three months. I'm staying until June," she said, "and I've already paid a month's rent."

I said, "Okay, if you'd like, you can go upstairs and choose a room. There're four bedrooms up there and my room is down here. And I don't charge people for staying in my home. You can move in tomorrow."

Two days later, Lesley did move in. A classmate helped her bring her things over from across the street.

As time passed, there was one situation and another with school, and things took a little longer than "until June." Lesley stayed through August. I had helped her out a bit financially as well as given her a place to stay. At some point, she mentioned that she had a pistol she had left back home in Georgia.

"You have a pistol?" I said, to be sure I'd heard her correctly. I was still fighting the fact that I needed to wear my hearing aids daily.

"Yes," she said. "Everybody back home has one. But I left it at home because I was told that they'll take it from you if they catch you with one in Illinois."

35

As Lesley was always short of money, and I didn't feel comfortable giving any more, I said, "Well, if you ever need the money and decide to sell it, let me know and I'll take it off your hands."

About a year later, Lesley called and asked me if I was still good for what I'd said about buying her pistol. I'd never owned a firearm, although I had been in the army and had done a fair amount of firing M14s. I told her, "Sure, I'm still good for it," and I sent her a check for $750. She sent the Glock 9mm pistol, of which I had no working knowledge.

My neighbor Phil Pippenger, on the other hand, knew all about the pistol, and he came over, pretty excited to see it, to show me how it worked. I got a Firearm Owner's Identification Card, and my next step was to buy a safe, because I'd read and heard so much about firearm accidents.

Oh, yes—and Ms. Shapiro refunded Lesley's two weeks of unused rent as she found her "stolen jewelry" where she had always kept it. New tenants—a couple—moved in immediately and stayed until the following year. Ms. Shapiro was simply using this ploy to "trade up" for more rent and a longer lease.

A couple of years later, Geri Shapiro would become a close confidante of Phillip Pippenger.

Maybe even a new best friend!

It's not entirely clear.

14
The Folding Cart

As per my usual, I began working on ideas to alleviate Cecilia's backpack issue. The solution would entail a device that would allow a student to pull their backpack to school on wheels instead of lugging it on their back, and then to fold and store it in a small space.

I researched the problem on the Internet (my version of high-tech) and found a number of articles and references to the problems backpacks were creating for young people. The health issue seemed to be that children do not have fully formed and hardened bones, so carrying backpacks laden with heavy books risked injury to their spines.

I began making models of various designs and configurations that would address the issue of hauling a backpack on wheels, and once at school, would collapse for easy storage in a school locker. Within a week, I had come up with a design I thought fit the bill. I was pleased, frankly, and scheduled an unveiling for my granddaughter and her parents. It was nothing formal, but it was, at that point, fairly important in my view. In my mind's eye, I could hear the exclamations of how wonderful this cart was and how much easier it would make life for Cecilia and her friends. I imagined making a dozen or so prototypes and giving them to Cecilia and Josie and some of their friends to test. From there, I would fine-tune and have the carts manufactured as quickly and inexpensively as was practical. The news would spread by word of mouth, like wildfire. In no time, students across the country would be effortlessly toting their heavy backpacks to school on wheels.

What a great idea.

There was a drumroll in my head as I entered the living room with the new creation to show the family.

I paused a moment to scan their faces for smiles and eyebrows raised in surprise and approval.

It wasn't happening.

I gave a demonstration showing its virtues and the ease with which it worked, how it folded so simply and would so easily fit into a school locker. I showed how the wheels were aligned and secured so the cart would always follow directly behind the student without zig-zagging all over the sidewalk. I demonstrated how absolutely functional it was.

And to top it off, I mentioned the colors I had in mind for lucky users to choose from!

Still they all sat, passively.

I looked at Cecilia and shrugged my shoulders.

"It's really good, Farfi," she said. "I mean, I can really see how it works. It's neat."

Politeness is a virtue, but I could pretty easily see she was just being kind and that my creation wasn't something she'd be using.

"Thanks honey," I said. "But you don't like it really. What is it you don't like?"

"Well," she said, "it's just that it's kind of, you know, so tall. It looks kind of awkward. I mean, it's just kind of … you know … it would attract a lot of attention. You know what I mean?"

"Oh," I said. "You mean it would be embarrassing. What if all of your friends were using one? What then?"

"You got it, Farfi. It would be embarrassing. My friends wouldn't use it!" She laughed a bit, imagining the expressions of her friends' faces when shown the cart.

Her parents sat and smiled at me with the look of, "Whatever made you think a sixth grader would be caught dead pulling this thing around?"

It was no big deal, and I was glad to have the input. I still thought there might be some value in it, even at the cost of some slight embarrassment.

I then realized that peer pressure was as strong, or stronger, now as it had been when I was a kid and had to wear my father's discarded shoes because we didn't have money to buy new ones. The shoes were a couple of sizes too large for me, and the teasing was incessant about me and my "spades," which the other kids labeled the shoes because of their pointed toes. From that vantage point, there was no way I wanted Cecilia to even test the trip to school with the great, new, but embarrassing backpack tote.

What I had to do was go back to the drawing board.

I began to rethink in earnest what it was I was doing and take a new and more informed approach. I thought about different ways to accomplish the same goal and yet have something that would blend in to the background, unnoticeable to the psyche of a young and sensitive student.

I looked on the Internet again and spotted some Igloo coolers with collapsible handles. They were ruggedly designed to be used out-of-doors, time and again. The handles were the same style as luggage handles. Next, I found a supplier where I could get such luggage handles. I managed to make fittings for roller blade wheels on the luggage handles, and I was almost in business.

I hit a snag with one part of what I was trying to create. I could not figure out a way to reduce the width of the luggage handles to allow the device to fit into a school locker and at the same time keep the width necessary for stability while pulling the unit up and down curbs and across uneven surfaces.

It was Michael who came to the rescue. He knew of a design engineer living on his block and he introduced us. The man listened and suggested a cohort of his, as he did not do this particular type of design. He gave me contact information for Jerry Zablocki, who came over to my place, listened to my descriptions, and saw the models that I had created.

He quickly came up with some suggestions that sounded right on target, including a way to fold the luggage tote unit to a smaller width when not in use, so that it would fit easily into a school locker. Jerry went a step further and made drawings of the unit as he envisioned it, and with a few adjustments to fit my concept, it was done.

The problem now was that I could not possibly, with tools at hand, create the prototype needed. I would have to search the Internet for someone to produce the prototype at a reasonable price. I found a family-owned company that could make what I needed affordably, compared to quotes from other prototype makers.

The end prototype was a "folding cart" that could carry a backpack and fold into a reasonably small 19" x 6" x 5" Unit. When folded, it could be carried in an over-the-shoulder bag, as the unit weighed less than five pounds. Since it was so convenient to carry, it could be used by public transportation commuters to shop for groceries after work, without worrying about too large a load. It could handle thirty pounds, and grocery bags could hang from the hook designed for the backpacks.

In May 2008, it was time to get serious in pursuing a patent for this idea destined to sweep the nation. The problem of choosing a company to do the manufacturing once I had the patent (from the many who would be interested), was the kind of problem we "idea guys" relish.

Given all the above, what better situation than to have a next door neighbor who was a patent attorney, who might appreciate having the work of writing up the patent application.

Therefore, I showed Phillip Pippenger the idea and asked him if he'd be interested in writing the patent. I signed on with his intellectual property law firm—Leydig, Voit & Mayer in Chicago—and paid a flat fee of $4000 for the patent application for the folding cart. Phil wrote the application, and it was filed on May 20, 2008.

Leydig, Voit & Mayer sent me a final copy of the patent application, the receipt for my payment to them, and the receipt from the United States Patent and Trademark Office, the USPTO.

Although I knew it would take some time for the USPTO to complete their examination of my application, I was excited to at least have a start.

15
Sharing a Secret

In past conversation, Phil Pippenger had mentioned that he had a master's degree in electrical engineering in addition to his law degree. I had run into a stone wall a few years previously when I tried unsuccessfully to find a way to implement my idea of using a phone system to notify people that it was time to take their medications. Now, the thought struck me that with his education in electrical engineering, Phil might know something about the equipment needed to present the idea to the patent office.

A quick debate with myself resolved this outstanding issue, as I saw it. I would offer Phil a 50 percent share of a successful patent in exchange for his knowledge of the equipment and for writing up the patent application. That would cover all my bases, and Phil would be getting a very good deal.

These thoughts occurred to me a few months after Pippenger had written and submitted my folding cart patent application. I invited him over one weekday evening, telling him I had an idea I wanted to discuss. He was a big fan of Pepsi in cans, so I tried to keep a few on hand for those occasions when he would pop over to "take a break," as he described it.

"Your home feels peaceful, like church," he said, as he sat slouched in one of the two big overstuffed chairs, looking at the artwork on the walls and up at the vaulted living room ceiling.

"I can't believe you made all these pieces yourself," he said, "pretty versatile."

I then told Phil as he sat, Pepsi in hand, that, "I have this idea ..." and I went on to describe the background of the idea, working in about the chemo and the pills and the transplant. I told him about my attempt to get something going at AT&T and of feeling handcuffed by my lack of knowledge.

I presented the idea of him writing the patent application free of charge and then splitting the patent 50-50 if it were successful.

He liked the idea and said, "Yes. I can do that. I'll have one of my people do the patent search on the idea and begin writing the application.

"Incidentally, you don't have to know about the electrical connections or the equipment involved. All you have to have for a patent is the idea."

Here I was in 2008, about to get a patent application started, yet I had had the idea since 2002. For six years, I had been sitting on this idea and not telling anyone except my family and a few close friends. I'd been harkening back to the Edison era when patent applications were accompanied by models to demonstrate what they were about. I thought if the inventor didn't have the model, he would at least have thorough working knowledge of all the materials and how everything connected with everything else. "Just the idea." Oh boy. Well, since I had made the offer, I wasn't going to try to backtrack my way out of it. I'd stick with the 50-50 split, and Phil could write the application.

We shook hands on the deal, and I asked when he could get started. My experience with patents is that the application process engenders some degree of anxiety. And now, even though I'd sat on it for six years, I was convinced someone must be waiting in the wings with the same idea, about to file their application too. Mine had to be done pronto—the sooner the better.

Phil said he'd have one of his people do some searches the next week, and then we'd get going if there wasn't anything that looked like a definite roadblock.

The next Wednesday or Thursday, I called Phil at his office to see if anything had been done regarding the patent search.

"Yes," he said, "I had," and he named someone, "do a search on it, and it looks good. It's a go."

Oh boy, what a stupendous day this was. This was going to be great.

A couple of weeks later, I called Phil again to check in.

"Well," he said, "it looks like we're not going to be able to get to this for a while, maybe not for a few months, anyway. We've got a lot of projects going all of a sudden. Other than that, I don't really know what to tell you."

"Oh," I said, and then I thought for a moment. "You know, I don't think I can wait that long. If it's okay with you, I think what I'll do is take the idea to Paul Hletko and ask him to write it. I'll just pay him to do it because I have to get this done. I really can't wait. I'll have to take the idea for myself."

"I think that's what you should do," he said.

In late September 2008, I called Paul at Cardinal Law in Evanston to set up a meeting. I told him the idea and gave him the background that Phillip Pippenger--whom Paul knew-- had done a patent search and nothing had shown up.

Paul and I then settled on an arrangement and I signed a Cardinal contract.

Paul submitted the patent application on October 9, 2008, and once again, I was able to breathe easier.

Here it is 2008 and I have two patent applications pending at the USPTO. I'm still alive. My only symptom is the feverish reaction I have my at my twelve-week check-ups, when the nurse flushes my port, and I've only had pneumonia once in the past two years. To top it all off, I'm working out regularly and playing tennis whenever I can.

Man, I'm alive, and life is pretty damn good.

16
A Friend Returns

The rest of 2008 ticked away.

The New Year arrived shortly after my December Solstice party. I been celebrating the arrival of the solstice since the 1970s as a way of looking forward to the longer days and shorter nights. Although we don't have the darkness in the winter months that is experienced further north, we get enough to more than satisfy anybody I know.

In the 1980s, I began to experience depression periodically during the winter. I couldn't grasp what was causing the problem.

In the 1990s, the cause became apparent out of the blue--literally. I had started a café in downtown Evanston in 1991, along with my son Michael and Lene, then his girlfriend, now his wife. One day in the early nineties, late winter or early spring, the weather had been overcast for about two weeks. I was working the morning shift, which spanned from 6:00 a.m. until about 3:00 p.m. I had felt generally depressed for a week for no discernible reason. I had had enough therapy by this time in my life to be able to fairly accurately assess my state of mind and where I was in relationship to my world.

I was healthy. My family was healthy. My friendships were intact and these friends were doing well. The café was thriving, and the community embraced it. So what the hell was wrong?

After those two straight dark, overcast weeks, the sun suddenly found a large gap in the clouds and broke through, bringing brightness to the street and a glimpse of beautiful blue sky above. Michael had just come in to handle the afternoon shift and take over the manager duties until 11:00 p.m. I said "Hello, do well," and added, "I'm outta here."

I wasn't all that conscious of what was going on as I left the café and went straight to the parking garage. I got into my car and immediately drove straight down to the lakefront. Once there, I quickly alit from the car and went out onto the pier at the boat dock in Evanston.

I stood on the pier, holding my arms out and looking skyward. I stared at this bright blue expanse sky and felt a physical surge of energy and joy begin to fill my skull. It was exhilarating to be alive! I was literally breathing in the power and thrill of life.

After fifteen or twenty minutes at the lakefront, there was no more depression. I felt light on my feet as I strode back to the car and would have liked to play some catch with someone, if I had a ball, or shoot a few hoops, if I could find a basket.

Over the next few days, I found some information on the Internet about "Seasonally Activated Depression." After finding it was referenced as a hospital treating SAD syndrome, I called Evanston Hospital and spoke with the psychiatrist who was involved with the program. He explained that the hospital had lamps that could simulate the sun's rays and stimulate certain nerve impulses in the brain to relieve the effects of the absence of natural sunlight. He said the hospital would rent lamps to patients following some interviews and tests.

I realized by the doctor's reactions to comments that I made about myself that he could see I was reasonably self-aware. "Yes," he said, after a few minutes, "it sounds to me like you would be a good candidate to rent a lamp."

Rather than wait the amount of time it would take to go through the hospital program, I went online and found a company in Canada that supplied the lamps. Within a week, after paying extra for speedy shipment, I was the proud owner of a lamp.

I still find myself periodically getting into a mental slump in the winter, or actually feeling depressed, and not remember why. Then voilà! I realize what is happening and out comes the trusty lamp. I can sometimes actually feel the physical sensation in my head of things changing and of a chemical reaction occurring. It's been a wonderful tool.

A few years ago, I went to Denmark over the Christmas holidays with my family. I took a small travel version of the SAD lamp I used it for half an hour to forty minutes every morning before leaving my room. In Denmark, the sun rose at about 8:45 a.m. and set at 3:45 p.m., a short day, not to mention that most of Denmark's daylight time in late December is enveloped in cloud cover. I remember one "morning" at 11:30, as we were driving to a shopping mall, there was a sudden break in the cloud cover. Every car on the road immediately had the front window visors down to block the sun, which sat barely above the horizon.

Therapists in Denmark and Sweden have different ideas about their suicide rates. Some say winter suicides are often attributable to the lack of sunlight. Others say not. Some say summer suicides are because of the lagging effect of the dark and dreary winter days catching up to the victim. Others say not.

I've always wondered if in Seattle—where many Swedes, Danes, and Norwegians settled in this country—there is a higher suicide rate than elsewhere. If so, is it genetic, nothing to do with the sunlight? Or is it because Seattle is so often overcast and dismal.

***

Phillip Pippenger continued to come over regularly and hang out. I guess my vaulted cathedral living room ceiling continued to hold its "churchlike" appeal.

Sometimes he came with one or two of his children.

17
Kids

I've always liked kids, the different sizes and shapes they come in, and perhaps more so, the variety of personalities that accompany those sizes and shapes. I don't know if it's because of my own childhood, or if it's built into me by nature. I experienced comparative deprivation throughout my childhood, and I intended never to visit that upon my children. It was a powerful burden, and it was there every day. It entailed much more than economics, although that may have been where it started.

I especially appreciate the naturalness that kids bring to the flow of their lives and the honesty with which they express themselves, in both words and actions. The ways their honesty can surface, without self-consciousness, can be intriguing and sometimes alarming. "Revelatory" is probably the best word to describe kids' innate innocence and integrity. Sometimes their revelations are intentional and sometimes not.

Back in the 1980s, there were a couple of youngsters from across the street who used to come over pretty regularly to "hang out for a while," during the summer. These two, David and Emma, would come in the house, and we'd talk about "stuff" for a few minutes. I think they were probably about ten and seven years of age, David being the elder.

In those days, I smoked and chewed gum. I didn't chew it nonstop, but I usually had a pack in my shirt pocket with whatever was left of the original five sticks. It would have been Wrigley's Doublemint. Never Spearmint. I chewed Doublemint for years. In fact, I'd chewed it for long enough that if asked, I probably couldn't have remembered the last time that I'd bought Juicy Fruit or Beemans or Blackjack or Fleer's Double-Bubble.

"Hey! Does anybody around this joint want a stick of gum?" I'd say to David and Emma after a few minutes. I was careful not to overload them with Pepsi or Coke, but a piece of gum seemed harmless enough.

They were always "willing partners in crime" with the gum routine. Usually, I would make the offer, but once in a while, if my attention waned or I was just too slow, David might provide a prompt, like, "Do you have anything to snack on, like gum?" But the usual routine was that I could tell by the degree of fidgeting when the time had come

Truth be told, although they liked me, an equal thrust of their visits might have been the availability of the stick of gum. And I often liked to throw in a positive admonition, "C'mon now, tell me the truth. This isn't gonna spoil your dinner, is it?" At this, they would roll their eyes and look at each other and giggle, then turn to me and offer full assurances that, no, their dinner wouldn't be spoiled by this one stick of gum. We did this same gum routine pretty much every time they came over.

One day, David asked me if I'd ever tried a gum called "Big Red."

"No, I haven't. I've never heard of it," I said.

As luck would have it, the next day at the kiosk in the lobby of the building where I worked in downtown Chicago, I saw some packs of Big Red.

From that point on, it was always Big Red that was the available gum on those summer stopovers.

I don't think the gum produced any negative consequences for either Emma or David; she is now a top-notch customer service bank officer and David teaches advanced high school mathematics and does private tutoring in Rhode Island.

But back to the kids in general.

51

Somewhere, as a spinoff of the gum routine and with the return of Michael and Lene from Denmark with my granddaughters Cecilia and Josie, I started putting out Tootsie Pops. I put them on a nice handmade wood tray that had been a gift to me. The tray sits on a small antique desk for hats in the entranceway inside the front door. The tray is made out of crosswise slats that leave open spaces in between. The Tootsie Pops can stand up on their stems when inserted into the open spaces on the tray. The array of colors of the wrappers, each corresponding with its flavor was a source of wonder and pleasure by adults, as well as by kids.

In 2009, Phil was over regularly with one or two of his kids in tow, as I've mentioned. Phil was not shy about digging into the candy, and in short order, his kids found that that they, too, had a taste for Tootsie Pops.

In the fall of 2009, Phil and Hilleory added a fourth child to the family, and the older ones grew more and more comfortable coming to the house on their own. They were direct about why they had come, "I have a friend over. Can we have lollipops?"

They were relaxed, knowing they were welcome to come in and help themselves. In fact, they would walk into my yard, come up to the deck, walk into my dining room, and head for the front hallway, where the Tootsie Pops lived. They were comfortable enough to do so even when I had company over for dinner. The dining room is small. There was just enough room for a Pippenger child to slide open and quietly close the screen door from the deck, then very quietly walk past the dining room table, without making eye contact with any of the four adults sitting at the table. We adults suspended our conversation and quietly watched this drama unfold.

Three or four Tootsie Pops in hand, the innocent intruder retraced his steps, eyes still averted from the guests and the host, as he exited the house by the same route.

Only after the young visitor had exited the gate at the far end of the garage and headed into the alley, out of earshot, did we indulge ourselves with the laughter we'd all been suppressing, and then someone said, "And is this a regular occurrence, Wendell?"

The wonder of it all notwithstanding, I realized I needed to make a change in the accessibility of my home. I hung a small chain from my sliding deck screen door and affixed a screw to the woodwork framing the deck doors, so that the chain could attach to the screw to allow for some privacy. It was a simple solution to any compromising situations that might occur, even while it pleased me to know that the kids next door felt comfortable with their next door neighbor.

18
Apps?

The summer of 2009 arrives without much fanfare.

The Pippengers' fourth child is born in September and named Asa.

I have the patent application in on the Folding Cart.

I have the patent application in on the Notification System.

I am over at Michael and Lene's hanging out one June evening. Michael says, "Hey Dad, you know Apple has come out with a new idea called apps. This might really be something you could use."

Not having a clue what he might be talking about, I asked him to elaborate.

"Well," he says, "an app is this new idea that Apple has figured out for their new phones. You've heard of the iPhone, right?"

I nod.

"An app is something you can do on an iPhone. You program your phone with, say, a video game that you've made up where you try to accomplish some objective, like knock the bricks off the top of the wall that somebody is building to keep you inside. Then you put this app in the Apple Store and people can buy it, download it, and play the game on their own iPhone. Get it?"

"Yeah, I get it, but I don't have an iPhone, and I don't like any of those kinds of games. I don't see how I could use it, really. What are you getting at?" I say.

Michael says, "Well, I was thinking that you could have an app programmed to do your phone idea. It might give you a chance to test the market."

I look at him with amazement. He is telling me there might be a way to test my notification idea without years of work trying to promote the idea to corporations. That's even if I do get the patent. This sounds too good to be true.

"Wait a minute!"

"That's right," he says. "People go on the Apple App Store site and buy all kinds of products. You buy it right off of your phone. Then they download it from satellites to your phone, and there it is. You might be able to do that. It might be a way to test market your idea."

I'm pretty low in the expertise hierarchy when it comes to what I call "the high tech experience," which includes computers, Internet-related functions, smart phones, Wi-Fi, or anything else digital. I often seem to be at the same technological level as auto mechanics; while their field has come to be dominated by computers. It's not uncommon to hear a mechanic lament, "You can't even tell what's wrong with a car these days until you hook it up to the damn computer and get a readout."

While I have no idea what Michael is talking about, I can see there is the potential for me to actualize an idea, even though I know nothing about computers, programming, or even the vocabulary used to communicate in this alien tongue.

In a flash, I had been introduced, in the broadest, to a world that existed within a new, self-contained set of parameters all its own. It's the world we're evolving toward more and more, with each passing day, and a world that has surely begun to manifest itself as big brother to the world we used to live in.

Not too long before this exchange with Michael, I was still dialing a phone number to get hooked up to the Internet. Plus, I'd seen a story somewhere that people living out in Montana sometimes spent as long as forty-five minutes waiting to get a phone line hook-up to the Internet. Kind of kills the fun of it all.

Back in the 1980s, a friend said he thought it wouldn't be long before computers were commonplace in most homes across the country. I was pretty sure that wouldn't happen. At the time, that same friend was dead certain about the existence of aliens in our ranks. I was having trouble with both.

By September, though, I had become very familiar with the new concept of apps; they came to mind several times a day. I had purchased my first iPhone. I wasn't an app freak, although I did download a couple, like "Buster," which allowed me to see when the next Chicago Transit Authority bus is coming, or when the next CTA El train or subway might be arriving.

Ironically, while I remained pretty much in the dark about how all this worked, I did have an idea that might take me more deeply in to it, as a willing explorer you might say.

I began looking for someone who could help bring my idea to fruition. Searches on the Internet revealed some people who worked on "building apps," but they all seemed to be on the west coast, where all the cutting edge progress was happening. I wanted someone from the Chicago area; it still seemed important to meet the people I might be entrusting my idea to. One of the things that made me willing to step things up and try to get my idea to market was the fact that I had a "patent pending" status, and I could reasonably hope to soon have a patent.

In November, as luck would have it, I came across a company in Chicago that programmed apps for clients. I was exhilarated, so I connected by phone with the owner and senior partner of Vokal Interactive and gave him a brief description of what I was looking for in the way of development. I made an appointment and went to Vokal's office, where I signed a nondisclosure agreement. Reid Lappin—founder, senior partner, and CEO—said he would research the idea over the coming Thanksgiving weekend and call me early the next week.

The news from Lappin was all positive. In early December 2009, Thomas & Sons, Inc. and Vokal signed an agreement. Monies were exchanged, along with a contract that stipulated the timeline and guaranteed a date for completion.

A few years prior to this, I had begun Thomas & Sons, Inc., as a family corporation, with the thought that if any of my ideas actually ended up with any value, I would have something to leave to my family. I had no idea, still don't, about my due date to depart from this world. I don't dwell on death; just take what comes how it comes. Death is just the last phase of life. We know nothing of what follows. We all prepare for it, each in our own way-- from the time we stop growing and start dwindling, which is usually in our twenties--whether we like it or not, know it or not, face it or not. Some people think death begins the moment we're born. Maybe.

Whatever your perspective, it's a long process. I spent many a night, as I lay in bed in my late thirties and early forties, trying to come to terms with my mortality and the concept of eternity.

When I was a kid, say, seven, eight or nine, I used to try to comprehend the distance from earth to the stars, which I had learned were as large as or larger than our own sun. In trying to conceptualize the immensity of the distance and the concept of eternity, I would have to halt the process, as I would become dizzy. Eternity would go on forever, and it was dark and empty. I would have to vacate that realm, as my body shuddered with a queasiness, and I would go quickly to something safe and secure, like a piece of bread with butter or just look at what might be in the refrigerator. I would do anything at that moment to get away from the vastly dark, frighteningly foreboding, and lifeless envelopment of where I was, which was my floating and drifting in space. Out there, lost in the dark of eternity.

19

A Contract

In December 2009, totally excited, I sign the contract with Vokal to develop the app which will allow my notification system idea to be implemented. I can't believe my good fortune.

They not only know how to do the programming, they also know a phone service company to do the work needed to get the calls through at predetermined times with the recorded messages that the user has made.

All of this will be done, as stated in the contract that we sign, in a mere eighteen weeks.

The only thing Vokal cannot guarantee is the acceptance of the finished product by Apple Corporation. This is not something I'm going to worry about. Apple is a forward-thinking company, very innovative.

Simply put, my idea is going to save lives.

It will alleviate a great deal of concern for millions of people regarding their adherence to their medication schedules. Thousands of adult children concerned about notifying their parents will benefit. It will reduce medical costs across the board. Fewer people will go to hospitals due to their own negligence. Fewer people will need nursing homes. It amazes me. The applications seem almost boundless.

The Notification System will call multiple numbers at the same time, with the same message for all. A little league coach would be able to send a message to cancel a practice by calling all of the players simultaneously. Either they would hear the coach's recording when they picked up the call, or the system would leave a voicemail.

A teacher could call all the parents of his or her class with a message regarding an assignment or an illness or anything else of importance.

This idea has to succeed. Not only is it going to benefit millions of people, it is going to benefit me, an obvious side effect being that I am going to become rich.

What would I do with all the money that was going to be coming in?

My thoughts turned to a life of luxury, a large mansion. Cars. I'd have a few cars. A Jaguar, a Mercedes, a zippy little Porsche that would be easy to get in and out of, since I would no longer struggle with lower back problems. My pale skin will take on a perpetual tan. I'd probably go around town in a casually expensive sport coat and a tie that blows over my shoulder as I drive.

My shoes are soft leather loafers like other rich people wear. The others, of course, will see them, and that will allow us to accept each other as equals. The shoes have thin soles, not really made for walking. Most of the walking for my exclusive set will be across thick oriental rugs as we head to the bar, or possibly the elevator, as we don't climb stairs. This club requires no membership card. There is automatic recognition of membership when one reaches our level. At the bar, I'm nursing a whiskey and ice in a short, stout, etched crystal glass that sits on a small table within easy reach. I'm perusing the New York Times, deciding which theatre I want to attend this evening and who else might be there.

I quickly tire of all these riches, content to remain where I am, as I am. I have a place to stay; it's my home; it's good shelter; and I now own it outright.

It has a basement.

It has a kitchen that is perfectly functional. I know where everything is. One of my daughter's-in-law tells me, "It really isn't very functional, and everything is so old."

Well so am I.

My car runs well. It's fifteen years old; not relevant. It gets me from "A" to "B," in comfort.

My estate is large enough. I tend my own lawn and shrubbery and would not want more than I have. I have little enough grass that my battery-powered lawnmower will cut it all before the battery runs too low, about twenty-five minutes. Of course, most people with homes have lawns. I basically do not. Most of my yard is taken up with natural prairie grass plants that my son Steve collected from within a three-mile radius of the house and planted some 25 years ago. He's a botanist and ecologist, among other things.

If I did come into money, which I don't expect ever to happen, particularly at this stage of the game, I would simply look to the best places for it to do the most good. This, of course, after I saw that my family was taken care of, and any friends who might need assistance. None of my friends accumulate for the sake of accumulation.

So you might say I was invested in the contract, both financially and emotionally. Eighteen weeks from signing, and after paying a rather substantial amount of money, the product would be on hand. This was going to be a grueling eighteen weeks, far from my original expectation of two or three weeks.

We went through a Phase One meeting, where everything seemed to be on target. By this time, I had committed more financial resources to the project, as there was a new phone system called "Android" that looked to be an important player in the marketplace. There are certain crossovers in the procedures with Vokal that make it advantageous to program Android at the same time as the Apple iPhone and iPad. I could not commit more emotionally to the investment because I was already at one hundred percent.

I talked with my friend, Rick in Healdsburg, California, about the agony of having to wait eighteen weeks for the completion of my product. He laughed and told me about the time he had to wait six months for the completion of a contract when he was the head of marketing at a Chicago manufacturing company. "I couldn't do it," I said, believing what I said to be true.

20
A Small Pleasure

It's now the spring of 2009, and the year prior, Phillip and Hilleory Pippenger gave me a key to their home. A lot of neighbors do that. I had given keys to neighbors over the years, to the point that I can't remember who has keys to my home and who doesn't. Many of my sons' friends knew we kept our extra key under the lid of the small garbage can on the deck, where I keep my charcoal briquettes. Sometimes, I would start to tell someone that if I wasn't home, and they would finish the sentence, saying, "I know, I can use the extra key from the can on the deck." It was hardly a secret, and if you knew where the key was, you were someone we trusted.

My house, with three young men and me, did not seem like the kind of house someone would target. No jewelry, no cash, regular clothes, a golden retriever—not too much a thief would be interested in.

Well, this estimation was wrong because my house has been broken into twice. The first time, I was out of town, and a friend was staying during my absence. He left the house for a few hours, and when he returned, the house had been torn to hell. The thief took anything and everything of value, including a stereo system, two television sets, leather coats, cameras, and other miscellaneous items. Then, so he would not be conspicuous pushing all this stuff down the sidewalk in a shopping cart, he packed up my garaged station wagon with all of my goods and stole the car.

The car was a diesel station wagon with two batteries, and it was eventually found on the south side of Chicago, minus the batteries, hubcaps, and one tire.

The second time my home was broken into was much less dramatic, and they, or he, left the car.

Sharing a key is not that extraordinary and the key I had for the Pippengers' home was so I could feed their cat and take in their mail when they were away. They went on vacations a couple of times a year, usually down to Tennessee, where, I think, Phil's father still lives, or to visit Hilleory's folks in a small town somewhere in the South.

Hilleory had told me at about this time that she was really anxious to get back to work: "As soon as Asa turns two," she said. I don't know what getting back to work meant because I don't know that she's ever had paid employment as an adult and Asa has passed his seventh birthday.

At any rate, the Pippengers were heading out of town, and I was to feed the cat and take in the mail. Easy enough.

On the day they leave, I go up the front stairs to get the mail from the basket next to their front door. As I climb the stairs, I notice feathers strewn about on the side of the porch. On a ledge, about eight feet above the flooring, is a bird's nest. I had noticed the nest before, and now, once again, I look at it. The nest is shredded and disheveled, no longer full, round, and compact. When I look back at the feathers on the porch, I also see the remnants of eggshells lying about.

I think I know what had happened.

Phil liked to put the cat out into the yard, or let her, on many an evening, onto the front porch, from which she would depart on her prowl of the neighborhood. He had told me that she liked to hunt, and I didn't think much about it. That's what cats do. It's what their genetics dictate. Since he, as far as I knew, let her out in the evening for an hour or so, I didn't think much harm would be done.

Now, though, what I see changes my mind.

I am pretty certain that their cat was responsible for all this damage.

For the duration of the Pippengers' absence, I dutifully take the mail in and lay it on their dining room table and feed the cat, but I don't let the cat out the door as I enter and exit their home.

Now, another slightly strange thing was happening, at least to me. I wouldn't understand this strangeness for some time.

When the Pippengers return, I tell Phil about the feathers and the eggshells, and his eyes light up. A smile creeps across his face curling the corners of his mouth, showing a certain appreciation of the deed. He seemed to like the imagery of what his cat has done.

I take a mental step back.

I swallow and finish digesting his expression. I explain to Phil how cats that were let loose in English neighborhoods and, to some degree, the existence of some feral cats had seriously decimated the bird population of Great Britain. I continue on with my opinion that it seems unfair to the birds to let the house cats loose, when they've already been fed at home and are now killing because that's what they do rather than because they need to eat.

I haven't seen the cat out since. Come to think of it, I don't know if they still have a cat.

21

Oops! ... Oops!

The United States Patent and Trademark Office rejected my patent application for the Notification System that had been submitted on October 9, 2008. Paul Hletko, my patent attorney, responded and overcame the first objection. Unfortunately, the USPTO came back with a final rejection. When the USPTO gives a final rejection to a patent application, it is really somewhat misleading in that the applicant is then given a period of some months to respond and overcome this final rejection. Obviously, a final rejection by the patent office does not really mean "final," like the last out in a baseball game.

The USPTO had found too many similarities between my application and that of an existing patent that belonged to Cisco Corporation. "Well, at least I'm in good company," I thought, even though I would rather have the patent than the good company.

In January 2010, the USPTO issued a second and final rejection to my Notification System application. Paul and I both thought that an answer to their final rejection would keep the application in "patent pending" status, possibly as long as an additional year. By that time, and with the protection offered, I felt pretty secure that I would have completed the iPhone and Android programming and would have, hopefully, secured a leadership role in the marketplace for apps.

In February, I sent the USPTO a "Declaration of Wendell Thomas under oath" saying I had conceived of the present invention at least prior to May 21, 2004, in the hope that the

USPTO would allow me to share in the patent held by Cisco. My hopes were dashed, along with any thoughts of getting a patent, when the USPTO issued a final rejection in June. To overcome this, I would be required to appeal.

Time had run out with this idea.

Paul had done a good job, as far as I was concerned, and he was honest in his assessment of the situation as it progressed—or, for me—regressed through the USPTO system.

I had another situation that felt more pressing than trying to maintain a patent pending status or latch on and share the existing patent with Cisco Corporation.

My project with Vokal was to have been completed before the end of April 2009, yet there did not seem to be any end in sight. April turned to May and May to June. I was getting frantic, as it was taking twice the time promised for completion, and, still, in July, no light appeared in the tunnel to assuage my anxiety.

From where I stood, ignorance was no longer bliss.

When I called the Vokal office and spoke with the representative handling my account, he would dispense a good deal of upbeat attitude on the phone. It felt somewhat comforting to know that the interface was very close to compatibility with the phone service that was being provided from Guatemala for the connections of the calling system. When the call ended, I soon again realized that all the lingo was from a world I knew nothing about.

I sat somewhat stupefied. I tipped back in the swivel chair at my desk, my hands, fingers laced, laid on my chest, and looked at the cedar ceiling of my den. I noticed the knots in the wood. I looked for patterns in their swirls, and I looked for animals and faces, as one might do with clouds. I sat in peaceful avoidance of the fact that I had no idea what I had just been told, even though the person on the other end of the line was speaking with perfect diction, and I had heard every word.

During this time, with regularity, I asked Phillip his opinion of what was going on, as I looked for support that the situation was not as hopeless as it seemed. With his considerable knowledge of the world of electronics, software, and hardware, I valued his expertise and overall comprehension of the situation.

Phil had told me he held a patent that was being used throughout Europe for safer airplane travel. If my memory is correct, he said that the program was a system that automatically sent a plane in distress to the nearest available airport. As I recall, I think that maybe his system was designed to thwart hijackings by superimposing an automatic pilot control. I am only relying on memory, and a sketchy amount of information given in the first place.

Phil informed me that sometimes programming and interfaces take a bit, or quite a bit, longer than might have originally been expected, even with experts involved.

"I'd just sit tight for a while longer," he would say.

While I could understand this, when I fed the data back into my own primitive processor, I kept coming up with thoughts like, "Hey! Wait a minute. They're 25 percent beyond the date they set to finish." Or, "What the hell! Now they're 50 percent beyond the time they were gonna be done."

I felt more urgency than anyone else involved. In fact, I realized I was the only one who seemed to give a damn. My sons cared, but mostly because they saw me getting more stressed out.

I was emotionally invested to the hilt.

Eventually, I saw that only a couple of options were available to me. Number one, I would have to look for a backup company to take what had been done and finish the project. Number two, I would then have to give Vokal a deadline to complete the project.

Once again, I wanted to find a firm in the Chicago area where I could meet the people who would be involved.

I found a company in Villa Park, a small suburb west of the city. The name of the company was Bolder Image. My son Peter and I went out and met with the team. They had proposed on the phone that they could finish my project. With all of the work that had been done, they didn't expect to have much difficulty tying up the loose ends that Vokal seemed unable to do.

I gave Vokal a deadline, they failed to meet it, so I pulled the work from Vokal and transferred it to Bolder Image. This was going to work, by hook or by crook. My compulsiveness had kicked in.

The switch came in August 2010, and I was now going to be going to town. I was excited to have a good team working on the completion. I felt secure about the switch, and I wanted the idea to become reality, and to hell with the patent. I just wanted my project completed.

The group at Bolder Image seemed a good lot, when I met them and signed a contract that August day. One of the things I appreciated was that the contract said very clearly that they did not farm out any of the work. All the programming and other work would be done locally. There would be no offshore work done by Bolder Image.

The only question I had about Bolder Image was the number of people in the office wearing tee shirts with messages of Jesus and Christianity. I have no religious affiliation, and if I did, I wouldn't announce it via my wardrobe, and I always have a mental caution light for those who do.

There are always naysayers for any new idea that comes along but I was pretty damned certain that my idea was gonna be a real successful shocker.

I suppose if you stood back and looked at my enthusiasm for my own ideas, you might say, "He's slightly overboard, yeah?"

Or, "Really?"

Or, "Is this guy bonkers, or what?"
Or, "Hmm, I'd like some of what he's smoking."

22
Phil Has an Idea or Two

Phil now has four kids and pops over at least once a week.

In late August 2010, he sits in my living room, Pepsi in hand, and a leg thrown over the arm of the cushioned chair in which he's made himself comfortable. He says, "You know, Wendell, I've been thinking about your app project, and I have an idea. If you're interested, you could apply for a patent with the same idea as before, when Paul wrote your application, but this time, because of all of the programming, I think an application would be successful as a software patent."

"Is that a separate category?" I ask. "I mean, you know, a software patent?"

"There isn't really a special category," he says. "It's just that with all the patents being issued for software concepts and programs, it's almost as though there is. And you're doing a lot of programming."

He's got his sizable frame slouched and canted to the corner of the chair. It's an oversized chair, and that's a pretty good thing because Phillip is an oversized guy. At this time, he's probably about six feet tall, and I would guess that his weight runs around 270 pounds. He's not "svelte" or "lean and mean."

With his can of Pepsi, his unbuttoned shirt hanging down either side of his belly, his legs splayed, his heels planted heavily on the floor, with his toes pointing up, he hardly looks the part of Cassius, as in Caesar's remark, "Cassius has a lean and hungry look. Such men are dangerous."

"You got your final rejection on the Notification System in May or June, right?" he asks.

"It was June," I say.

"If you have the application that Paul wrote, I'd like to take a look at it. I think you still might be able to get the patent," he says.

I go to the den and rummage a bit in the Cardinal Law file and there it is. When I bring it to the living room, Phil is ready to read through it and is also ready for another Pepsi.

I sit quietly with my coffee, and Phil looks through the application. This sounds to me like it might be a pretty good deal if he can pull it off, like going to an entrance on the other side of the stadium when one side is too crowded.

What do I care if it's a software patent or some other kind of patent? All I want is a patent. I could worry once I had it in hand. It would give me a sense of power to defend my invention. I would expect there to be many infringers, on an idea as good as this.

When Phil finishes looking at the rejected application, he nods his head and says, "I think this is definitely patentable at this point with, as I said before, all of the programming that's being done to implement your product."

We then talk about how to get the patent accepted by the USPTO and decide that we would be best off if Phil writes the new application, as he is already fully versed in all aspects of the idea.

Phil suggests that he could write the patent on weekends as a neighbor and friend rather than have me go through Leydig, Voit & Mayer, which in this case might cost as much as $15,000. He says that he could write, submit, and do anything else that the patent application required, aside from the fees that the patent office charged, for $4000.

I want to know that I'm not on slippery footing with what is being proposed. I ask him if it would matter to Leydig if he is

71

doing this on the side, and he says, "No, they wouldn't care. You couldn't afford to pay what they would charge for this anyway. Companies like Microsoft or Caterpillar, they don't care what they spend for an application. Leydig might charge twelve or fifteen thousand for something like this, if it were for a corporate client. On the other hand, they really wouldn't care if I did this for you. Of course, if you want to, we could do it through Leydig."

I am quickly okay with him doing his writing on the upcoming weekends and with covering all of my bases for $4000.

I pay Phil on August 28, 2010, and he begins writing my patent application. We talk regularly on the phone and pass ideas back and forth on emails as to what should go into the application and what might be left out now, to be used for a later version. I was going to be using the date of my first and rejected patent (October 9, 2008) with the USPTO on this application in order to give myself a two-year edge, just in case others were now applying for the same idea. It seems well worth giving up two years on the patent to ensure that I would have the two-year edge on the application end of things.

My son Steve is living in Michigan and is very preoccupied with his work as an ecologist both in the field and the office, assessing the projected impact of proposed construction on wetland parcels in given areas. Because of the hours he works and the time his job requires, I avoid sending him copies of Phil's emails that I send to his brothers, either for their approval or to question any of the ideas Phil and I are working on.

Michael and Peter generally go along with what is being proposed, but do offer inputs and additions. It is helpful to me to have these youthful minds on my side for insights into things I might be missing.

On September 3, 2010, Phil sends me an email:

"Wendell, Just an update—I'm still working away on the draft, and will have it done tomorrow afternoon or evening if that is alright for you. I know I previously guessed that it would be this evening, so I wanted to give you the heads up so you didn't think I had forgotten. We can go over the draft this weekend and decide what changes/additions we need.

Alright, just wanted to keep you in the loop, Wendell, talk to you soon. Phil"

The next day, September 4th, Phil catches up to me as I am working in my garage, and he hits me up for a loan of $10,000.

"Could you see your way through to do this? It would help if you could," he says. Then he adds, "This is kind of embarrassing, and I understand if you can't."

It surprises me because only the week before that, I had given him $4000 to write the new Notification System application (of which he had decided to change the name to "Localized Message System").

Luck is with him, because when I switched from Vokal to Bolder Image, I transferred some funds and happen to have the money in my checking account.

I never give a thought to the right or wrong, or whether it violates of rule against lending money to one's lawyer. He is my neighbor, and he says he needs help. We nod our heads in agreement on the interest-free loan.

Phil explains something or other about how Leydig altered their accounting procedures and how the bonus that he had expected in September would not be coming until later, probably in December.

From my side, I think, "What the hell, I can tide him over, I guess."

So I lend him $10,000 and write the check on September 4, 2010.

The following day I would be leaving on what is generally my annual trip out to visit friends in California. Rick is my oldest and dearest friend, and I like to try to spend some time with him at least once a year. When I say "oldest" friend, I suppose I should clarify that as Rick is a full five months younger than me and is not nearly older than other friends. He is my friend of the longest duration; that's what I mean to say. We became fast friends in the fifth grade at Evanston's Lincoln School, when he moved to Evanston from Rogers Park in Chicago during the fall semester.

Rick and I spent a good deal of our childhoods together, doing what kids do when they are growing up. In our case, it seems our lives revolved around playing sports, talking about girls, and never having enough time for either.

Tongue firmly in cheek, I have to say that of all the kids I've raised, Rick has been the most challenging.

Rick can harbor some fairly strong opinions about things. The problem with his strong opinions versus my strong opinions is that his are often backed up with fact, or an argument that would make you think he knows something--or everything--about what he's espousing.

Most of my life seems to be governed by feelings. If it feels right, then I'll find all the reasons to back up a decision. The result is that there are times when I am astoundingly accurate and way ahead of the curve and other times when I do something colossally stupid.

Rick never had the difficulties with school that I experienced. In later years, I have been able to look back and see that some of my problems had to do with my family's structure and function, or lack of it. School did not inspire me. It was a place to be that wasn't home, and so that's where I spent my time.

Rick had an easy time learning and was always one of the brighter bricks. In addition to his bachelor's degree in liberal arts and sciences, he ended up with a master's degree in business administration, and a few years later, an additional master's degree in education.

Rick and Judy now live in Sonoma County, and Rick does some farming. I wouldn't call it "gentleman farming"; it's virtually all done by hand, laboriously, and often on knees still tender from the previous day's abuse in the hard, rocky soil. When I visit, I like to help with the labor and pass the time catching up, philosophizing, gossiping, and whatever else comes to mind.

Anyway, when I'm there, Rick pretty much gets the free use of a mule for the days we spend in the field. If not a mule, at least a workhorse who's still trying to show he's as strong as a bull.

So when it comes to my travails, if Rick makes the statement, "I want to be candid with you," I can pretty well assume I'm in some kind of deep shit.

You realize when you hear those words that it's time to dump your fiancée or to make some major behavioral modification to the way you've been conducting your life, or if you insist, you can choose to remain in the completely sub functional, self-abusive state in which you are currently mired.

There are a couple of things that I've appreciated about these infrequent occurrences when Rick "goes candid" on me. Number one is that he is oft-times accurate. Second, I appreciate his willingness to risk shaking the foundation of the relationship to speak his truth. That, in turn, makes Rick extraordinarily trustworthy.

"Well," I might say to myself before I begin to digest what he has just said, "We all have room to improve," as I look at him and wonder what it is that I might feel like being candid about in return. Whatever I think of, I just let slide because I know Rick well enough, and have for long enough, to know he's not trying to hurt me.

If it happens to be at dinner that something candid gets said, I'll just nod and ask him to pass the chicken, and I might look to Judy for some support or defense of my latest foible. I love it when a woman steps in to save me.

So Phil was working on the patent application, and I had paid him for that. Then he had borrowed $10,000, and the next day, I take off for California to visit Judy and Rick.

Oh brother, I can hear it already...

23
Things Move Along

While I was at the Markoffs' in Healdsburg, I had access to the Internet on their second computer in one of the upstairs bedrooms.

After our "patent group" (Michael, Peter, and me) had gone back and forth a couple of times with rewrites and changes to the Notification System application, Phil sent the following email on Monday, September 13, 2010:

"Wendell, thanks for the quick turnaround, that's a nice point about 'message' vs. 'reminder.' I'll make that change wherever it appears, and we'll plan on filing Wednesday absent any big issues from the others. Phil"

On Thursday, September 16th, I sent Phil an email:

"Phil,

I'll be travelling starting early am and will get home mid-evening. Thanks for your great help. I'm thinking that our patent app went in on Wed. Manana, W"

Ten minutes later, Phil responded:

"Wendell, good to hear you're coming back, hope you had a great time out there. And yes indeed, you are now the proud applicant-inventor with the USPTO. I don't have the new serial number in front of me, but will get it from Susan tomorrow and send it over to you. Have a safe trip, Phil"

***

Susan was Phil's secretary at Leydig, Voit & Mayer. It struck me that it must be okay with the firm, just like Phil had said, that he was doing some moonlighting.

At this point, my spirit remained unbroken even though I had had the disappointing experience with Vokal. I was plowing through the unknown fields of high-tech electronic development work with the ease of a passenger on a fast-travelling, larger-than-life, luxury liner heading for new horizons, without any knowledge that, in fact, there loomed ahead icebergs that were many times larger than the vessel I was on.

Vokal had not done their work as per our contract, and I had paid money in advance. While they wanted to collect a "mere" additional $5000 to call our situation even, I wanted a return from them of considerably more than that—the monies paid for work not completed. I thought they had pretty thoroughly failed to keep their end of the contract.

I did not consider Vokal to be an evil entity. I saw them as young and aggressive, prone to bite off more than they could chew, like, "Get the business now, and worry about how to do it later." I thought they got in over their heads with the concept I was pushing; with the contract they had signed; with the reality of being able to make the proper and reliable connections with the platform(s) that they tried to work from (whatever that means); and with the third-party phone service company they had subcontracted and were passing on to us. Vokal did do their work locally, and I appreciated that, but I was leery regarding the phone service company, which was operating from Guatemala. From early indications, they were certainly in no rush to get things done

So, I now had my patent application reentered, using the previous date of 2008, and I had a new contract with Bolder Image to do the remaining programming for the phone system app.

One of the positives of all this was that the contract with Bolder Image stipulated that they would do all of the work using local employees. The contract guaranteed there would be no offshore work. I had been concerned about having the work done locally, so I felt the decision to go with Bolder Image was a sound one. I didn't want to have my work done where there might be problems understanding instructions or delays in communications.

November brought what I was waiting for. We got into the Apple App Store with our app. I was only concerned about of couple of things. First, I was hoping that the phone system we were using would be able to handle the volume I expected, and second, my shoulder was killing me.

The unveiling of our app in the Apple Store did not, as I had anticipated, take the app world by storm. The day after it went on sale, I threw a celebratory dinner. It wasn't a big affair, but it was significant to me. To have a dream become reality was important. It felt like an accomplishment, even though my contribution was limited to ideas and money. I had Peter and his wife, Leila, Michael, Lene, their two daughters, and the Pippenger family of six. Rather than try to cook for this mix, I simply ordered out a number of deep dish pizzas.

In the next week or so, we had a few downloads, and I gave away several freebies that Apple Corporation makes available to developers. Certainly it would just be a matter of time before customers would begin spreading the word, and our app would catch on like wildfire.

Didn't happen. Momentarily, at least, it was a flop.

One of the benefits of this slight failure to get thousands or even hundreds of downloads was the discovery that our phone company connection proved totally unreliable. One day in November, there was a rainstorm in Guatemala, and we lost the phone connections within our system. A rainstorm? The manager of the company was vacationing and unable to access the system to fix it. We were without a connection to our system for three days. I absolutely could not ask people to download and rely on our system for medication alerts when they might not get the call. We would be putting people at risk, and I would not do that. I still believed fully in the idea, but our system had to be made as reliable as possible.

In early December 2010, just before some repairs to my shoulder, I fired the phone team from Guatemala. I was left without any product and would have to begin again, hopefully having learned a couple of things. The thought of not being able to teach an old dog new tricks had not even entered my mind.

At this same time, it became clear that Vokal had no intention of returning my money. Maybe a lawyer could make a phone call or two and help out. Phil stepped in and did some negotiating with Vokal. They told him they could return $6500, but that anything more would cause them to go bankrupt. I didn't believe them and asked Phil, who had offered to take the case for $2000, to go ahead and file a lawsuit to recover unearned deposits for work not completed and for some work never even begun.

"It's a piece of cake," he said. In fact, it was so tilted in my favor, he did not need any more than a copy of our contract to look at, no figures, nothing else.

It sounded to me like this was going to work out fine. I told Phil, "I'm partial to three-layer chocolate fudge."

I'd taken up tennis in 2005 and found that I loved the game. I wasn't really able to play singles; my mobility was limited by my hip replacements. But how I loved playing doubles. I worked at it and enjoyed improving my game until I think that I was actually becoming a decent player, not good, mind you, but decent, really. Well, as happens with some players, I blew my shoulder out. In my case, that means I tore two tendons. My arm became less and less functional. Not only could I not serve well, I couldn't even lift my dinner plate.

The surgery to fix my shoulder was scheduled with Greg Portland, M.D. for December 6, 2010. Greg did an excellent job, but I would be off the courts until May. Shoulder surgery requires a rather lengthy rehab, and the rehab can be ever so slightly uncomfortable... as in "a twinge painful."

On December 9th, I sent Phil an email:

"hi p, I'm doin' all 'o my stuff left-handed. pretty cool, eh? I'd like to go ahead and   begin our suit against vocal. or, are we suiing an individual? either way, I'd like to begin. thanks, w"

I don't recall if this was that time in my life when I was sending emails without using capital letters, or if I used all small letters because I couldn't depress the "shift" key, as I was using only one hand.

I gave Phil a check for $2000 on December 14th, and he told me a few days later that he had filed the suit on December 15th.

It seemed all I had to do now was find a replacement for the unreliable Guatemala phone system and I would once again be in business. Of course, in business after the new programming was done. Oh yes, and I had to find a phone relay company willing to take on the project, with their only hope of cost reimbursement coming from future revenues. I would not be able to finance the programming for whatever phone system I hooked up with.

24
I Get It

On January 3, 2011, Phillip repaid the $10,000 loan I had made to him in September. I sent him an email that evening to thank him:

"phil,

thanks for your integrity. Wendell"

Two minutes later, he responded:

"Hey, thank *you* Wendell for trusting in me.Phil"

It was pleasing to learn that Phil was trustworthy that way and had stuck by his word in repaying the loan. Maybe Leydig, Voit & Mayer had had some accounting difficulties after all. It still did seem, though, that a firm that large, with somewhere between eighty and a hundred partners, would have a better handle on their accounting procedures. But who am I?

On January 4th, I sent Phil the following email:

"p, I'm re-sending [not rescinding] because I don't think I heard back from you. w"

Attached to this brief email was the email I was re-sending:

"hi phil

i think you said you'd check with reid this week to see if he got the notice from the court.

let me know, please, what he says and blah blah blah. thanks w"

Once again, I did not hear back from Phil explaining anything, so on January 14th I sent him yet another email:

"how long (would you guess) before   something begins happening in the court(s)?"

I did not get a response from Phil, so I sent him another email on January 18th:

"i'm not trying to pinpoint you on the court date. i just wondered... is it like, 3 weeks? 8 weeks? 4 months? generally...?."

This time, Phil sent a reply:

"Wendell, I'm going to try to get a more definitive schedule from the clerk so we can   know better what the time table will be. But as far as actual substantive action by the Court, they tend to take their time. At any rate, I'll give the clerk a call today to see if we can   get a timetable – they don't always give one, but we'll see."

That was somewhat of a relief. It's not that anything to be done in court would require anything of me. It simply put my mind at ease to know it might be a while before anything happened with the lawsuit. I had enough going on at that point and really didn't need more.

The whole Vokal situation had messed with my mind. I had no product. They didn't want to refund my money. Because of the degree of my emotional investment, at times I felt on the verge of "overload." I needed to stay steady and maintain what balance I could.

25
Traction and Ice

Where I began in my relationship with Bolder Image and where I ended changed dramatically. It went from up-front and trustworthy to deceitful and dishonest over the course of many months.

As January 2011 arrived, I had a couple of obstacles to getting my app back into the Apple Store. I had stopped the app in its tracks because of the phone system failures. The Guatemalan phone service was obligated to maintain service for the customers that already existed, but I didn't want any more users headed in their direction.

I had undertaken a blind search of the Internet, hoping to find a source to fulfill our phone service connection requirements. A number of companies came to light that I thought might be in the compatibility ballpark--a pleasant surprise. Another surprise was that the first company I called, Call-Em-All, based in Texas, expressed an interest and seemed open to the opportunity.

The surprise of all surprises was that within a month, I was able to introduce the key people at Bolder Image to the key people at Call-Em-All. By mid-February, the two companies had worked out the nuts and bolts and were ready to begin work in earnest.

My main point of contact at Bolder Image was Marc Cain. I asked Marc about the programming situation with the new phone company and whether or not John, who had finished the incomplete work from Vokal, would continue to do the programming. He told me, "Yes, John will be doing the work. At least to begin with."

Marc also told me he estimated the work would probably take around one hundred hours, a hundred and twenty max. We all know how that goes, so I prepared mentally for a hundred and fifty hours.

Thus, in March 2011, the work began. Or perhaps I should say the Bolder Image rip-off began. Is that okay to say?

[The little guy who sits on my shoulder and watches everything I do whispers loudly into my ear, "Yes, it is!"]

I don't want to get mired down in the story of ineptitude that Bolder Image demonstrated from March 2011 until January 2012. To maintain respect for myself and my product, I had to dump Bolder Image at that juncture.

I will touch on a few things about how they functioned.

In direct violation of the agreement they had made with me, Bolder Image did not do the work locally. They hired a company from India to do the programming. When, after six months, that company didn't work out, they hired a different company from India.

They conveniently forgot the stipulation in the contract that the work would be done locally, by their employees.

During 2011, I would occasionally see a name on an email that looked Indian--not a big deal. I thought it was probably someone who lived in or near Villa Park and maybe worked out of their home.

From the time the work with Call-Em-All ostensibly began in February, things went awry. It wasn't until the end of March that Call-Em-All was made aware of the things Bolder Image was trying to implement on Call-Em-All's platform. Call-Em-All had some very legitimate concerns that Thomas & Sons, Inc., through their developers, Bolder Image, was about to institute a new and auxiliary phone calling service through their system. I became aware of the problem when Call-Em-All required a contract to be drawn up which would cover the usual business arrangements that companies have with each other. Because of all this, some of the production was slowed down.

When I was working out the contract with Call-Em-All in August 2011, and had a question about some phrasing they had used to protect themselves, which I feared might compromise my patent pending situation with my phone Notification System, I turned to Phillip Pippenger for some advice. Phil had been kept aware of the contract negotiation as it proceeded, so I asked him: "P

> I changed comment a-7 from "abive," to above. Thanks much. Now I will attach it and send it to Brad. Are we going to wait to say something about our patent pending? W"

In the email, "Brad" is Brad Herrmann, President of Call-Em-All.

> Phil responded:
>
> "Wendell, regarding the patent, I would work it in something like this:
>
> Dear Brad,
>
> Thank you for sending the draft agreement. We have made a few changes, with comments added   to explain the changes or ask a question. Hopefully the changes look OK to you, but feel   free to let   me know if you see any problems.   Regarding   the proprietary information of   Thomas, the restriction on using the Thomas   code is probably not strictly necessary in view of the patent pending status of the Thomas code and   product, but we'd still like to have it in there as a normal business term. Thanks, Wendell"
>
> In return, I emailed to Phil:
>
> "P You are very-VERY GOOD! W"

Phil was an excellent letter-writer and helped me on three separate occasions with letters. While Phil's status was "next door neighbor," I was not particularly comfortable with the fact that he would not give me a bill for any of the extra help he provided. I explained that I would much prefer to pay him for any help he gave as the help was given, rather than to receive a bill at some point for a cumulative amount. I didn't want an unexpected bill for $1000 or $2000.

Phil's response was always, "Don't worry about it. I'm happy to help." In late August 2011, after Phil had met me in downtown Chicago to discuss the progress of the app with Marc Cain and Brian Meyers of Bolder Image, I did, however, go with him to an Apple Store and buy him an iPhone. I was pleased to do this.

As we walked toward the Apple Store, Phillip let me know he had decided to accept an offer from a small intellectual property law firm, Miller, Matthias & Hull. He said he had been invited to join them as an equity partner and would be the fourth member of the group.

Phil had kept me up to date on his situation at Leydig, Voit & Mayer, and this seemed like a well-thought–out move. I told him as much and offered my congratulations.

Phil eventually made that switch in October of 2011.

But back to the Bolder Image situation.

Marc Cain was pretty well able to keep me in the dark, but I believe the real problem for me at Bolder Image was the man behind the scenes who was the master puppeteer. His name was Dave Gruen, and I suspect he was the one pulling the strings.

I think Marc was being as honest as he could be and still keep his job. That's what it boils down to.

The notification system idea was an idea I felt was going to bring some real benefits to both me and the public, so I was an easy sale on any positives offered. There were many times during the ostensible programming when I was told that I would have a download in a couple of days. For example, on June 9,

2011: "... I hope to have that worked out by tomorrow, and I can give you a test app on Saturday. Cross your fingers!"

So, again, I would buy into that. "Ah," I would think, "we're almost there!"

But it didn't happen. But almost!

Then on June 15th: "It is now finished and just testing. I hope by tomorrow I will have a [sic] app for you to put on your phone."

Didn't happen.

On June 21st: "I am hoping it will be any day now that they get these things working..."

I continued to buy in to what I was told. I never knew when to pull the plug. I had such high hopes for a successful and socially beneficial product, with so much of myself invested, that I was never able to take a step back and look at the situation from a different perspective.

In the meantime, I knew next to nothing about what was being done. Bolder Image never told me that they had farmed out the work to India, where they might have been paying as much as $18 per hour, while they charged me $135 dollars per hour. On the monthly bill they sent, I began receiving "discounts." On final analysis, my payments to Bolder Image averaged about $99 per hour. The rip-off is painful to think about.

At the end of the day, Bolder Image did not get the work done. At one point, they charged me for eight hours of work to post a notice in the App Store adding the availability to purchase "100 Calls" with a price attached. It never showed up in the App Store! I had to pay this bill, or they would not release the programming of the product, which they were holding. Rip-rip-rip.

I completed the project with a new programmer after I fired Bolder Image. He was absolutely honest and efficient. He started my project from scratch and built the product on a solid platform. His name is Michael Frederick. Michael is a gem. He was what I was led to believe I would get from the first two developers. Finally!

As an example, when I asked Michael Frederick about how much time it might take to put a notice in the App Store with a new purchase availability for 100 calls, he said, "Oh, that's no biggie. Ten minutes at most."

Stephen Barclay was the person at Call-Em-All with whom I had the bulk of my contact, and he was as honest as you could wish and competent to boot.

I still consider myself a pretty complete dunce with regard to computers. Programming? Now you're talking very mysterious stuff.

I didn't fire Bolder Image until January 2012. By then, I had more and bigger irons in the fire that, once again, were not of my making.

26
Fissures in the Ice

On May 9, 2011, having received notice of an Office Action from the United States Patent and Trademark Office (USPTO) that gave objections to my pursuit of the Folding Cart patent application, I wrote an email to Phil:

"Phil, As a reminder, I would like to continue to pursue the patent for the collapsible cart.

Would you write the response to overcome the inspector's objections in the first office action?

And, more importantly, does our application still look viable to you? Thanks, W"

This was the "early middle" of what was turning into my continuing mess with Bolder Image,

Phil responded with a return email on May 10th:

"Hi Wendell, yes on all counts. The application does still look viable, and I will take care of the response. I just finished another application prosecution for another client, where the examiner kept rejecting the claims, the supervisor then rejected the claims, and then I appealed it all to the Patent Board of Review and ...Smack! We won, and the Board reversed the examiner 100%. So I don't worry too much about the rejection in this case, examiners get things wrong sometimes, but even when they stick to their guns, they're not the last word. Phil"

The first rejection the USPTO offers is generally not the be-all and end-all of the process. I believe, from a layman's perspective, that it is unusual to be awarded a patent without having to overcome objections. I also think that applications often go to the Final Rejection stage before they get approved.

I wasn't worried about this Office Action, and Leydig, Voit & Mayer soon sent me documentation that the objections had been overcome.

My ongoing frustration with Bolder Image did not warp my attention to the extent that I forgot about my lawsuit against Vokal. On August 18, 2011, I sent Phil the following email:

"P,
Would your guess still be, "anytime now?" Is there a way to check without offending the judge? W"

Phil did not respond by email but, rather, by phone. In our conversation, he did reiterate that it could be any time from this point forward. He did not consider it a good idea to make an attempt of any sort to speak with the judge. "They tend to look askance at that type of behavior," he said.

In October 2011, I became concerned with the status of the books of Thomas & Sons, Inc. In the past, I had always done a cursory job with the accounting processes for our family corporation. In fact, not only had I done a cursory job, but an advisor from the state of Illinois had told me some years prior that I could stop filing any Illinois tax returns because the corporation had no activity. "We don't need the extra work of nothing," he had said. Following his suggestion, I hadn't filed with the state for, as a rough guess, about five years.

Now though, the corporation was about to embark on fulfilling any number of thousands upon thousands of customers who could use our app to improve their lives. When the development of the app was completed, I did not then want to be too far behind in having proper books and proper legal records-- have some knowledge of where the corporation stood. Along these same lines, I did not want to be building a future problem for myself with the IRS for negligence.

I called the firm that I had used many years before and was able to re-connect with the accountant with whom I had last worked. He gave me some instructions as to how best to straighten out my books. Actually, "straightening out" would be inaccurate. Since I had never done a decent job of bookkeeping, there was nothing to straighten out. What had to be done was to set up the books from scratch and get things laid out properly.

In the late fall, November I think, I couldn't find a copy of the Notification System ("Localized Message System") application that Phil had submitted for the phone system in September 2010. In the past, I had always been given a final copy of a patent application that had been filed. I thought that maybe I had misfiled what he had given me, and I looked for it sporadically. Because I was also doing other things, it wasn't something I thought much about. It was most likely an email attachment that I had printed out and then promptly misplaced.

November rolled into December, and I began wondering about the status of the lawsuit Phil had filed against Vokal the previous December. How long was it gonna take the damn thing to get to court?

Wait a minute. I have no record of the lawsuit. I'd better ask Phil for copies of the patent application and the lawsuit. I did not, at this juncture, have any idea what I might be given as a record regarding the lawsuit against Vokal. There probably is some kind of paperwork that the court issued that I might be given a copy of, or there must be some paperwork that Phil has that he could give me copies of. There had never been anything in my life that involved anything like a lawsuit, or any court proceeding.

My contact with the courts came on two occasions. The first contact was being a witness in a criminal case where the criminal I had identified in a lineup, and then testified against in court, was given an eighteen-year prison sentence. At the criminal's sentencing, the judge said, "You are a menace to society."

My second contact was considerably more involved. I served as a jurist in another criminal case, and the defendant was found guilty. In this case, I was the foreman, and much to the chagrin of my fellow jurists, I was the last one to acknowledge the defendant's guilt. I wanted to be absolutely certain there were no loopholes left uncovered, that we had explored every possibility that existed. For my own stability, to be able to live with myself, I could leave no stone unturned. In the final analysis, I could see the light, and we found the defendant guilty.

Briefly, I found the situation to be very convoluted. It was a Chicago policeman whom we found guilty of armed robbery. He was off-duty at the time of the incident and had his weapon on him. He was out to dinner at a restaurant with his brother-in-law, who was a convicted felon and with whom he was to have no contact. There were gangs and illegal aliens involved. Did he take less than twenty dollars from someone he thought was member of a gang that had confronted him earlier that day when he was out of uniform? Did he then drop the money, or some of it, on the ground for the man to pick up? Was it armed robbery, when he never showed his weapon but had it with him?

The long and the short of it is that we were required to look at the facts and not make judgements of our own regarding different possibilities. For the jurist, the law is the law and is based on fact only.

I found the jury duty to be an emotionally draining experience, and it stayed with me for many a day. The irony was that we were supposed to only look at facts and not allow emotion into our decisions. I thought it was an enormous responsibility; we jurists had to honor our judicial system as peers of the defendant and then accept the responsibility for sending him to prison. Prison!

It's a hard concept for me. I can more easily accept being a prisoner of war than being a prisoner in my own country. Confinement. A small space. Of the four sides of the cell, three are concrete. The one side that isn't concrete has bars and a securely locked door. The corridor outside the space echoes with sounds, which are sometimes screams. Human screams.

But let's get back to my lawsuit. While I had had two experiences in "court," I really knew nothing of procedures for court filings, briefs, motions, responses, subpoenas, or affidavits.

The bookkeeping aspect was tedious, but as long as I was going to persevere and do it correctly and then keep it correct and current, I might as well follow through on all the other recordkeeping loose ends as well.

I was really going to get things up to snuff. Johnny-on-the-spot.

First, I wanted to get my money back from Vokal. They'd been holding money of mine for about a year and half. I wanted it returned.

In early December 2011, in a phone conversation with Phil, I mentioned to him that I couldn't find any record of my Notification System ("Localized Reminder System") patent application. I asked if he would mind sending me a copy, or if he had back in 2010, would he mind sending me another copy?

He said he would do that shortly, but it didn't happen.

In mid-December, I made another verbal request for the information about both the patent application and the lawsuit receipts or court filing information or whatever it was that I was supposed to have, and Phil said that it would be forthcoming.

But, it wasn't.

On about the 20th, I made another verbal request, and I was once again told that it would be sent over to me. That meant the magic of the internet via an email with an attachment. Although I had never sent an attachment at that time, I was becoming, ever so slowly, comprehending of certain high-tech lingo and its' intents.

The email did not come.

In addition to teaching college level English, my son, Peter, is also a playwright. I began suggesting to him, "What if I never received the information that I sought? What could be made of that? Why wouldn't the person in question give up the information? What kind of a mystery story or mind-bender could this be? Did I only think I had a patent application and a lawsuit? Was I dreaming it? Was I out of touch with reality in toto? Was I living in a dream world? Franz Kafka?"

At any rate, Peter and I playfully kicked around various ideas and concepts to try to create something out of the vagueness of the oblique responses that Phil gave to my requests. I knew that Peter would not take what I was suggesting as an idea because when the creative process exists, my experience has been that it exists in an isolated form and cannot attach to the ideas of others in a conscious state of mind. If something is the idea of someone else, then the creative process does not allow for it to be pursued because it would be untrue to itself. Many is the time that people have suggested to me that I should make a "this or that." While I might well have responded that it sounded like a great idea, I really couldn't make it or become involved because I did not create it. Instead of taking someone else's idea and making it, one might as well buy a book with a title (if there isn't already one), "Creativity: Making Someone Else's Ideas Into Your Own... Drawings and Plagiarisms Included."

Peter was in the same boat with me. If it were to be a play, I'd have to write it.

On Thursday, December 22nd, I had gone the half a block down the street to Michael and Lene's home to have dinner, break my isolation, help them with a few holiday chores, and visit. We had dinner, and the granddaughters were upstairs preparing for whatever they were preparing for. I think school was still in session, so they were probably doing their homework while we three adults sat at the kitchen table talking. There was a knock on the front door.

It was Phil, and he had his two-year-old son, Asa, cradled in the crook of his arm. We welcomed them in, having no idea why they had come.

Phil began, while he looked at Asa, "Can you say 'Wendell?' 'Wendell?' Can you say 'Wendell?'"

Asa responded as best he could, which was pretty good, and said the name. Phil looked at him with pleasure and then at us. It was not the first time I'd heard the youngster say my name. Phil usually had him do this when he was with Asa and I was nearby. Sometimes, and rather cutely, Asa would announce me on first sight without being prompted.

"I wanted to get you something for Christmas," he said, as he looked at me, "and I wasn't sure what. Then I came across this in the store the other day, and I thought, 'Ah, yes, that's what he'd like.'"

He pulled from the lapel pocket of his leather motorcycle jacket a small wrapped gift and gave it to me. I opened it then and saw a pair of somewhat unusual looking gloves.

"Gloves that you can use in the colder weather that have a particular sensitivity in the fingertips. Now you can use your iPhone in the winter without getting your hands cold," he said.

The gloves were red and black. I thanked him for the thoughtful gift, and there was a minute or two of small talk before he and Asa left.

I thought the gift probably had something to do with not fulfilling my requests for copies of my information. Giving or receiving Christmas gifts to or from the Pippengers, or Phil, was not something I would ever have thought of.

The year ended on a high note with our family Christmas Eve dinner hosted by Lene and Michael. Lene spends the day cooking a dinner for fourteen of us while Michael helps out by socializing. Lene makes a traditional Danish dinner with all of the trimmings. There is a large roast of pork, specially cut at the Swedish butcher shop in Chicago, which, when roasted, has half an inch of chewy, crunchy, delicious fat covering the meat. There are two roasted ducks. There are browned potatoes with a sweet caramel liquid coating, which is to be spooned or ladled out of the pan, and there are browned potatoes without the sauce. There is salad, and there are vegetables and a sour beet sauce to go with the pork.

For dessert, there is the traditional Danish rice pudding and cherry sauce, with a large quantity of broken, halved, and only slightly broken almonds mixed in the pudding. "Would anyone like to dress up their dessert with some fresh made whipped cream?" Lene says.

Among all of the broken almonds is one unbroken one. After a huge and delicious meal, the pudding, has to be eaten until one lucky person finds the whole almond in their mouth. This sometimes requires second, or even third, helpings, with all of the jokes and laughter that accompany this type of "punishment." That lucky almond recipient is given a prize, a table game of some sort which a few courageous members of the family then begin to play.

Some of us attempt valiantly to ambulate outdoors for a short walk, while others do various things, none of which require any quick movement. I generally sit, gently rubbing my stomach in small circles and asking myself, as I moan quietly, why I don't have more self-control.

Of course, included with the holiday dinner has been an array of drinks of choice.

Resolutions would be made in a week and others would be found in January.

27
The Titantic Hits Something

Uh-oh . . . Phil had a baluster from his stairwell break, fall out, or do something or other, and he wondered, in early January 2012, if he could borrow my lathe.

On January 5th, I sent Phil an email:

"Hi P,

Is your garage heated? If not, you can use my basement. I have to clean up some first, so get back to me on this.

Also, can you send me that notification system patent information, please? Thanks, W"

The next day, I sent him another email:

"P, ... also, are you coming to do lathe work?

And, can you send me a copy of the patent application? Thanks, W"

He then sent me a response:

"Hey W, ... On the other stuff, yep, I'd love to do some lathing this weekend if you're available, and we can move it to my garage for the day to avoid junking up your basement and air ducts with wood dust, and on the app, I'll get that off the home PC this evening as well. See you! P"

Phil came to my home that Sunday and did his lathing for the baluster. I had cleaned up the basement and made room for him to work freely. Also, since I had worked a number of hours preparing the basement to once again be used for some lathe work, I mentioned to Phil that since we each do different things for each other, I considered that I had contributed equally with what I had done for him in return for his pro bono work for me. He agreed.

More than a week later, on January 16th, I send another email to Phil:

"Hey P,

Can you send me that patent application file?

You're too young to be acquiring the attributes of my brain.

I knew this was gonna be about somethin' as soon as I typed in your address. W"

That same evening Phil responded:

"Hey W,

No, I'm not going senile yet. I have it on my second laptop next to me and I'm trying to locate the charger so I can boot 'er up (we filed with a nonpublication request, so its not online or else I would just grab it there). Anyway, if I can't find a suitable charger here tonight I'll grab one from the office tomorrow. P"

As the fulfillment of my requests continued to not happen, I sent another email. On January 18th, I said:

"P, Did you get your laptop charged? W"

No response, once again, so I began taking things into my own hands to try to solve the problem. I sent Phil the following email on January 20th:

"Hey P,

I'm tryin' to find out something about the suit against Vokal. Like when it might come to court. I went to the circuit court site and tried entering, 'Thomas & Sons, Inc.,' and got nothing. Then I tried 'Vokal Interactive,' and got nothing. The site says they can bring up the info if I give them the name. Do you have a number for the case?

I know a gal who works in the clerk's office (Dorothy Brown). Should I try to call her to get some info? Or am I at the wrong court?

Also, the patent stuff, please. I think the USPTO usually gives some kind of filing number along with the date if my memory serves me correctly.

I'll pick up a charger for you if you need one. Just tell me the model number.

I really want to get this stuff in my files.

I had a, 'not too good,' blood test and I don't want loose ends hangin' around. Thanks, W"

My exasperation grew. I was in the position of needing to haul the very heavy fish onboard the very small rowboat that I was in, without tipping the boat over. I didn't want to flounder any longer, and at the same time, I didn't want to become accusatory and be a bad neighbor, friend, and client to someone in whom I had built a good amount of trust. Or, someone in whom I wanted to have a good amount of trust.

On January 22nd, I found a rough draft of my patent application on my computer by hunting out some of the history that computers carry and was able to print it out. While it was not the actual application, it did provide some solace that at least I had something. When I thought about it, I realized that Michael and Peter would each have a copy of the same thing somewhere on their computers.

Phil and I talked, and he said he was going to have everything to me on Tuesday, January 24th, when his computer returned from the repair shop. It turned out he had to take his computer to PC Solutions, the fix-it people.

It did seem a bit odd to me that Hilleory, out of the blue, would tell Michael and Lene at a Christmas party that Phil had taken his computer in to PC Solutions to get it fixed. But then I thought, "Who knows?" and shrugged my mental shoulders.

In the meantime, Peter and I spoke on the phone, going over different scenarios for the play I envisioned. Why would a lawyer do this to a client? Why string someone along? Was he stringing me along? Is there something going on, or am I just insecure and I going off the deep end?

This Phillip Pippenger episode, though, did not really seem to be a case of me running off the deep end.

Tuesday arrives, and while he did not send the information I wanted, Phil did send an email:

"W, the PC Solutions guys are awesome—too bad they don't do app development huh? Anyway, I've got all my data transferred over to my new computer and also on a backup external drive, and I've been going through it tonight putting everything in its proper folder, killing redundant files, etc. I've got all your materials as well, and I'll put those on a disc or email depending on how big the final collection is. I've got some agreement drafts, letter drafts, and things like that that you may want to have as well. I have to turn back to an application I'm filing tonight, but will shoot/bring your stuff over to you tomorrow.

I'll give you a call tomorrow as well, I wanted to go over a few strategy items.

Alright, talk to you soon, P"

I had no idea what strategy he was talking about, but I was glad to know that I would be getting my information the next day.

I was getting to be Phil's best email client, I was sure, because on January 25th, I sent him another email:

"…Please send (unless you put it on a disc…disk?…) the court "stuff" and the patent application 'stuff.'"

Ah, what a relief to receive his response at 10:51 that same night:

"Hey Wendell, just wanted to scoop up a few of the word drafts before I sent, here are the patent docs attached. I'm also gathering some agreement drafts, not sure if you have a file for those or not.

I am sorting out my litigation files for everybody to the right folders, and then will send those as well.

As far as strategy, its probably too late to call right now but maybe we can talk in the morning if you're available (say 10 or so?). We have a little movement in the case, so wanted to discuss with you.

As far as Bolder Image, we should talk to them and get whatever we can before talking to IRS etc., so we should plan to get together and call them next week given that time table..."

After six weeks of waiting, nudging, cajoling, wishing, and wondering, I finally had it. I was so relieved, I didn't bother to look through the patent application itself because I had just printed it out from my own computer a few days prior.

I took a brief look at the USPTO Electronic Acknowledgement Receipt, which Phil had also attached, and was pleased.

So I went to bed that night, reassured and a little contrite for having doubted Phil and making fun of the situation with Peter. And generally for being wimpy, for feeling threatened when nothing was, in fact, wrong.

Of course there wasn't... was there?

28
The Ship Shudders

The next morning, Thursday, January 26th, Phil and I had a phone conversation. The "strategy" that Phil mentioned and wanted to work out had to do with Vokal.

Phil had received a phone call from the Cook County Circuit Court Clerk's Office letting him know that the judge handling the Vokal lawsuit wanted to have a meeting with Phil.

Our phone conversation flowed something like this:

"I got a call from the clerk's office," Phil said, "and the judge wants to meet with me *ex parte*."

"What are you talking about? The judge wants to what?" I asked.

"He wants to meet with me *ex parte*," he said.

"What is *ex parte*?" I asked, never having heard the term.

"Oh," he said, "*ex parte* is when you meet with a judge on your own, just the two of you."

"So, what does he want to meet with you about?" I asked.

"Your Vokal suit, of course," he said.

"Is this how it usually goes with something like this?" I asked.

"Not usually," he said. "Actually, I've never had an *ex parte* meeting with a judge before, and to tell you the truth, I'm kind of excited."

"Is there something I should do?" I asked.

"Not really," he said. "The meeting is scheduled for tomorrow afternoon in the judge's chambers. I'll give you a call about it when I get home."

"Okay," I said, not knowing quite what was going on, "and just so you know, I have a tennis match tomorrow night, and I have to leave the house before six. If I don't hear from you before I leave, I'll call you when I get home. Or, why don't you call me at like, say, nine-thirty. I should be home and settled by then."

"Okay," he said.

As the day was fresh and I had a tennis match set for the next evening, and with Phil to call with the judge's information, I felt like things were turning more positive. I didn't know what the judge might say, but I wasn't worried. I remembered how convincing Phil had been with his opinion about the case being "a piece of cake." Maybe Vokal had gone to the judge and asked if they could settle. I had no idea, really, how any of this court stuff worked, and I didn't have much interest in finding out. Phil knew how things worked, and that's why I had hired him.

With my comfort level restored and some time on my hands, I went back to Phil's email from the night before and downloaded the attachment from the USPTO. It was the receipt.

I printed it out.

As I looked at it, I could see it was a standard USPTO receipt. Kind of. There was something that looked a bit odd to me. Maybe it was my printer.

A USPTO Electronic Acknowledgement Receipt is printed out on letter-sized paper. The receipt has a rectangular border, within which is one centered vertical line and about fifteen horizontal lines, spaced unevenly, that go across the width of the bordered paper.

There were small specks that looked like someone might have taken a quill pen with ink and made tiny dots here and there on the form. As I looked more closely at the form, I thought I could see that the border lines and intersecting lines were sometimes smudged, with one horizontal line appearing to have a duplicate line tapering off on either end and beyond the vertical border line.

The whole sheet had a fuzzy-looking appearance to me.

Our government does a lot of bungling and mangling. Yet, in other ways there is a great deal of precision and efficiency. One of the precise ways that the government performs is in the presentation of its forms. When the government creates a form, however long the behind-the-scenes work might take, it's done with precision.

The form I was looking at looked sloppy at best: lines that didn't meet, lines that overlapped, smudges on a report, and a general grey appearance to what I would normally expect to be crisp and white.

I called Michael and, luckily, caught him at home. I asked if I couldn't beg a couple of minutes for me to hurry over and show him this to get his "take" on it. I didn't tell him any of the particulars I was wondering about.

When I arrived, I got straight to the point, not wanting to interrupt what was probably his usual day of appointments, email responses, phone calls, and whatnot. Busier than me, that's for certain.

Michael looked at it and then at me. "So what's the question?" he asked.

"Does this look okay to you?" I asked.

"What do you mean?"

"Well look at it. Is there anything about it that looks odd? Does this look legit to you? Phil sent it last night, and I just printed it out, and there's something that just doesn't look right. It looks messy. What do you think? Look at all the smudges. Something's wrong," I said.

He looked at it again and said, "I can't see that something's wrong with it. I see what you're saying, but I can't tell if there is actually anything wrong with it."

I thanked him and left to walk the half a block back home, thinking there was something he just wasn't seeing.

The rest of the day went smoothly, as I worked on one project or another. I still had a number of irons in different fires and probably my biggest concern, now that I had the patent submission information and the lawsuit information that would come to light tomorrow, was what to do about finding a developer to wrap up the Bolder Image snafu/rip-off.

In my mental wanderings and Internet searches, I had come across a site called, "Elance." The company supplied names of programmers, freelance developers, and ostensible experts in all kinds of high-tech electronic and computer fields.

I got in touch with Stephen Barclay, one of Call-Em-All's founders, and he said he would assist me in interviewing anyone I thought might be a good fit to finish up the work I needed done. Stephen might be genetically predisposed toward computers and their applications. Much of his family has been involved in computer systems for two or three generations now. In fact, his uncle was involved early in the space program, coordinating communications with NASA's astronauts. Stephen comes from the same seed, and is absolutely honest to boot.

This was how I was came to hire Michael Frederick, our great programmer, with interviewing help from Stephen, after I found Michael's listing on Elance.

Friday morning faded to afternoon, and then to an early dinner, as I prepared to head halfway to downtown during rush hour for my tennis match. I once read a first-person story about a famous tennis player who had won a number of national doubles championships, and a number of the top world tournament matches, with his partner. In the article, while he mentioned having played thousands of sets in hundreds of tennis tournaments, he could only recall four sets that he had played error-free.

Of course, I never do play error-free or even up to my expectations.

The truth is that sometimes I make a good shot. More often I do not. As I get older and play less, my game gets worse. Instead of waiting for the ball with poise, I often reach while in motion just trying to get my racquet on the damn thing. How could my team lose when we are quite obviously better? Sometimes, when we rotate partners, my team loses again. "What's goin' on here," I'll think to myself. "These guys doin' this on purpose? Messin' with my head?"

Of course, they're not. Of course, it's just me not quite willing to accept the ability that I have. Or rather, the ability I am playing with at the moment. In my mind, I'm almost always much better than I just played. Then I can't wait to go back for more. "So, when are we playing again?" I say, as the matches end, and I've been given a drubbing.

The drive home after tennis was usually about tennis. On this Friday night, though, other thoughts came to mind. It wouldn't be too long now, and I would have the second of my "urgencies of late" resolved, i.e., knowing what the judge had said regarding my case. I hoped the judge had told Phil that the other side just wants to pay what we're seeking, realizing they made mistakes they hadn't previously been willing to admit.

I got home at around 9:20 p.m. There was no message on the machine. I had a snack and waited for the phone to ring. I sat around, doing nothing special, particularly nothing that would require any kind of commitment on my part. When the phone did not ring by 10 o'clock, I decided I'd wait until 10:10 p.m. and then give Phil a call.

I called him and the gist of the conversation was as follows.

"Hello," I said.

"Hey Wendell. I didn't know if you were home."

"I am," I said.

"How was the tennis?" Phil asked.

"Oh, my usual. I just didn't play as well as I wanted to. On the other hand, I never do. I'm really a Wimbledon champion just layin' in the weeds. You know, I don't want to frighten anybody," I said.

"So, did you talk with the judge?" I asked.

"Yeah, I did. It went really well. We talked for a few minutes about lawyers and judges, and then a little bit about some famous court cases. Actually, he was a pretty cool guy. I'm glad I had the chance to…" he said, and I cut in.

"What was his name?" I asked.

"Oh, yeah. His name. It was Randy Stevenson," he said.

"Stevenson?" I repeated, as I wrote the name on a scratch pad.

"Yeah, he was." Phil started out, but I cut him off again.

"What did he say?" I asked.

My six or eight weeks of waiting not-so-patiently was starting to show.

"Oh, you mean about your case?" he asked.

"Yeah, what did he say?" I asked.

"Oh, yeah," he said. "But here's the thing."

I could picture the judge sitting in his chambers, wearing his black robe. Recessed to his right is the dark engraved woodwork encasing his window, which has a crank for opening. The panes on the glass are small and diamond shaped. There are many of them, a Tudor-style window. The afternoon sunlight is streaking through, shooting rays of sunlight into the dark room. I imagine two leather couches sitting on a large oriental carpet that lies in front of his mahogany desk. There are a couple of large glass ashtrays sitting in wells of the brass ashtray holders that stand about eighteen inches tall near the arm of each couch. The judge and certain of his select cronies, some of whom are lawyers, oft-times enjoy a late afternoon bourbon and an expensive cigar.

Phil continued, "Like I said, he was a really cool guy, actually. I liked him. I mean, that kind of surprised me. He wasn't stuffy at all.

"What he said was, actually, for one thing, he thought your idea and how it came about was really cool. I mean, you know, he was impressed by what you're trying to do.

"And then what he said was that he didn't really think that you had a lawsuit here. He said, 'I'm sorry, but your elderly client doesn't really have a lawsuit in this situation because he stayed with Vokal for too long. If he had stopped using them when they didn't complete the work on time and then filed a lawsuit, he would have had a case. As it is though, he simply stayed with them for too long a time.'

"So that's what Judge Stevenson concluded," Phil said.

It took about a nanosecond for all of this to register with me.

I was leaning against the doorjamb that leads into my kitchen from the front room.

I fumed.

I yelled into the phone. "Well, fuck that son of bitch! This is a bunch of bullshit. I sure as fuck do have a case!"

And I went on.

"This is Chicago bullshit! Somebody got to that bastard. This is a fix. I'll tell you what. I'm not gonna take this kind of crap. I'm gonna go to the media about this bullshit. I'm gonna get some fucking attention!"

Phil came back right away with, "Now, wait a minute. There're other solutions. This doesn't mean it's the end of the line with this. We can submit it to another judge and see what he says. This doesn't have to be final."

"You were gonna give me the docket number for the case. Do you have that?" I said.

"No, actually, I couldn't find it. I know I've got it here somewhere. I'll find it, really," he said

"I don't want to start shopping a lawsuit around to see which judge is gonna take it. If one doesn't take it, then that's the deal. I'm not shopping. You said it was cut and dried. 'A piece of cake.' This is a fix. Somebody got to that bastard, I can tell you that," I said. I was no longer yelling.

Phil said, "Okay, we'll do something. But don't go to the media tonight, okay? Why don't I come over to your house in the morning, if that's all right. I'll come over, say, at ten, tomorrow, and we can talk about it. Just tell me that you're not going to the media tonight. Let's talk about it in the morning. We'll get this worked out. Would that be okay?"

"Yeah, okay, I guess. We'll talk about it," I said.

I had no plans for that night, at that hour, on trying to call any of the media people I know. And I do know some people who can make waves if they choose. They carry a lot of weight.

Phil went on, leading me into a conversation about morals and morality and how he doesn't do things to get rich and how he doesn't want to be that way and how he knows people like that and he doesn't respect them.

We got off the phone at about 10:30 or 10:40 and I sat up for a while, hating that son of a bitch, Judge Randy Stevenson.

29
Listing and Sinking

I didn't sleep soundly that Friday night. For months, I had been trying to deal with one inept developer after another. Of necessity, I was dealing in a field I knew nothing about, just trying to turn a simple, straightforward idea into reality. An easy description, a contract, payments, and, yet, no satisfactory product had come of it. I continued eating into monies I had saved for retirement. Of course, I was the one making the decisions on how to spend the money; nobody was twisting my arm to take the path I had chosen.

I still believed in the idea and that it would help reduce various costs throughout the healthcare industry, if I could find a way to expose the product to potential consumers. It remained a win-win hypothetical situation. The obvious downside was if it was a complete failure and did not benefit anyone, including, of course, myself.

Now, to make matters worse, I had run into a bum of a judge who was most likely being paid off by somebody. This was a dirty deal.

So I lay in bed, tossing and turning.

Sometimes at night, while I laid in bed, when my sons were still at home and quite a bit younger, I would have what I call "night thoughts." I might lie there, and for some reason unknown to me, a dark thought would pass through my mind. It might be a thought that one of my kids was in a dangerous situation, an illness, say, or an automobile accident, or some other infernal occurrence. In these night thoughts, I was always in the position of not being able do anything or change anything. I knew, of course, that nothing had really taken place and that

111

my son would be home pretty soon, safe. Yet, the dark fear would persist, and the story line of what could happen would continue. It was like a large, dark shroud covering me, and I couldn't shake it off.

Night thoughts set in this night, thoughts of the judge, Vokal, and the recent firing of Bolder Image for their lack of performance and questionable ethics.

On Saturday, long before the first morning light began to appear, I was out of bed, had brushed my teeth, dressed, and was making coffee.

I realized that I had a friend who was habitually up early and who happened to be an attorney. I jumped in my car with my to-go cup of coffee and headed toward his home in the hope of seeing his kitchen light on, which would mean that he was up and about. When I arrived, sure enough, from the alley I could see him standing at the sink. I approached the back door and knocked gently. He was surprised to see me and motioned for me to come in quietly, as his wife was still asleep.

I quickly explained about my next door neighbor and yesterday's *ex parte* meeting with the judge.

My friend told me right off that this sounded fishy. He said that judges don't usually have an *ex parte* meeting with an attorney in a situation like mine. He then suggested looking on the Internet for this particular judge. He had never heard of him, he said, which didn't mean that he didn't work in the Cook County Circuit Court. My friend handled many lawsuits and had for years, so he thought it a little unusual that he had not heard this particular judge's name before. He also suggested I do myself a favor and have a witness present when Phil showed up for our 10:00 a.m. meeting.

As I was leaving, he wished me "Good luck," but with raised eyebrows, meaning he was skeptical of the situation and the guy I was dealing with. Daylight was just breaking as I headed home.

I parked in the garage, went into my kitchen, had another cup of coffee, and decided to wait quietly for Michael at his house. I went there, let myself in, removed my shoes, and tiptoed to the kitchen to wait for him to come down.

He was surprised to see me, of course, and after assurances that, yes, I was okay, I told him I needed him to be at my house by 9:45 a.m. this same morning.

He said he could do that, and I went home.

I looked up the names of judges on the site of the Clerk of the Circuit Court, Cook County, Illinois. There was no Randy Stevenson listed. There was no Randall Stevenson listed. There was no Randy Stephenson. There was no Randall Stephenson listed.

I am a bit hard of hearing, so I generally give the benefit of the doubt to the other party when there is a disagreement about what had been said. In this case, even though I was quite certain that I had distinctly heard Phil say Randy Stevenson, there was always the possibility of error on my part. Having just had my doubts assuaged with regard to the USPTO documents, I thought it best to give Phillip some leeway again. It might be something very innocent, and I didn't want to damage my relationship with Phil by making what might turn out to be off-the-wall accusations or insinuations.

I got off the Cook County site and fiddled around a bit, waiting for Michael to arrive.

Michael arrived at my back door right at 9:45 a.m., and Phillip showed up at the front door at about ten.

Phil was in his customary attire: unbuttoned white shirt hanging down well below his waist and white tee-shirt, untucked, that occasionally reached below his belt.

Michael and I were hanging out in the kitchen, so that's where I directed Phil.

Phil was a little surprised to see Michael, but there was no scene.

I sipped my coffee as we made small talk for a minute or two, and then Phil opened up the conversation he was there for.

"Well, it's a good news/bad news thing," he said, and briefly looked at Michael and myself and then back at the counter where he fidgeted with the coffee mug he had brought with him. "The good news is, I found the docket number for our case against Vokal. The bad news is that the number the clerk gave me for the case is a nonexistent number. I just found that out this morning from a friend."

I said, "No-no-no. What are you saying? Are you saying the court gave you a case number or docket number or whatever it's called and it was no good?"

"That's right," he said. "I've been scammed. The clerk's office scammed me."

"No," I said. "That's not right, Phil. You're saying the Cook County Clerk of the Court gave you a phony case number?"

"Yeah," he said. "That's what happened."

"No, Phil," I said, "this isn't right. This isn't the truth. C'mon tell the truth, man."

"This is the truth," he said.

Michael and I periodically caught each other's eye as the conversation unfolded. Neither of us showed expression.

"Do you have a receipt?" I asked.

"No," Phil said. "I often don't keep receipts when I file a case."

There was a lull of about ten seconds. Phil was standing there big as life. He didn't look like he was insane, but his story wasn't making any sense at all.

Phil said, "The other thing is, I found out the judge I met with yesterday was an imposter."

I said, "What? No, Phil, I mean wait a minute. What are you saying? Are you saying that the judge you met with in the judge's chambers was an imposter?"

114

"That's right," he said.

I said, "No, Phil, this isn't the truth. C'mon, man, tell the truth. What's going on? I mean, this stuff you're saying just isn't true."

"It is the truth," he said.

Michael was quiet this whole time. I stood still, as did Phil. He was looking down at the counter.

I said, "Do you have the docket number? You said you'd have the docket number."

He said, "Yeah," and I wrote down on a scrap of paper that I had on my kitchen counter, "2010-1-5199," as he gave those numbers to me.

I later recalled that in my ignorance about the court system, when I repeated the numbers back to Phil, I said each number individually. I later learned that the "2010" was actually the reference to the year in which the case was filed.

"This is the number?" I asked, as I showed him what I had written.

"Yeah, that's it," he said.

Michael and I were sitting on kitchen stools, and Phil was standing. His head was tipped down towards the counter.

"Phil," I said, "I think I'm gonna have to get another attorney to handle this lawsuit. I'd be better off doing that, I think."

With head still bent, almost inaudibly, he said, "I don't blame you."

Shortly thereafter, Phil left and Michael and I stayed on in the kitchen. It wasn't as though we had to catch our breath from a hard game of basketball or a series of wind sprints. It was more like a fog had settled in and you really had to focus on things to discern what they were. Neither of us felt any need to get emotional about what had just taken place.

Quietly, so as not to disturb the mood, I said, "Wow. Holy cannoli. What do you think about that?"

Michael said, "Unbelievable. Just unbelievable.

"It's like he came over here with this idea in mind to pull this off on you. And then I'm sitting here, and he doesn't have the ability to change his plan or alter his story. He was fixated on doing this. You know, Dad, you've told me many times how bright you think he is. You say, 'exceptionally bright.' You don't say 'genius', but you come close.

"But I have to tell you, Dad, in my opinion, every time I see him and he opens his mouth, he gets dumber and dumber."

Where the hell have I been? I thought.

It's always been a source of pride to be able to look to my sons for their insights and their honesty. This was another case in point.

It was now about 10:30 a.m., Saturday, January 28, 2012.

30
Deeper Down

By 11:00 a.m., I had driven back to my attorney-friend's home to give him the low-down on what happened with Phil and to show him the copy of the acknowledgement receipt from the patent office that looked odd to me.

It didn't take long to tell the story, and he looked at me and just shook his head.

"I'll tell you this," he said, "If the ARDC heard this, they'd have him on the psychiatrist's couch in about two minutes. This is unbelievable. He's off his nut.

"Does he do drugs? He must do drugs or something."

"No," I said, "he doesn't do drugs. I guarantee you he doesn't. I don't even think he drinks. Maybe he has a beer once in a while, I'm not sure. He's not a drinker though, I'll put it that way. What's the 'ACDC' or whatever it is you said?"

"Oh, it's called the ARDC; it stands for Attorney Registration and Disciplinary Commission. All lawyers are registered with the commission. Every state has its own. They oversee what we do, with rules and regulations. You've heard of the Bar Association. It's the bar, basically. Essentially, they punish lawyers who violate the rules."

"You mean for stuff like this?" I asked.

"Yeah, for stuff like this, except this is crazy," he said.

"And here, look at this," I said and handed him the copy of the receipt.

He looked at it and asked, "Is this some kind of receipt from the patent office?"

117

"Yeah," I said, "it's what Phil sent me a few days ago, and it doesn't look right to me. What do you think?"

He scanned it and asked, "What's wrong with it?"

"I don't know," I said. "It just doesn't look right. Here," and I ran my finger up and down the page, "look at the smudges. Like a mist of ink on the page. And, look at the way the lines at this corner don't meet. This all looks odd to me."

He looked some more and then said, "I can't tell that something's wrong with it. You know, computers and printers don't always work the way we want them to. Especially if it's important," and he laughed. "Sometimes, we just get a bad copy on an email or on an attachment. This was an attachment, right?"

"Yeah, it was," I said.

"I really can't tell that something's wrong with it," he said. "It could just be a bad copy."

We talked some more on much lighter topics, taking turns trying to one-up the other with some pithy philosophical point about society or people. It's a regular thing we do, each attempting a humorous slant on some current event. While we don't keep a score card, it does sometimes get pretty competitive. If asked, I would say that I probably come out on top and he would certainly say the same of himself. So, maybe it's a draw, with me being just slightly ahead.

When I got home, I called Michael to get the phone number of a friend of his who is a lawyer. Perhaps his friend would be interested in taking on the case. Instead, Michael said he would make the call and get back to me, which he did.

It was good luck for me as it seemed, at first blush, that his friend Chris Gibbons would take on the work that I had just fired Phil from. Chris was home when I called, but just on his way out. He said I happened to live in the direction he was going, and he would stop over to hear the situation.

When Chris arrived, we had a coffee, and I filled him in on the situation with Vokal, and that I thought they owed me a reimbursement. On the surface, he said it did sound like I had a potential lawsuit. I gave Chris the information about Phil and where his office was and that I had told him I was going to get other counsel to handle the Vokal lawsuit. Chris ended by saying he would be able to pick up any information Phil might have at his office on Monday.

It sounded pretty good to me. I had gone from the frying pan into the fire and then back out again. I have known Chris since he was a youngster and a playmate of Michael's, and they have remained friends since. In fact, dear friends.

Before Chris left, I did want one more thing from him besides his commitment to take on the lawsuit. I wanted him to look at the USPTO Electronic Acknowledgement Receipt and give his opinion as to its authenticity.

I asked him to look at it, and I said no more. He looked it over, and then he looked at me, as he slightly shrugged his shoulders.

"So," he said, "what about it?"

"Do you think it looks kind of odd?" I asked.

"No. I don't get what you mean. It's a patent office receipt, right?"

"Yeah, it is," I said. "But look at it. Look at how it looks like there's tiny ink dots all over the place. And look how those two lines," as I now had my finger on the page to show him, "don't even meet. I mean, this is a government form. They're gonna have the lines meet on one of their forms. C'mon."

"You know, Wendell, sometimes you get a bad copy as an attachment or the printer is smudging one thing or another. I mean, I have this kind of thing happen from time to time, and I'm on the computer most of the day. It happens. I can't really say that there's anything wrong with this. It might just be a bad transfer. This stuff isn't always perfect, you know."

We left it at that and Chris took off for wherever he was headed.

I was left with myself, and my mind was jumping around a bit.

I had waited for more than a year to get my money back from Vokal, and now I had to start all over again. At least I knew Chris would do a good job. But what had happened to Phil? Did he flip out this past week? I knew he didn't do drugs. Or at least I thought I knew. Maybe he needed a break. Was he having a walking breakdown? Where'd he come up with all that stuff? What's he doing? He needed something. But now, okay, Chris would take care of it. It's all going to work out. What the hell happened with Phil?

Jesus.

I probably did some house cleaning in the afternoon, or maybe I went to the local YMCA where I'd been a member for most of the past sixty-five years. I was pretty diligent about my exercise, always feeling better when it was over. So much of my youth was spent playing sports that exercise was just a part of life by now.

Early Saturday evening, I found an email from Phil, sent that afternoon:

"Wendell, there IS [sic] an action, and I didn't have it, looks from the mailing date that it probably got through Leydig's docketing around the time I left on my 2wks notice. At any rate, no drop dead but we should respond in the next few weeks (by 2/16). I am attaching a first pdf that includes from the top (1) the latest action, (2) our claims and arguments and (3) the earlier office action.

As you can see from the first action in the pdf, we overcame the first rejection—the initial patent Shourek is no longer an asserted reference. However, the Examiner has asserted new art instead, in a 103 combination. These patents, Chen and Shavitz, are attached. As you can see, neither has all the features of the invention, and even combined they would not meet the limitation of the claims. For example, neither meets the limitation that "the open cart is flat" i.e., no protrusion under the carried item. See the lip in Cheng that carries the item, without which Cheng would not function.

If you're available tonight or tomorrow, we should discuss how to respond.

Best, Phil"

I read the email again. Then, I read it a third time.

In the email, he said, "At any rate, no drop dead but we should respond in the next few weeks (by 2/16)."

The notice of the office action by the USPTO was a notice of Final Rejection status for my patent application for the Folding Cart, and February 16th was just nineteen days away.

I had been ignorant about many things to do with the filing of patent applications and ignorant about many other things in life, it's true. But one thing that I was aware of, because I'd been in this situation before, was that when the USPTO gave an office action that was the notice of a "Final Rejection" status of an application, the applicant then had a time limit to respond. The time limit was five months from the date of the notice.

When I counted backwards, I figured out that the "Final Rejection" notice had been issued on September 16, 2011. Now, here it was January 28, 2012, and Phil is telling me that this notice somehow slipped through some cracks?

Cracks in what? I had some questions!

Somehow, Leydig had not given Phil the notice that would have been sent directly to him from the USPTO? If Leydig, Voit & Mayer had received the notice, somehow his secretary, Susan, would not have given the notice to Phil? Somehow, Susan would not have put the letter on his desk? Somehow, she would not have forwarded the email to Phil? Somehow, the notice was sent to someone other than Phil?

Somehow, the USPTO knew that Phil was leaving Leydig so they sent the information to Leydig with the hope that the firm would have the good sense to give it to someone who might take responsibility for this? Somehow, Leydig had intercepted Phil's emails from the USPTO because this is the way they did business?

This was all a little much.

Something had definitely gone awry with my neighbor.

Wait a minute. Maybe he'd just been negligent!

That was it. That was probably it, I think. I mean, that could have been the problem. He was just negligent and embarrassed as hell to tell me about it since the debacle of this morning. Did he even know what he'd done this morning? He's probably overloaded with too many Microsoft applications, or Caterpillar applications. I think he makes trips to Peoria on occasion. Caterpillar might have a gazillion applications a year. Maybe he's really just embarrassed himself.

I muddled over this for an hour or two. There had to be some explanation I wasn't getting, maybe even something pretty obvious was missing.

Phil has a master's degree in Electrical Engineering from Rice University. He has a B.S. in Physics from Wesleyan University and a B.S. in Electrical Engineering from Cal Tech. He has a law degree from Cornell and he's a patent attorney. The writing of patents requires a certain expertise. In my opinion, you have to have some special kind of brain to do that work. I mean, I can write some basic stuff, and I can do some things and create some things and have some ideas, but I could never write up a patent application. Not a good one, anyway.

At about 8:30 that night, I emailed Phil and said that I could meet him on Sunday at the café a couple of blocks from our houses. Better there, I thought, than him coming to my home or me going to his.

I said that anytime would be okay with me.

In the email, I was less than enthusiastic about attempting to overcome the notice from the USPTO. I had a sour taste in my mouth and didn't necessarily want to sit with Phil and ignore what had happened earlier that day, while we tried to work out something together to assure my future success.

I didn't hear back from him on Saturday, and I didn't hear back from him on Sunday.

I left it at that because at this point, I didn't care that much. I wanted the patent, sure, but it's not the easiest thing to overcome a Final Rejection. It seemed to be too much of a long shot. I was satisfied to leave things where they were for the moment and keep Phil at arm's length.

31
The Ship Hits Bottom

With the exception of being inside my head all day, trying to make sense of the situation, Sunday was relatively quiet.

There was one thought, though, that I couldn't shake: that damned electronic receipt from the USPTO just didn't look right. Never mind that everyone I had shown it to was disinclined to see anything odd. Oftentimes, when I have a question about something, I'll run it past one of my friends. I then take in what they say, figuring their perspective might be more accurate or their thinking clearer than mine. This time, it wasn't happening.

That afternoon, I had an epiphany. I could go to Paul Hletko on Monday morning and show him the receipt. Paul was someone I knew; in fact, he had been my patent attorney for my first patent. He would be able to look at it and tell me if it was legit.

I called Michael and asked him to call Paul at home, even though it was a Sunday. Getting Paul's opinion now took on grave importance for me. The questionable receipt had moved to front and center of my mind.

Michael called back and said Paul would be at his distillery in the morning and we could stop by at around 9:00 a.m. This put my mind at ease knowing I might soon have some resolution. I hoped the people who couldn't see anything amiss would turn out to be correct. I wasn't looking for more trouble.

Again, Sunday night, I couldn't get Phillip's behavior out of my thoughts.

I tossed and turned and tried to slow down my mind, but without success

On Monday morning, I got up at about six, once again earlier than usual for me by a couple of hours.

I made coffee and waited for the light, which in late January is well past six. I sat wondering how Paul would view the USPTO receipt. I was still sitting at the kitchen counter, doodling designs on a scrap of paper, when I heard a motorcycle. It was 7:15. Phil didn't usually leave for work until sometime between 9:00 and 10:00. Even in the cold winter months, he would often ride his motorcycle to work if there was no snow on the ground. His engine roared as he gunned it down the alley. He was in some kind of hurry. In the early morning quiet, I could hear him as he took off down South Boulevard, and for several blocks more.

A few minutes later, I realized I had begun fantasizing that Phil's conscience had caught up to him and he was going to do away with himself. I suppose the combination of confusion and lack of sleep over the last three nights was causing my mind to wander this way.

I called Michael at a few minutes past 7:30 a.m. and told him what I was thinking.

"Hey, Dad," he said, "slow down. Nobody's gone anywhere to commit suicide. Forget that. You're projecting."

When Michael said this to me, I understood where these thoughts had come from. If I had been deceiving someone for no reason, someone I had led to trust me, and I didn't own up to the truth, I might feel so ashamed and humiliated that maybe I'd consider ending it all. If I had done what I suspected Phil had done to me, I would have felt morally bankrupt. Probably despondent.

Never mind. Things would work themselves out. Here I was, going off the deep end.

Michael was right about Phil. My own mother committed suicide, but that never entered my mind, at least not right then.

At 8:10 a.m., twenty minutes after my conversation with Michael, the phone rang, and I picked it up.

It was Phil.

"Hi Wendell," he said, "it's Phil."

"Yeah," I said.

"I just wanted to tell you some things," he said. "I wasn't really honest with you about what happened with Vokal."

He paused. Was he going to tell me he had taken a payoff from them and beg my forgiveness?

"I thought maybe that was the case," I said. I waited.

He picked up again and began to explain.

"What happened was that back then, in 2010, the economy was in such bad shape that I really thought they might go out of business if I filed the lawsuit.

"I mean, I know that you wanted your money back and all of that, but I didn't think you'd get it back in court. I mean, I didn't think they had the money."

As Phil talked, I remembered that shortly after I began working with them, Vokal expanded their office space into a whole floor in a heavily secured building. It was probably twice the size of their previous space.

"Here they were," he said, "a few young guys trying to make a go of their ideas for business with high tech development, and they got caught in a downdraft.

"I thought what I'd do is, let the economy pick up a bit and then go after them when they might have stabilized and when things in general were just better."

The more Phil talked, the more my guard went up. I think of myself as a forgiving person, and I don't want to stress other people. I am typically amenable to compromise, even when it favors the other side. Certain things in life are not negotiable, such as matters of a person's character or "substance." The rest I don't care too much about.

"So things have not been recovering as fast as I had hoped, and I've gotten myself into this situation with you, of all people. I really wanted to do what was going to be best for everyone, and now, oh boy," he said, and I could hear his voice start to crack.

I said to myself, *"Don't you dare. Do not say a word."*

Usually, I would respond to someone experiencing an emotionally difficult situation by offering some kind of comfort. I did not want to do that this time, to tell him to forget it, or to say, "Don't worry about it." I preferred not to offer any solace. I wanted him to work out of it on his own.

He went on, and he began to choke and gag as he cried, struggling to speak.

"How I could do this to one of my few friends… in fact my only friend… my best friend," in between sobs.

I kept telling myself, *"Mouth shut."*

Phil gained his composure and began to speak in his normal voice once again. It didn't take him long.

I wondered, never having been to his office, if he had a door and a private office. I imagined him with the door closed, if he had one, sitting in a large swivel chair with his back to what might be the large plate glass rectangles that fronted his office into the hall. I could see, in my mind's eye, someone walking past the office and glancing over without realizing that an emotional upheaval was taking place, because Phil's voice had been fairly quiet throughout the call. I'm sure his modulated weeping would not have been heard through a closed door.

When we hung up, I was left wondering about the economy and Vokal's expansion. I wondered about someone who only has one friend. An "only friend," would have to be, by definition, or at least by logical progression, a "best friend."

What I was left with at the end of the conversation was that I had been able to hold my ground and not cave in to all those years--since childhood--of caretaking. I had stayed within myself and was pleased about that. I allowed Phil to take himself on without covering for him.

I accepted my kudos.

32
Turning Surreal

I was packing some pretty heavy-duty emotions when I went over to pick Michael up at 8:50 for our three-block walk to Paul's distillery, F.E.W.

To name his company, Paul had used the initials of Frances E. Willard, an American temperance leader and educator. She was an Evanston resident and president of the Women's Christian Temperance Union. She lived in the 1800s and was known throughout the world. A statue of this heroine still stands at the United States Capitol Building, a hundred and fifty years later. She was also an early suffragette and a leader in that struggle.

In fact, owing to her influence, Evanston was a "dry" community from her time until sometime in the 1970's, when economic pressures prevailed. Evanston now has bars aplenty.

While Paul makes whiskey and gin, we weren't heading there to get anything more than Paul's knowledge of the patent office and his assessment of the receipt I had concerns about. It was too early in the day to imbibe, anyway.

The phone call from Phil that morning had not made me either more or less concerned about the receipt and its validity.

When we arrived, Paul was at his desk near the huge stainless steel kettle-shaped units used in the distilling process, although, in what way, I do not recall, even though Paul explained it all. Paul is a good and successful distiller and markets his high quality products well, as evidenced by the continued growth in both national and international sales of F.E.W.

Paul was also a hard-working patent attorney, who had been attentive to my back-and-forth with the patent office. I was looking forward to his assessment of this receipt. It was time for the unveiling. Paul started.

"Mike said you have a question about a patent office receipt or something like that," he said, looking at me.

"Yeah, that's what it is. I'm wondering," I said, as I pulled my canvas shoulder bag in front of me and reached in to get the receipt, "if you would look at this electronic receipt and tell me if it looks okay to you."

I handed the receipt to Paul, and he began looking at it. Michael and I stood, waiting.

"What in particular are you wondering about?" he said, looking up.

"Well," I said, "I'm just wondering if it looks okay to you. I mean, is this the kind of receipt you might get from the patent office? It's got a smudge here and there, and it's got those tiny ink dots all over the place. I'm just wondering if you think it looks normal. Everybody I've shown it to says they can't tell anything. I thought you might be able to."

"I'd be in the group with everybody else," he said. "I don't know how the examiner might send the receipt and with what information he might put down. He could be in a rush and leave something out, or the printer might make smudges when the paper is sent through. I can't say that there is something wrong with this. There could be, but there might not be. Either way.

"But, if you're concerned, you could call the examiner."

"How would I know who the examiner would be?" I asked.

He said, "The chances are about ninety-nine percent that the examiner we had when I did your first application would be the same examiner doing this one. He would be familiar with your prior application. That's usually how it works."

I said, "Okay. So I should get the examiner's name from the other application and then try to call him?"

Then, I realized that I might be able to cut that corner.

"Do you think you'd mind calling him?" I asked.

"No, I can't call him because I'm not the attorney on this application, but I can give you his number and you can call," he said.

Paul did something on his computer and then said, "The number is," and as he said it, I wrote it down on my scratch pad.

"Do you mind if I call him from here?" I said. I was already affixing my earbuds to my iPhone.

"Help yourself," he said.

Paul and Michael began conversing, and I began my call.

To my surprise, the examiner, Gerald Gautier, answered the call and even announced his name. I introduced myself and told him the number of the patent application I was calling about.

I said, "I'm concerned about the status of this application, and I'm wondering if you would be able to tell me who the examiner might be."

Gautier responded, "There is no examiner. It hasn't yet been assigned."

I was aware at this point that Michael and Paul had stopped with their conversation and were looking at me.

My mind raced.

"Not assigned yet? How could that be?" I said. "It was submitted in September of 2010. It hasn't been assigned yet?"

I was amazed. I began heating up, although I kept my tone with Mr. Gautier well-modulated. This wasn't right. I was losing years from false assumptions and expectations. Something had gone wrong.

Because of my age and my terminal cancer, I have been given what is referred to at the USPTO as "the fast track." It had been my understanding that my priority status would move any

131

application I submitted through the system much faster than what I was now being told.

Mr. Gautier's voice came through again, "No, I'm sorry, but it was not. It was submitted January 25, 2012."

"Oh, no!" I said. I took a deep breath, while Mr. Gautier remained silent. "Mr. Gautier, would you mind sending me the patent office receipt? Something's going on here."

"Yes," he said, "I could do that."

"Here," I said, "let me give you my email address. This is impossible." I proceeded to give Mr. Gautier my email address, asked him to repeat it back to me, which he did, and thanked him for his help.

I turned to Paul and Michael.

"Pippenger submitted the application last week. He never put it in before. The examiner is going to send me the receipt. Holy shit! That dirty rat!" I said. "What's wrong with him?"

Everybody voiced an opinion about the situation, and all of us also seemed to realize there was nowhere to go with any of the information that we now had. Michael and I thanked Paul, and we wished him well in the new business. He, in turn, wished me well with whatever might be going on.

On the walk back to Michael's, I told him about the phone call that morning, and I told him about Phillip's confession. About Phil's weeping. About his "Oh boy," and his "Here I go," followed by more weeping and gagging.

Fifteen minutes later, I was wandering around in my house, as well as my head. These things had happened, and I had no answers for any of it.

The email from Mr. Gautier had already arrived; I downloaded and printed it. I noticed immediately a number of differences between the authentic receipt and the receipt Phil had given me. They were apparent at first glance. Otherwise, I didn't feel like studying it at that moment.

I had a coffee and sat, looking out of my living room window into the backyard. I have an unusual layout, in that my living room looks into the back of the property instead of toward the street. On the street side of the house are my bedroom on the northwest corner and the den on the street side, or the southwest corner of the house.

It all looked so peaceful in the backyard, with an occasional bird appearing. Otherwise, it had the look of winter. . . quiet. My phone rang.

"Hello?" I said.

It was Phil calling again, at about 11:00 a.m. on Monday, January 30th, only about an hour since my recent discovery about him.

"Hi Wendell," he said, in his normal voice.

"You know, you didn't seem too enthused about overcoming the examiner's Final Rejection of your Folding Cart application, but I think we can do it. So, if it's okay with you, I went ahead and made a phone call appointment to talk with her for tomorrow at ten o'clock, and it would really be good if you would be there for the call. They kind of like to have the inventor participate. It earns you some points.

"I have to call her back with a confirmation. Can you be at my house at ten?"

"No," I said, "I can't make it tomorrow."

"Oh, too bad. Can you make it Wednesday? I could try to make the appointment for Wednesday, if you can make it then," he said.

I thought to myself for a moment. Yeah, for sure I didn't want to be around him, but I did want the patent, even if it meant spending a little time with him.

His vibes had turned negative.

"Yeah," I said, "I could make Wednesday."

"Oh, great!" he said. "I'll call her back and try to set it up for Wednesday at ten o'clock. That's great."

Within the hour, Phil called back and the appointment was set. I would go to Phil's house a couple of minutes before the hour, and then we'd call, each of us using one of his portable phones.

I said nothing to him of my discovery at the patent office regarding his seventeen- or eighteen-month late submission of my application.

It had been a bamboozling long two and a half days.

I recapped the weekend in my mind.

The picture it painted blended with the subtle passages of hues into the fast clashes and stark changes of colors, making a perfect portrait of surrealism. I was there, somewhere in the painting looking for myself, or looking out for myself—it was hard to tell the difference.

I was emotionally and intellectually overwhelmed, and it would take me some weeks to digest what had happened this weekend.

"I wish I had a wall to hang this portrait on," I thought. I rummaged through the clutter of my mind, but I couldn't find any space to hang it.

33
Saying the Right Thing

On Wednesday, February 1, 2012, I went next door to Phil's house, at a few minutes before ten o'clock in the morning, for our joint call to Mrs. Katy Ebner, an examiner at the USPTO. Phil was nervous. Probably for a couple of reasons.

I was sure that the first reason was that he knew what he had done was unacceptable by anyone's standards of decency, and more particularly, for the standards a lawyer would be expected to maintain with a client. My recently acquired awareness that there was a governing body for lawyers, the ARDC, led me to this conclusion, and he was probably afraid he had put himself in jeopardy.

Secondly, he probably hoped to overcome Mrs. Ebner's objections, to put himself back in my good graces. Then again, it wasn't my good graces that he really cared about. If there could be a good outcome to the USPTO call, then maybe I would forget about the other things he had done.

He had done some serious shit to me, and I had to take some time and decide how to respond.

It was complicated. He was my next door neighbor and all. I'd have to do the right thing. To get there, I'd have to mull it over.

At 10:00 a.m., Phil called Mrs. Ebner. She picked up and Phil introduced himself. He said that the inventor was also present, so I took a moment and introduced myself. She asked me a couple of questions about where and how the idea had originated. After I answered, I turned the call over to Phil and turned my receiver off, as it was buzzing and it had been difficult to hear clearly what Mrs. Ebner was saying.

By this time, Phil had emailed the Final Office Action notice to me, and I had been able to look at the objections Mrs. Ebner had raised to issuance. Along with her written assessment, there were two presentations in pictorial form, references to other patents with similarities to my submission.

As I looked at the pictures, I noticed some differences between their carts and what my idea was. The differences were important to me because they were the very reasons my cart was unique.

Phil was going around in circles, unclear in whatever he was trying to say. It didn't sound like he had anything substantial to overcome the objections Mrs. Ebner had given. When he circled around for the third time, I mouthed to Phil that I wanted to talk.

Psychologically, he was in a tenuous position. He didn't want me on the phone, yet he couldn't deny my request. His look expressed his reticence.

I refreshed Mrs. Ebner's memory by stating my name once again and then quickly cut to the chase. I spoke with her for no more than two minutes, as I explained what I considered to be the substantial differences between my cart and the carts she had referenced as objections. When I finished, Mrs. Ebner said, "Oh, I didn't understand that part of your application. You've clarified it. If you can put that," and then she described some USPTO procedure for amending the application that I failed to understand and closed with, "in the amendment, I can issue the patent."

Being certain that Phil had heard me, I said, "We should make a correction in amended form, and then you'll issue the patent?"

She replied, "Yes, then I can issue the patent."

I said, "Thank you, Mrs. Ebner, let me hand the phone over to Mr. Pippenger, so he can understand from you what he is to do."

With that, I got out quickly. The phone call was done and Phil had been instructed as to what he should write in amended form for issuance of the patent.

At home, I realized that I would not be filing ARDC information against Phil until the patent had been issued. I had understood that while a patent was in the issuance stage by the USPTO, the only person who could have the issuance withdrawn was the attorney who had filed the application. I was afraid, of course, that, if I filed anything with the ARDC, Phil might pull the patent or stop it from being issued.

Obviously, I could no longer trust Phillip. He was too adept at speaking not just from both sides of his face, but from the many sides of his many faces.

I felt gratitude, however, toward the USPTO examiner, Mrs. Ebner. She listened and took in what I said about the differences between my application and the patented carts. I appreciated the precision of her concentration, as well as her willingness to accept the differences I pointed out without stubbornly and unduly defending her original position.

I went home, grateful to both Mrs. Ebner and myself.

Now I'd have a few weeks of downtime. Enough time to decide what to do. Time to talk with my family and mull things over with myself.

34
Mulling

As I thought about what Phil had done, I was unable to find any ground that felt comfortable. It didn't feel right to just let the whole thing go.

Every angle I explored left me thinking this was not going to be one of those situations where you just say to yourself, "Oh, to hell with it all," and then forget about it and go on with your life.

But then another voice, forgiveness maybe, would whisper, "So he made a mistake. Big deal. Everybody makes mistakes."

However, the voice of that little "mini-me" guy on my shoulder seemed to be making the most compelling case.

That little voice, which only I could hear, would say, *"He did it on purpose. He was trying to hurt you. He was going to steal your patent. He might have taken a payoff from Vokal. He's a bad guy. All done with intent. No accident. Justice."*

The thing about the mini-me voice is that it doesn't lie. It might not advocate what is most comfortable, but it never lies. Because that voice is my own and because it values the truth as the basis of all human interaction, I have to listen to it, and I have to do what that voice says.

After a couple of weeks of deliberation, trying to understand, considering forgiving and turning the other proverbial cheek, I was still left with turning him in to the ARDC.

The truth was, there had been too much intentional dishonesty, years of deceit. Nothing that had happened had been an accident. It had been done systematically, with forethought. This guy was a dirty player for sure.

It was a big decision because it would affect someone's life besides my own.

Let it be justice.

Right in the midst of all this came spring break from school, and the Pippenger family took off for wherever they were going, somewhere down south. While they were gone, I dutifully collected their mail and took it back to my home, where I kept it in a plastic bag until I would deliver it to their door when they returned.

I wanted to maintain an outward impression of neutrality until the expected date of issuance for the Folding Cart patent by the USPTO.

Obviously, because I wasn't going into their home, I wasn't feeding the cat. I couldn't go into their home. I needed distance from them. Everything about him began to feel unclean, and the house a place filled with bad vibes.

Notwithstanding the social implications of a next door neighbor who professed I was his best friend, who had family members closely tied to members of mine, and whom I saw on a daily basis, I couldn't wipe the slate clean.

I bounced the idea of turning him in to the ARDC off of several different people. I knew what felt right for me, and I wanted others' take on it in case I was missing something important.

I talked with my sons about my decision and what, if anything, I should do. The consensus was, "Turn him in."

I happened at that time to have a series of doctor appointments with various doctors, all of whom I've been with for some years, and with all of whom I am on a first name basis. That being the case, and considering I tend to share personal matters with my doctors, I asked their opinions, after giving each of them a brief description of the situation.

To a person, and without hesitation, they responded, "Turn him in."

I checked it out with friends and neighbors who had been apprised of the situation as it had unfolded. To a person, they said, "Turn him in."

There were only two people who suggested I should let it go and just forget about it. One of them said, "Revenge is a dish best served cold," and he misattributed the quote to Shakespeare. I was not going to hide in the weeds or disguise things and ambush Phil at some later date. This was a time to stand up and be counted. This was about justice, and I wanted Phil to know what I was doing as I did it.

The decision made and seconded, I made the trip downtown to the ARDC office to see if there might be some information that would help me proceed.

The offices were on the fifteenth floor. I went through a couple of large plate glass doors. Inside, I came face to face with the seal of the Illinois Supreme Court, hanging on the wall above the two receptionists' large, shared space. It was an embossed disc three feet in diameter. The carpeting in the office was wall-to-wall, and sounds were muted with the exception of some symphonic music coming from the overhead speakers.

The furniture was padded. Square, polished-marble columns supported the expanse of ceiling.

The room was strong, quiet, and serious.

It was a hallowed space.

I asked the receptionist, who had nodded in my direction, what the procedure might be to register a complaint, and she briefly explained it to me. She also gave me a small brochure which explained the ARDC in general terms and what happens when a complaint is filed.

For one thing, the ARDC would respond in two to four weeks.

I was glad to get out of there. Actually, it all seemed too serious to me. I would not want any disciplinary involvement with that office and could understand why lawyers who heard from the ARDC, questioning their behavior, might feel uneasy.

Back at home, I would be able to write my information carefully. As long as I was going to submit a complaint, I did not want questions or confusion due to negligence or oversight on my part.

Another reason I had plenty of time to do a proper job was because I intended to wait to send it until after I was assured that Phil would not be able to interfere with the issuance of my Folding Cart patent.

Only three weeks prior, I knew nothing of the ARDC. Now I was going to turn in an errant attorney to them for judgement.

In the next few days, I began writing my letter of complaint. I wrote a draft and then read and reread it. I wrote another draft. And another.

Putting together the drafts compelled me to review everything that had transpired with Phil over the past few years. As I picked apart each situation, I came to realize and to acknowledge, once again, that everything had been done with intent. I still wondered about the "why" of it all and still came up with no answer.

Phil not only threatened to destroy everything I was working on, he also threatened to destroy any chance I might have to leave something to my family.

The writing of my complaint never felt quite good enough.

Then I remembered a guy who I've played tennis with. He was a good solid guy on the courts, and I recalled he was a law professor connected with the Bar Association. I gave him a call and an almost fifteen-minute nonstop account of the situation. And I asked him for some editing help. He said he would read what I had written, and to that end, I sent him an email with the latest draft attached.

After his first read through, he said, "This is disbarment stuff. I would guess that is what will happen."

Let the chips would fall where they might. I did not set out to hunt Phil down and try to hurt him; it was simply that he must be held accountable. If I didn't force him to answer to an authority, there would never be any acknowledgement of what he had done, nor would he likely acknowledge it. I needed that acknowledgement.

While I ended up very satisfied with what I was submitting to the ARDC, I will say that the fine-tuning, absent all my emotional add-ins, was due to my tennis friend. He did excellent editing on my behalf.

When I finished, I was fully aware of having given my best, and it was solid. I had covered my bases.

35

The ARDC Letter

Dear Sirs/Madams:

I would like to lodge a complaint against Phillip M. Pippenger, a registered attorney in the State of Illinois.

The complaint I am lodging encompasses the following: Dishonesty; Fraud; Deceit; Forgery. Mr. Pippenger did not engage in the work he promised to do, did not tell me the truth and engaged in deception regarding the work he had done."

The letter went on from there, with all the appropriate information. The professional relationship Phil and I had begun in the spring of 2008 and lasted until March 2012, when I was finally able to totally disengage from him. At that time, the USPTO had given me a delivery date for my patent on the Folding Cart, and I no longer felt obliged to stay neutral.

There were many facets of the relationship that I had had with Phil.

He and his family had been to my home for dinner, albeit pizza that I had ordered out.

He had borrowed some of my tools, as he had needed them, before he was fully organized as a homeowner.

He had gone with me to one or two archery shoots.

Although going downtown to have lunch with Phil on his expense account was something I always declined, he had invited me a few times.

I had his wife and his kids over so they could meet other kids in our immediate neighborhood. I had invited the other parents along with their kids. It seemed like a good gesture for the neighborhood, since the days of letting your kids out of the house in the morning and expecting to see them in time for dinner are a thing of the past.

These days, the trend is "play-dates." The first few times I heard this term, I thought I had misheard what had been said. Kids made dates to play?

Phillip had borrowed money, when he needed funds, having found that I was good for a loan. He probably knew it wasn't cricket for a lawyer to borrow from a client.

In between the time that I paid him to write a patent and three months later when I paid him to file a lawsuit, he had borrowed the money. When he paid it back, he emailed me, saying, "Hey, thank *you,* Wendell, for trusting in me." The irony could not be more profound, by hindsight.

I had given Phil a number of hand tools that I had brought back from a friend who was in the process of cleaning out her garage before moving.

The letter to the ARDC did not get into any details about tools, or dinners, or additions on the house that weren't to be, or the cat feasting on the neighborhood's nesting birds. It didn't mention the perverse pleasure he had shown. None of that was covered.

The letter covered the chronology of what can now, laughably, be called our professional relationship. That being the case, it only covered the basics of deceit, fraud, forgery, and dishonesty.

While a letter of complaint to the ARDC seems like an easy black-or-white decision, it wasn't, as I have explained.

Should I have known sooner? Well, there are some who would say, "Yes." Maybe I should have. Except, I have a problem with the word, "should."   It implies judgment. It suggests failure and is easily associated with guilt. It conjures up expectations, often assumed—not explicit--and to not meet those expectations is tantamount to hell. If not hell, then the person should, at the very least, be judged by society as worthless.

Given the makeup of my life, there is no way I could have known what had taken place sooner than I did. If, in fact, I am willing to work with a person, trust becomes part of the deal. I trust you; you trust me. I trusted Phil. That is the assumed relationship between a lawyer and a client. It is called a *fiduciary relationship*, and it has everything to do with trust.

My friend Rick and I were partners in business. We each found it to be somewhat humorous that when we announced to our families that we were going to into business together, each of our fathers, out of earshot of the other, suggested to his respective son that he retain a lawyer.

The fathers had both been involved in partnerships in which they had ended up on the short end of things. It was so bad in my father's case, he claimed that his former partner hired a bodyguard to accompany him daily--for some time.

I don't recall ever having a partnership agreement with Rick during our seven-year partnership, with the exception of a schedule of how and when I would, if I could, pay back money I had borrowed from him in order to be his partner.

So, I am trusting by default because of my makeup. And Pippenger screwed me. It became a bewildering experience because it had never happened before.

How's this? Perhaps he had set out to steal my Notification System patent. Was he going to rewrite it and submit it using a new title for the application? Might he give it to a relative who did not have the same last name? It's all conjecture, no evidence. Yet is there another explanation for his behavior?

Did he maneuver Vokal into paying him some cash, in exchange for not filing the lawsuit? Was he able to convince them he would be able to keep me out of it? Who would believe he was actually acting on behalf of the global economy, as he asserted on the phone while weeping?

Was it just the simple pleasure, as when the cat killed the birds, of seeing me denied forever a patent for my Folding Cart, letting the time pass with no response to the USPTO by the due date for Final Rejection?

As the ARDC said in the brochure I was given, "Our principal purpose is to assist the Supreme Court (of Illinois) to determine a lawyer's fitness to practice law in Illinois." That said, as the ARDC described itself, I had every reason to believe I would hear back from them, and I would then give them any other information required to back up my statements.

I sent the letter of complaint on April 2, 2012.

Since I had no official contact with anyone at the ARDC, I used the brochure as a guideline. The brochure said, "We will notify you in writing of our decision whether to investigate about two weeks after we receive your request. If we determine there is not sufficient basis for us to investigate, our letter will explain the reasons for our decision." All I had to do was to bide my time.

36
The Waiting Game

With the embarrassment and humiliation any normal human would feel after doing what he had done, I halfway expected the Pippengers to move to a neighborhood where nobody would know them. However, no "For Sale" sign was forthcoming in February of 2012. A month later, still no sign. I began to resign myself to the idea that they would probably wait until the school year ended, then put the house up for sale and close in the summer.

In the meantime, I was moving ahead with what I had to do and had filed my complaint with the Attorney Registration and Disciplinary Commission.

I received a response from the ARDC in a letter dated April 5, 2012. The letter read as follows:

"Dear Mr. Thomas:

We have received your communication regarding Phillip Pippenger.

We will request that the attorney submit a response to the matters you have raised. A copy of the attorney's response may be sent to you for your comments. We will then determine whether further investigation is warranted.

We will contact you if we require additional information from you and will advise you of any decision we reach in the matter. Please notify us of any change in your address or telephone number.

The enclosed brochure explains how our inquiry will proceed. Thank you for your cooperation."

The letter was signed by Myrrha G. Guzman, Senior Counsel.

The brochure, which was a copy of what I already had, explained that the time involved until I would hear again from the ARDC might be as long as six weeks.

Only six weeks? Interminable, sometimes.

I tried to encourage myself by recalling how long I had already waited to get my app product up to snuff and how long I had monitored it on a daily, and sometimes hourly, basis.

Within just a few days, on April 11, 2012, at 8:13p.m., I received an email from Phil. The following is what he sent:

"Wendell,

I regret the state of things between us, and I want for all the world to go back to how we were as neighbors. Since words can be tossed around without being meant, you can never know for sure if a person means what they say.

But some things are not tossed around as easily, and it struck me that if I put my money where my mouth is, you would see that I mean what I say. So in that light, I know that you want to have more funds for Thomas and Sons, i.e., for expenses, to share with the boys, etc., and I would like to help in that regard in a substantial way. I have some figures in mind, but would like to sit down with one or both of you and Mike so we can reach a final decision on it.

I know it wouldn't mean that you would be inviting me over for coffee anytime soon, but I think it would help show that this whole thing is just a terrible mistake and misunderstanding and not a product of any evil intent on my part.

Please let me know what you think.

Thanks, Phil"

I responded with the one choice I could have:

"Phil,

No thanks for your offer.

Wendell"

And that took care of that. I was not then, nor would I ever be, open to accepting an offer of money in a situation of this nature.

Money is not justice.

The information from this latest email could not, of course, have been included in my original letter of complaint to the ARDC.

What was he thinking? That he would give me some money and I would then withdraw my complaint?

If he wanted to give me money, why didn't he just do it? What had to be decided?

When I have made donations to charity, or to a friend or someone who needed help, I haven't asked that they sign a contract, or that we sit down together so that we can reach a final decision on it. I have never given something to someone that entailed any decision on a mutual basis. To give is to give freely, no strings attached.

What decision had to be made? What was going to be signed by me, or Michael, or both? Were we going to sign on to a "deal" where I would choose not to respond, with evidence, to his letter of response to the ARDC?

What did he mean by, "...it would help show that this whole thing is just a terrible mistake and misunderstanding and not a product of any evil intent on my part."

You don't work as a patent attorney for someone and then allow their patent application to drift off into eternity, never to be issued, as had been the case with the Folding Cart patent application.

There had to be evil intent. Otherwise, why did he not file the lawsuit against Vokal to recover some of my money. His far-fetched story of waiting for the economy to turn around was quite possibly an attempt to cloud the issue and sidestep his negligence.

As I have said, the question regarding Vokal was did he accept money from them in exchange for keeping me at bay? Did he convince them that the amount of $6,500 was acceptable and he'd pass it on to me? What was his "planned negligence" about? I don't think I'll ever find out.

April is one of the short months, and it was taking forever.

I was "waiting for Godot." The days passed slowly as I waited for a response from the ARDC.

On the other hand, I looked forward to speedy closure once the process began. I envisioned an admission of guilt for the things he had done, which he knew he had done. In fact, there was not a reason to expect otherwise; I had all the information that I needed in just a few emails.

If there was any doubt as to what I was saying about his introducing an imposter judge, or the Clerk of the Court of Cook County scamming him, I had a witness who could corroborate everything.

I thought the whole thing would get resolved pretty quickly, but the days were interminable.

"Hey, Michael," I said one day, as I tried to bolster my hopes, "I think he'll just say, 'mea culpa.'"

"No, Dad. I don't think so," he said. "He's going to be fighting for his life. He's going to do everything he can to fight you. I don't know what that might be, but it'll be everything he's got. And whatever he can make up that you can't prove. I think that's who you're dealing with."

Well, Michael is a pretty astute "people-person," and his take is most often accurate. He routinely sees things more clearly than I do—although that might not be much to boast about. Still, I was comforted by the fact that the information I gave was all

150

straightforward. It would be difficult to make something more of it than what it was, no matter how hard he might try.

By the end of April, I had begun to wonder what was going on. "How hard can it be to read a letter, feel ashamed, and respond?" I had little doubt that after his disbarment, he would be able to find employment somewhere doing something. He has a good mind, and even though he screwed me around on everything he had done on my behalf, there had to be companies out there who needed a good high-tech person, or a good software salesman, or one or another of the "new economy" jobs that I kept hearing were being created.

Disbarment would definitely not be the end of the road for him.

May arrived with the usual flush of greenery and some of the early flora, like tulips. The buds on the trees became small leaves, curled and tight, then unfolding and stretched out a little more each day. Some of the more aggressive--or attentive-- lawn services had begun their seasonal work on the neighborhood lawns. As a breeze blew, the aerating, reseeding, and fertilizing wafted to the senses and a deep breath brought the knowledge that life begun again in earnest after the long, dark winter months.

While I tend my own lawn and property, most of my neighbors employ one of the lawn services to tend theirs. My front lawn is only about a six- or eight-foot strip of grass on the house side of the public walk in front. The rest of the front area is taken up with prairie grasses that my son Steve collected from within a three-mile radius of my home. They might be among the last of these grasses in the area.

Another thing growing in my front yard is a burr oak tree. Back in the early 1990s, Steve had collected some twenty or thirty acorns from Calvary Cemetery, about two blocks from my home. He brought them home and put them out for the squirrels.

As luck would have it, I now have a burr oak growing in both the front and back yards.

As if that isn't enough, on my parkway, surrounding the hackberry tree that the city put in about thirty years ago, grows a wealth of woodland sunflowers, which bloom for a number of months, beginning in late spring and lasting until the tail end of summer. To keep some history of the plants that used to thrive throughout the area, and with the hope that more neighbors would return to what the area supported years ago in way of natural selection, I share roots and cuttings with anyone who wants them.

Also with the longer days, which were sunnier and milder, I went to the tennis courts on all days the weather allowed.

And still, I received no word from the ARDC, and the days of May ticked away. Soon, early June was upon me.

37
Bedlam

By June 5, 2012, I had run out of patience, so I picked up the phone, dialed the ARDC's phone number, and was connected to one of the women there. I can't say for sure it was Myrrha Guzman, but it might have been. I said who I was and that I was calling to find out the status of the situation regarding my complaint against Phillip Pippenger. I mentioned the ARDC brochure had stated that I would probably hear back within four to six weeks, given consideration for the time allotted for an attorney response to a complaint.

"So, could you tell me, please, what's going on?" I asked.

Whoever it was told me that the file had been closed.

"What?" I said, with emphasis, as in a near shout. "How could that be? I never even heard back from you!"

The other party then informed me that a letter from the ARDC was sent to me on May 10, 2012, offering me the chance to respond to the attorney's letter. Since they had never heard back from me, they had closed the file.

"Oh! Wait a minute, ma'am. I never got any mail. Are you aware that the attorney that I complained about lives next door to me? Have you been aware of that?"

She said, "Oh my God! No. No, I don't think we have been aware of that."

"This is insane," I said, "I don't get a chance to respond to whatever he said? I never got any mail."

"I'm sorry," she said, and then added quietly, something like, "I'll have to see."

That afternoon, coincidental to my call, I received the letter from the ARDC stating that the case had been closed. It took one day to get from their Chicago office to my home.

I realized, too, Pippenger would also have known, within a day or two at most, the turnaround time between his letter of response to my receipt of the ARDC letter giving me a chance to respond.

Ah, what an easy thing to see in my mind's eye. He waits at home for the mail to arrive. After leaving mail at the Pippengers' and then my home, the mailman would continue north on his route. I wouldn't be home because I would have left an hour or two ago for one of my tennis matches. It would only take a few strides from Pippengers' front stairs to the side of my house, where my front door and mailbox are. Easy pickings in a neighborhood where the mailman is often the only person out and about in the late afternoon, and he's a few doors north by now and out of sight.

Something else clicked into place: The letter wherein Pippenger offered me money. If I had taken the money, would I then have agreed not to respond to the Pippenger letter to the ARDC? Was that what "had to be arranged" with Michael and myself to "reach a final decision." With either scenario, Pippenger can say anything he wants to be rid of the problem, because I'm never going to have the chance to respond to his letter. Clever.

"And, yes!" I was thinking, "if I don't agree to accept the money and any attached contingencies, I won't receive my letter from the ARDC. Clever again. How very-very clever."

I opened the letter from the ARDC. It was hard to take it in after all the expectations I had harbored.

"Dear Mr. Thomas:

"We have concluded our review of the above-referenced investigation and have determined that further action by this agency is unwarranted.

"You told us that you hired Phillip Pippenger to assist you in obtaining patents, and to pursue damages against a company that you claimed failed to perform the service you sought from it. You told us that Mr. Pippenger misrepresented to you the status of your patents and dispute with the subject company.

"Mr. Pippenger advised us of the legal services he provided to you. He denied many of the statements you attributed to him, but acknowledged that there may have been some misunderstanding or miscommunication.

"As you may know, Supreme Court Rules require that this Commission establish all elements of a violation of the Rules of Professional Conduct by clear and convincing evidence. It appears that the only evidence we would have regarding the representations that Mr. Pippenger made to you regarding your matters would consist of only your word against that of the attorney. Under these circumstances, we have determined that we would be unable to probe your allegations of misconduct against Mr. Pippenger. Accordingly, we are closing our file in this matter.

"Please understand that our decision to close this file does not mean that we found either you or Mr. Pippenger to be untruthful or that we believe Mr. Pippenger's statements over your statements. Our decision simply reflects our conclusion that a formal disciplinary prosecution, given all of the conflicting testimony, would not be successful.

"Thank you for bringing your concerns to our attention."

The letter was signed by Myrrha B. Guzman, and for the rest of the day and the evening, I was in a mental fog.

I got on the phone and called family, friends, and neighbors who had been made aware of the situation. It was not something that anyone I spoke with could understand.

Comments ranged from, "Well, that's the system" to, "Fucking lawyers," or, "You know, the ARDC is on the lawyer's side," or, "You've got to have money," or simply, "Sorry."

"That doesn't sound right," said the law professor who had helped me by editing my letter of complaint. "This isn't proper. Somehow, we're going to have to look into this. I can't do anything right now," (it was early in the evening), "but I'll get in touch with some people soon to find out what's going on with this."

There I was, all dressed for the party, and I found out I wasn't invited. How could everything that had happened, all that effort, suddenly be null and void? I have ample evidence to back my complaint and now, for some reason, the whole thing evaporates.

Why hadn't the ARDC sent the mail registered or certified, or whatever it is that requires a signature for receipt? How many other people has this happened to? This stinks. A Pippenger stench. What's wrong with this country?

With that, I went to bed for a good night's tossing and turning.

38
Getting to Work

The disappointment I had felt on June 5, 2012, was supplanted by exhilaration the next day when I opened another letter from the ARDC. It said:

"Dear Mr. Thomas:

"Enclosed is a copy of the response of Phillip Pippenger to the matters about which you have complained.

"If you believe the response is inaccurate or if you wish to provide additional information or documents for our consideration, please write to me within fourteen days.

"We will evaluate the matter and advise you of our decision. Again, thank you for your cooperation."

This letter was also signed by Myrrha B. Guzman.

I don't recall what expectations I might have entertained, if I were asked at the time, regarding what I thought Pippenger might say in response to my honest, straightforward, detailed letter.

What I would not have expected was what he did, which was to write a six-page letter, in small type, with not an iota of truth about any situation he described. He wrote a six-page letter of lies, and I had been given fourteen days to respond to the ARDC.

If he had painted, even with the clumsiness of a grade schooler working with oils and canvas for the first time, some of the situations in an effort to put himself in a more favorable light, that would have been one thing. It would not have been acceptable, but I would have had some comprehension of what he was doing.

What he, in fact, did became more unbelievable as I read his letter for the second and then the third time.

I was catapulted into a different realm. Justice had become JUSTICE.

While the ARDC was giving me fourteen days to respond, I really didn't have even that amount of time, because on the eleventh day, the following Friday, I was leaving for a family wedding in Colorado. A favorite niece, Courtney, was going to be getting married in the mountains, and my whole family was going. It was not something I was going to miss.

I almost began to get to work. There was only one thing stopping me.

First, I had to return the Pippengers' house key. After reading his letter of response and the blatant lies, I knew I would never want anything more to do with him. There was something very, very wrong with his outlook I had never thought of him as mentally ill. He was too sane in too many ways. It was something else, and I couldn't put my finger on it.

I remembered how he looked when I told him his cat had been killing the birds nesting on their front porch.

I remembered his crocodile tears when he offered his confession about the Vokal lawsuit and at the same time how he neglected to inform me of the belatedly filed patent application for the communication system.

The out-of-the-blue Christmas gift to me, the pandering to see if he couldn't help me start my snowblower, sharing a secret family issue with me before he had told his father, hanging out in my home that he said "feels like a church"—all these things now came together in my mind. I began to wonder if this person could even be dangerous.

At about 10:30 a.m. on Thursday, June 7th, I returned the Pippengers' house key. I went up the front stairs and rang the doorbell. When Hilleory answered, I handed the key to her and left without saying anything.

Hilleory said, "What? What's going on?" I kept on walking, went down the stairs, took the step across from their property to mine, and then up my brick walkway into my home to begin my work in earnest.

That was the last time I set foot on the Pippengers' property.

It did not take long for a response from Phillip, in an email at 11:01 that same morning:

"Dear Wendell,

I know there has been some tension between us, but I am writing as your neighbor and friend, so I hope you'll read this in that spirit. As you know, I would love to have some way to show you that I am the same person you always knew and am not the bad man you seem to have come to see me as. I offered a substantial contribution to your company (and as a working man with four young children, I am not rich), but you rejected that, so I have to accept that. I don't have much besides that to offer. I have other albeit smaller ideas, but I don't want to insult you by offering something that you may think is stupid or worthless, but if you could let me know what I could do I would gladly do it.

The reason I'm writing today is because Hilleory called me this morning in tears. She thought you were dying when you dropped off the keys, so I had to bring her up to speed on our tensions and issues. I accept that you and I aren't magically going to become buddies again in the near future, but if my peace offering is enough to get you to treat Hilleory and the kids as the innocent parties they really are, I would be grateful.

So please, let's work it out to that level at least, and I will hope that my peace offering helps you see that we are not bad people over here on the other side of the fence.

Thanks, Phil

p.s. I think your computer may have a virus or some sort of problem, I received some emails saying they were from you but that were obviously from someone else."

I responded six minutes later:

"Phil,

I have not in the past, nor do I have plans in the future, to treat Hilleory and the kids as anything but the innocents that they are and have been. Wendell"

Pippenger's email was written two days after receiving the case-closed letter from the ARDC. He thought that the case was closed and that he could now be declared the winner.

I looked at his email and pondered.

Here's a guy who has committed heinous acts and can continue to think of us as friends, and he wants to think of his offer of money as a "contribution?"

He had to "bring his wife up to speed" on the tension between us. This struck me as just more dishonesty. It was a given that he would not tell Hilleory the real story.

Unfortunately, Hilleory seemed content to keep her head buried in the sand and acquiesce to Phillip's whims. She didn't really have to question much of anything: The UPS truck, with another package or two, was a familiar sight in front of their home. I felt pretty certain that he "brought his wife up to speed" in a meaningless and inconsequential sentence or two, if even that.

Regarding the line about, "get me to treat Hilleory and the kids as the innocent parties they really are", was of course insulting and insincere. I had always treated Hilleory and the kids with kindness. To suggest otherwise is simply "twisting the landscape to fit his garden."

Moreover, though, this most recent email told me he wasn't aware that I had received the "go ahead" from the ARDC

160

to submit more evidence. And you can be sure I wasn't gonna spill those beans.

For me, that just meant staying in the saddle and working the horse harder, not a difficult vision to fulfill, since we were one and the same, the horse and I.

39
By The Skin of My Teeth

On May 8, 2012, Pippenger had sent his letter of response to the ARDC, regarding my letter of complaint. As I mentioned, he didn't have to worry about not telling the truth because he knew I would never receive the May 10th ARDC letter giving me the chance to respond with evidence.

When I finished and presented my evidence to the ARDC, they told me it was one of the finest presentations they had ever seen. That was satisfying to hear, a high compliment.

While I often tend to be casual in the things I make or do, there is one area in which I have never been casual—why, I can't say. That area is the retention of emails that have anything to do with business.

Casual can be functional, expedient, and even efficient.

Take my dining room table, for instance. It looks like a table, a good fit for my small dining room. It has four legs, which are similar in appearance. It has a top with five-inch-wide beveled boards, and it is sturdy, more than sturdy; it is as solid as a rock.

The table is something I made in a day, for Michael and Lene's coffee roasting operation and retail outlet, which they ran for a time in addition to the Unicorn Café. Michael needed a display table for some of his coffee and tea related items, and I was game to put a table together in a hurry.

I took four 4"x4"x4' posts and lathed them into rounds with contours receding and billowing up and down their length, matching each successive post's lathing to the first one I had done. When I finished the four legs, I cut them to equal lengths.

Next, I clamped six 2"x6"x5' pine boards together using dowels and glue and let it sit for a few hours. Then, I sanded the table top and added rails on each side, once again using glue and dowels. The project was almost completed.

Affixing the legs and staining the table did not take long. It dried overnight, and I was able to take it to Michael's store the next day. The one thing I would change, if I had it to do over, would be to make the legs removable. I have done that on other tables I've made since.

So precision and care, as demonstrated by this table project, is not really my forte. Casualness is, and sometimes it's useful.

But that exception of saving every business email, seemed the prudent thing to do. I mean, after all, I was about to have a huge amount of business at any moment. (I'm still waiting.)

While Pippenger's behavior was reprehensible, I have to believe that if he had even the slightest inkling that I saved emails, and if he thought there was even an outside chance I would ever have an opportunity to respond to his letter, he would never have written what he did.

It took quite a bit of thought as to how to organize and present the information and evidence, and I ended up with the idea of two separate binders.

The first, and smaller of the two three-ring binders, would show a reprint of Pippenger's six-page letter to the ARDC, broken into excerpts, each followed by my detailed analysis, indented to differentiate my work. Within my responses, I would cite references to the evidence, contained in the second three-ring binder, under six appendices: Evidence of Financials, Evidence of Folding Cart, Evidence of Localized Reminder System (the Notification System), Evidence of Vokal Lawsuit, Evidence of Conflicts, Evidence of Receipt of the Offer of Money.

Each of the six appendices would be organized by sequentially numbered tabs, labeled, "Item." Since the significance of his lies was the whole basis of my complaint, the evidence countering each lie comprised Items 1through 40.

On June 5th, the problem for me was the amount of work that I faced and the tight time constraint, which was overwhelming.

With the idea now set as to how I would organize my work, I began.

I felt some major time pressures to complete the work before leaving for Courtney's wedding. I sensed that in this case, "a bird in hand" was what I needed. I had until Tuesday, June 19th, to respond. I was not scheduled to return from Colorado until late Sunday night, and if I hadn't finished the work for the ARDC, it could mean disaster for my case. What if my plane was rescheduled? What if I didn't get home until Monday? There were too many potential hazards. What if - what if - what if. *I had to get it done before the wedding.*

Reading and rereading his letter, carefully, familiarized me with the nuances. I began marking up the letter, making notes, question marks, and statements on the paper. This was the first of a series of sixteen-hour days and a couple of eighteen-hour ones. By the third day, I was punchy and felt as if I had been staring at the computer screen and the paper shredder for infinity. And the maddening sound of the printer, the sound that only a "buy your ink from us and we'll give you the printer" printer can produce.

Pippenger's letter was consistent in only one thing, lies.

As his letter of response is too long to include in its entirety, I will show a few excerpts to demonstrate some of the lies and absurdities therein.

He opened by thanking the ARDC for sending my letter, conveying my "criticism." of him.

He continued: "While a quarrel apparently exists between me and Wendell, the facts will make it clear that it is not a legal or ethical issue, despite Wendell's choice to use this forum to leverage his issues."

Everything in my complaint was a legal or ethical issue. He then added: "I truly don't dispute that it was poor judgment on my part to work with or advise a person that was my neighbor and best friend.

"I obviously should have kept my relationship with Wendell purely personal, especially in light of the ongoing disputes that I knew existed with other neighbors."

Now, while I don't much care for one of my neighbors, Geri Shapiro, and while I challenge her illegal house sales, I had no idea who the other neighbors were with whom I was having "ongoing disputes." But I only had to keep reading to find out.

Regarding his negligence on the Folding Cart patent application, Pippenger said, "I have a letter indicating that Wendell was notified of that (USPTO) Action by me in early October of 2011." As I mentioned earlier, I did not find out about the Action until he emailed on January 28, 2012, "...there IS an action and I didn't have it...looks like it got through Leydig's docketing around the time I left (in October 2011)..."

Pippenger had received the notice on September 16, 2011, and had intentionally, I submit, failed to send the letter notifying me. Leydig Voit & Mayer validated to me, when I spoke with them, that Pippenger had the USPTO's Final Office Action in hand on September 16, 2011.

Regarding the Notification System patent application, he claimed:

"I became aware of a prior system just like Wendell's, and I researched it in greater detail. In short, Wendell's application had to do with setting reminders on one's iphone, [sic], cell phone, etc.; the prior system, called NotifyMe, did the same thing and did so with the same interface for setting dates and times. Unbeknownst to me at the time, Wendell's interface was not created by Wendell at all, but was actually a template provided for setting dates and times."

None of this is true, and there is also some rather absurd humor in a part of his lie. Pippenger had claimed to me earlier, of course, that he had filed my patent application for the Notification System on September 15, 2010. The app to which he refers, "NotifyMe," was not made available to the public until March of 2011. Even though the "NotifyMe" app was nothing at all like, or remotely connected to, ideas of my Notification System ("Localized Message System") patent application, I don't think Phillip was claiming to be clairvoyant, or that he had an inside track at the Apple Corporation and knew fully about "NotifyMe" before it was released…Or was he?

Actually, one of Pippenger's tactics was to say things that someone not familiar with the patent process might consider a reasonable explanation.

Keeping that in mind, this is the crux of Pippenger's rebuttal to the ARDC. It was a series of false presentations that he could embellish with an array of colorful adjectives to position himself as just a good solid guy who happened to try to help out a problematic neighbor and best friend.

The idea entailed deluging the listener, or reader, with a smattering of legalese, warped storylines designed to obfuscate the facts in the hope the reader would just nod in confusion and appreciation of the "packaging."

Obviously, before my fortuitous phone call to the ARDC a few days earlier, his letter had worked like a charm. They swallowed it hook, line, and sinker.

As for me, I stuck to my guns and kept "pounding away" at the computer, copying and printing, appending, cataloging, itemizing, sorting and finally entering the information into the two binders on Friday morning, June 15, 2012. When the binders and two copies, for me, were complete, I got in my car and headed immediately and lightheadedly for the ARDC office.

With the job completed, my feelings were positive with regard to both the effort and the results. I thought my work would withstand any kind of scrutiny: It was straightforward and totally honest.

I returned home and prepared to head for Midway Airport that afternoon, heading to Colorado for the family wedding, sleep-deprived zombie that I was.

"Justice," I thought and drifted off to sleep as the plane climbed.

40
A Neighbor I Don't Know

In his letter of response to the ARDC, Phillip Pippenger, appropriately, had a "Conclusion." After multiple readings of his letter, this "Conclusion" became more and more transparently inaccurate in content and feigned sincerity. I think the ARDC must have thought the same thing, considering the steps they took to discover who they were dealing with.

The "Conclusion," read as follows:

"In writing this response, I came to realize my falling out with Wendell was almost inevitable. He appears to be in conflict with each person or company that he sees or works with regularly. Even including just the disputed [sic] I know of, the list is impressive: Neighbors Priscilla and Jerri [sic], Attorney One, Vokal Interactive, Bolder Image, many I'm sure I don't know, and now me.

If there is any doubt that his ARDC complaint is anything but a calculated retaliation, consider that he 'transferred' his backpack cart application to me by an email dated Friday March 30 – only to file his ARDC complaint the very next business day! Clearly, his belated 'transfer' to me was not an honest attempt to have me handle anything; it was done in preparation for filing his ARDC complaint the next business day. Consider also that he complains I delayed his suit against Vokal; yet now, months later, he still has not filed such a suit. Consider that he did not even mention his attempt to sue Bolder Image, nor my refusal to assist in that endeavor, and yet it appears to have been the trigger for his complaint.

In short, while I sincerely regret the colloquial manner in which I conducted myself with Wendell, and apologize deeply for that, I feel that I looked after Wendell's best interests at every juncture, and it hurt me profoundly to receive his complaint. I look forward to any and all questions you may have about any of these matters or my relationship with Wendell Thomas."

So this is the guy who lives next door. The "neighbor guy." Given all the time he spends in isolation, working on his motorcycles or hanging out in his house, I wasn't aware he was close to any of our neighbors. You live and learn, I guess.

Of course, he might have mentioned the neighbors only because he thought, for one reason or another, I would not respond to his letter to the ARDC.

The neighbor, "Priscilla," to whom Pippenger refers, is Priscilla MacDougall. I do know who Priscilla is. I have never had any contact with her except to politely decline the annual invitation she extends for her garden party. I'm sure Priscilla is a wonderful person and that those who do attend are happy to purchase one of the books she sells at these affairs. I know that for some years, the book being sold was written by her now-deceased husband who, I believe, had at one time been a newsperson or commentator.

Priscilla's father was a renowned professor of journalism at Northwestern University. One of his graduate students who later became a news commentator met Priscilla when he was close to thirty, and she was a rambunctious two and half year old. That graduate student later became Priscilla's husband. I have no idea the age at which Priscilla married the newsman. Of course, I have no idea how old she was when they were first smitten with each other.

Priscilla, I think, is a retired professor of law at the University of Wisconsin.

As did her parents, I believe Priscilla runs the home she now owns as a boarding house.

I did know Priscilla's parents.

When my youngest son, Peter, was a third or fourth grader at Lincoln Elementary School, he had a playmate who lived a block and a half away. His playmate was a tall child who seemed to be as energetic as Peter was, which, I might say, was quite energetic.

After Peter had played with his classmate, Milton, a number of times both at our house and at Milton's, he said to me, "Dad, Milton doesn't have a bed."

"No bed?" I said.

"I think they're poor. He doesn't have a dresser, either," he said.

"Well, okay," I said.

Soon after, when the kids were in school, I went to Milton's house to speak with his mother, "casually." She was at home, as I thought she might be. I had figured that she was probably unemployed, and I was correct. Milton, his two sisters, and their mother lived on the second floor of a wood frame house. As I went up the stairs, I made a mental note that the handrail was loose. On the walls, the plaster was exposed here and there, and in a couple of places, the plaster was absent so that the wood lath was exposed.

Their apartment was worse than the hallway. Here, only a block and a half from my home, which is in a nice neighborhood, these people are living in slum conditions. Plaster and lath was exposed, floorboards uneven here and there. Bare bulbs in the light fixtures. Until that moment in the spring of 1978, I didn't know that places like this existed so close to my home.

170

She nodded occasionally as we spoke, and I was able to get her to agree that it would be a good thing if Milton had a bed. There was no floor covering in the living room, only a couple of wooden chairs and a small Formica-topped table with three aluminum chairs placed around it. It looked like they could use a sofa, to which she also nodded her agreement.

When I inquired who her landlord was, she said it was the MacDougall's from over on Judson.

I went up to Foster Street and Maple Avenue to a used furniture store, Crost Brothers, and I got the things I thought they needed most, which was a bed and a dresser for Milton and a sofa for the family. I delivered the goods in/on my station wagon. The mattress was new, as even a used furniture store was not allowed to sell used mattresses.

Professor MacDougall was liberal politically, or so I'd been told at the time. He may have run for president or the senate a couple of times, either on the Communist Party ticket or the Progressive Party, which I guess back in the fifties was considered about the same as the Communists.

At any rate, it left a bad taste in my mouth because I would not consider renting out property in the condition of the Milton place, particularly if I espoused "equality for everyone," and, "each according to their needs."

It's about walking the walk.

Regarding Geri Shapiro, who Pippenger also mentioned, let me quote from a letter I received from the City of Evanston when I complained about Shapiro's house sales, since she uses her home for a retail business:

"Good Afternoon Mr. Thomas,

"This is an ongoing problem with this lady…The property owner EVERY YEAR has been notified for converting her garage into a "resale shop." I will cite her for violations(s), and, if compliance (garage cleared out/cleaned up) is not met, I will issue a ticket to appear

171

in zoning court where a judge may fine her up to $500.00/day for each day she is in violation. If you would like to keep in touch for an update, please feel free to do so."

The letter was signed by the Zoning Officer of the City of Evanston.

"Attorney One" in Pippenger's conclusion is Paul Hletko. I never fired Paul and I never had a problem with him. He left the patent business voluntarily and became a distiller, and we are still friendly. As I covered a few pages back, I consulted with Paul before moving forward with my complaint to the Illinois ARDC.

As for the Vokal lawsuit that Pippenger never filed, he neglected to say that a competent attorney would have researched the situation and then acted if it were appropriate. The attorney I ended up hiring did think it was appropriate and filed a lawsuit which was satisfactorily settled out of court.

In light of the evidence I submitted to the ARDC, and with the subsequent validation of every single thing that I had said in my lengthy letter, coupled with the extraordinary inaccuracies, some of them blatantly false, that Pippenger had presented to them in his response, the ARDC reopened the matter for further investigation.

They wanted Pippenger to respond to my response, including every piece of evidence that backed up every single thing I had claimed.

When I received the response from the ARDC that they would pursue the matter, I went next to the Evanston Police Department and told them of the situation. I explained to them how my next door neighbor had been behaving toward me, both as a neighbor and as my lawyer, and how he had offered me money.

The person I spoke with asked for my phone number, adding, "We'll put the number on our 'Fast Response List.'"

I had come to realize that I couldn't trust what Pippenger might do next, and I wanted some kind of backup.

41

Slow Motion

The ARDC works at their own pace.

My original idea of how the ARDC procedure might work was slightly off base. That's probably one of my propensities that does not serve me well: I decide what makes sense to me and presume that that's how a particular situation will play itself out.

I would probably not have been a very good lawyer, if I were ever inclined in that direction. First and foremost, I never would have been accepted by any law school. My grades in high school and college were always borderline. A "C" for me was "doing very well." It went down from there.

My expectation of things taking a few weeks were unrealistic. It wasn't just the time it took but that Pippenger proclaimed innocence throughout while acknowledging through his lawyer the truth of what I had presented.

The ARDC unveiled its procedures quite slowly and with absolute deliberation. It is my belief, they didn't want to step on the toes of a dues-paying member, a "lawyer who is registered with the ARDC," which includes every lawyer in the State of Illinois. Not to be forgotten, because of their commitment to justice, they wanted to ensure he got due process.

"But what about me," I wondered, back and forth with myself. *"I'm the one who got totally screwed."*

"Well, you know you're not a Boeing or even a Caterpillar and still, you're being protected under the auspices of the Supreme Court of Illinois."

I was supposed to feel good but as I looked over my shoulder I could see that the bus was on its way. It drew nearer and nearer.

The ARDC sent me the letter that they were reopening the complaint for investigation on June 19, 2012, saying, "We will request that Mr. Pippenger submit a response to the matters you have raised."

On August 31st, the ARDC filed formal charges against Phillip McKinney Pippenger, the Attorney-Respondent. The charges seemed to me to be adequate to cause Pippenger to be disbarred, but the ARDC neglected to acknowledge a number of the things he had done or to charge him with them.

The charges of the ARDC in their Complaint are as follows:

"Count I (Lack of diligence and dishonesty-Localized Message System)

"In October, 2008, Wendell Thomas ('Thomas') filed a patent application with the United States Patent and Trademark Office ('USPTO') for a notification system that was designed to remind a patient when it was time for them to take medication. In June, 2010, the USPTO notified Thomas that his application for a patent on his notification system had been denied.

"In August, 2010, Pippenger agreed to represent Thomas in filing a new patent application for the notification system described in paragraph one, above, which would then be referred to as 'Localized Message System.' Pippenger requested and received $4,000 to complete and file the patent application. As of September 16, 2010, Pippenger had not filed the patent application for Thomas' Localized Message System.

"On Thursday September 16, 2010, Thomas sent Pippenger an e-mail message in which he stated:

"'I hope this will put us in the proper position to get the contract completed. I'll be travelling starting early am

175

and will get home mid-evening. Thanks for your great help. I'm thinking that our patent app went in on Wed.'

"On September 16, 2010, Pippenger sent an e-mail to Thomas that said the following:
"'Wendell, good to hear you're coming back, hope you had a great time out there. And yes indeed, you are now the proud applicant/inventor with the USPTO. I don't have the new serial number in front of me, but will get it from Susan tomorrow and send it over to you.' (Susan refers to Respondent's secretary)
"Pippenger's September 16, 2010 statement to Thomas, referenced in the above paragraph, was false and intended to mislead Thomas, in that as of September 16, 2010 Pippenger had not filed Thomas' patent application for the Localized Message System. Pippenger knew that his statement was false.
"Between January 5, 2012, and January 24, 2012, Thomas sent Pippenger at least five e-mail requests for a copy of the patent application he had believed had been filed on his behalf, and for the related receipt from the USPTO for the Localized Message System. Pippenger did not respond to the requests.
"On January 25, 2012, Pippenger submitted Thomas' application for a patent on the Localized Message System to the USPTO.
"On January 25, 2012, Pippenger sent Thomas an e-mail that contained an attachment that purported to be the electronic acknowledgement receipt from the USPTO for the patent application for the Localized Message System, filed by Pippenger on behalf of Thomas. The receipt was purportedly for application number 13358505 and was assigned confirmation number 8487. The receipt did not list application filing date, but was time stamped for 13:35:32.

"On January 30, 2012, Thomas contacted the USPTO to inquire about the status of his patent application the Localized Message System. Thomas learned that his application was still in processing and had been filed on January 25, 2012.

"Shortly thereafter, Thomas terminated Pippenger as his attorney in this matter.

"By reason of the conduct described above, Pippenger has engaged in the following misconduct:

a. Failure to act with reasonable diligence and promptness in representing a client, in violation of Rule 1.3 of the Illinois Rules of Professional Conduct (2010);

b. Failure to keep a client reasonably informed about the status of a matter, in violation of Rule 1.4(a)(3) of the Illinois Rules of Professional Conduct (2010);

c. Engaging in conduct involving dishonesty, fraud, deceit, or misrepresentation, in violation of Rule 8.4(c) of the Illinois rules of Professional Conduct (2010);

d. Conduct which is prejudicial to the administration of justice, in violation of Rule 8.4(d) of the Illinois Rules of Professional Conduct (2010); and

e. Conduct that tends to defeat the administration of justice, or to bring the courts or the legal profession into disrepute.

"Count II (Lack of diligence and false statements – Vokal matter)

"The Administrator re-alleges the allegations made in paragraphs shown above.

"In December, 2010, Pippenger agreed to represent Thomas in matters relating to a contractual dispute with Vokal Interactive LLC, ('Vokal'), a digital design consulting firm, which had been assisting Thomas in developing a mobile phone application for the notification system referred to above. Thomas paid Pippenger $2,000 towards anticipated legal fees and costs. Pippenger never filed a lawsuit on behalf of Thomas against Vokal or anyone associated with Vokal related to the dispute.

"Shortly thereafter, Pippenger told Thomas that he had filed Thomas' lawsuit against Vokal in the Circuit Court of Cook County. Pippenger's statement to Thomas that he had filed Thomas' lawsuit was false and intended to mislead Thomas, in fact, Pippenger never filed a lawsuit on behalf of Thomas against Vokal or anyone associated with Vokal. Pippenger knew that his statement was false.

"On January 14, 2011, Thomas sent Pippenger an e-mail requesting information about his lawsuit against Vokal, which stated:

"'How long (would you guess) before something begins happening in the court(s)?'

"On January 18, 2011, in response to Thomas' e-mail reference above, Pippenger sent Thomas an e-mail which stated:

"'Wendell, I'm going to try to get a more definitive schedule from the clerk so we will know better what the time table will be.

"'But as far as the actual substantive action by the court, they tend to take their time. At any rate, I'll give the clerk a call today to see if we can get a time table-they don't always give one but we'll see.'

"Pippenger's statement in paragraph above was false and intended to mislead Thomas, in that at the time that he sent the e-mail message to Thomas, Pippenger had not filed Thomas' lawsuit and could not call the clerk's office to get a timetable on the court's resolution of the non-existent lawsuit. Pippenger knew his statement was false.

"On January 25, 2012, Pippenger told Thomas that there had been progress in the lawsuit against Vokal, that the Clerk of the Court had requested that Pippenger meet *ex parte* in chambers with the judge presiding over Thomas' case, and that the meeting was scheduled for January 27, 2012.

"Pippenger's statements referenced in the above paragraph were false and intended to mislead Thomas, in that Pippenger had not filed a lawsuit on behalf of Thomas and had never been contacted by the Clerk of the Court to have an *ex parte* meeting with a judge. Pippenger knew that his statements were false.

"On January 27, 2012, Pippenger told Thomas that he had met with 'Judge Randy Stevenson,' who had purportedly been assigned to preside over Thomas' lawsuit against Vokal and that 'Judge Stevenson' told Pippenger that 'his elderly client didn't have a case at this point because he had stayed with Vokal for too long a period of time.'

"Pippenger's statement referenced in the above paragraph was false and intended to mislead Thomas, in that at the time that Pippenger claimed to have met with 'Judge Randy Stevenson,' he had not filed a lawsuit against Vokal on Thomas' behalf, there was no sitting judge in the Cook County Court system with that name, and Pippenger had not had the purported conversation about the supposed lack of merit to Thomas' claim. Pippenger knew that his statements were false.

"On January 28, 2012, Pippenger met with Thomas and Michael Thomas ('Michael'), Thomas' son, to further discuss the status of the purported lawsuit against Vokal. During the course of that meeting, Pippenger stated that he was embarrassed because the Cook Country Court system had scammed him; that case number '2010-1-5199,' the case number that Pippenger claimed to have been given when he filed Thomas' lawsuit was non-existent, and that he believed that the person whom he met with that was purportedly a judge was an imposter.

"Pippenger's statements referenced in the above paragraph were false and intended to mislead Thomas and Michael, in that Pippenger never filed a lawsuit or received a docket number for Thomas' claim and never met with anyone who was purportedly a judge presiding over Thomas' lawsuit. Pippenger knew that his statements were false.

"On January 30, 2012, Pippenger met with Thomas and revealed that his story regarding meeting with a judge had been false, and that he had not filed Thomas' lawsuit. At that time, Thomas advised Pippenger that he was terminating Pippenger's services in this matter.

"By reason of the conduct described above, Pippenger has engaged in the following misconduct:

a. Failure to act with reasonable diligence and promptness in representing a client, in violation of Rule 1.3 of the Illinois Rules of Professional Conduct (2010);

b. Failure to keep a client reasonably informed about the status of a matter, in violation of Rule 1.4(a)(3) of the Illinois Rules of Professional Conduct (2010);

c. Engaging in conduct involving dishonesty, fraud, deceit, or misrepresentation, in violation of Rule 8.4(c) of the Illinois Rules of Professional Conduct (2010);

d. Conduct which is prejudicial to the administration of justice, in violation of Rule 8.4(d) of the Illinois Rules of Professional Conduct (2010); and

e. Engaging in conduct that tends to defeat the administration of justice, or to bring the courts or the legal profession into disrepute.

"Count III (Dishonesty in relation to an ARDC disciplinary matter)

"The Administrator (Jerome Larkin) realleges the allegation contained in all previously presented paragraphs.

180

"On April 2, 2012 the Administrator received a request for an investigation of Pippenger from Thomas, alleging that Pippenger had neglected three cases that he had handled for Thomas and had made false statements about the cases.

"On April 3, 2012 based on the allegations contained in the above paragraph, the Administrator sent Pippenger a letter requesting that he respond to the allegations made by Thomas. Pippenger received the letter shortly after it had been mailed.

"In responding to Thomas' allegations about Pippenger's conduct related to the patent application for the Localized Message Center, Pippenger stated the following:

"'Although the patent application had been drafted, I informed Wendell that his chances of obtaining a patent on the interface, while not precisely zero, were very low in view of the NotifyMe application that already existed. In other words, patent pending could be guaranteed for a time, but actual patented status was not likely to occur. While this communication was a verbal communication over the telephone, my wife was sitting with me as Wendell and I talked. As such, she can attest to the fact that Wendell was aware of his low chances and agreed to stop or at least wait on the application in order to defer the likely rejection and to extend end date for the patent pending status for the interface.'

***

"'Eventually, Wendell was pressed by a friend or acquaintance to show them a receipt or other evidence that he had a patent pending. The best I could do for him was to file the application and provide the details to him and leave out the filing date so he could raise that in his own time which I did.

181

Although I of course copied the relevant information to provide to Wendell, the filing information was provided by me in a format that is fairly different from the PTO receipt format (as Wendell himself noted) and was not meant to be a facsimile of the receipt.'

"Pippenger's statements in the two above paragraphs were false and intended to mislead the Administrator, in that Thomas never agreed to delay the filing of his patent application, had been told by Pippenger in September, 2010 that the application had been filed, and was not being pressed by a friend or acquaintance to show evidence of a pending patent. Pippenger knew that his statements were false.

"In responding to Thomas' allegations about Pippenger's conduct related to Thomas' dispute with Vokal Interactive, Pippenger stated the following:

"'Wendell rejected Vokal's $6500 offer. He stated that driving Vokal into bankruptcy and making no money at all would be better that accepting even a penny less that he though [sic] he was entitled to. I counseled Wendell to wait to file any suit against Vokal, since making money in court is a proper use of our system, but simply using the courts to force a party into bankruptcy is both unproductive and inappropriate.

"'Wendell did wait; however, he eventually hired another attorney to handle the suit when the time came. While my wife was not present for each and every one of these conversations with Wendell, she was present for enough that she can attest to the circumstances, including the fact that Wendell was always aware of all relevant details.'

"Pippenger's statements in the previous two paragraphs were false and intended to mislead the Administrator, in that Thomas never agreed to delay the filing of his lawsuit against

Vokal; Thomas had previously been told by Pippenger that the lawsuit had been filed; and Pippenger provided Thomas with false progress reports regarding the lawsuit. Pippenger knew his statements were false.

"By reason of the conduct described above, Phillip McKinney Pippenger has engaged in the following misconduct:

a. Making a statement of material fact known by the lawyer to be false in connection with a lawyer disciplinary matter, in violation of Rule 8.1(a) of the Illinois Rules of Professional Conduct (2010);

b. Conduct involving dishonesty, fraud, deceit, misrepresentation, in violation of Rule 8.4c of the Illinois Rules of Professional Conduct (2010);

c. Conduct which is prejudicial to the administration of justice, in violation of Rule 8.4(d) of the Illinois Rules of Professional Conduct (2010); and

d. Conduct that tends to defeat the administration of justice or to bring the legal profession into disrepute, in violation of Illinois Supreme Court Rule 770.

WHEREFORE, the Administrator respectfully requests that this matter be assigned to a panel of the Hearing Board, that a hearing be held, and that the panel make findings of fact, conclusions of fact and law, and a recommendation for such discipline as is warranted.

Respectfully Submitted,
Jerome Larkin, Administrator"

***

So, this episode of my life was ending with the main character coming across more like a caricature, with the six "changes" he made of a patent office receipt; possible attempted theft of the Notification System patent application, also made unpatentable with his 16 omissions of Claims when he submitted it seventeen months late, and with his pocketing and never returning $4,000 of funds that I had paid him for the same application; not to forget "Randy Stevenson," the invisible judge. Then the attempt to have my Folding Cart patent application drift into oblivion by not notifying me of the Final Rejection from the patent office, his clumsy attempt of "offering" me money, and the grand finale, not placing my monies paid to him in a segregated account, which is required of lawyers. Never mind the years of deceit in the e-mails that he sent, and the fact that he borrowed money from his client. Also, as reliable as I've always found the United States Postal Service to be, it's unusual that the only piece of mail that I'm aware of ever missing since I've lived in this home was the letter from the ARDC giving me the chance to present evidence to validate my claims against Pippenger. And his wife, who overheard all these nonexistent conversations he had on the phone, to which she will testify at the hearing. It seems that from the presentation that Pippenger has made that she would be ready to testify in his behalf. I was left asking myself, *"Would she really be willing to perjure herself that way?"* What happened to the truth throughout this cavalcade of transgressions?

Jerome Larkin was the Administrator for the ARDC, and he had an ARDC lawyer, Meriel Coleman, acting as "Counsel for the Administrator" in the ARDC proceedings against Pippenger.

This all meant that Meriel Coleman would be the lawyer gathering the information and putting it into prosecutorial form for the hearing that would determine Pippenger's guilt or innocence.

When I looked at the ARDC charges against Pippenger, they appear to be enough to warrant disbarment, even though the ARDC left out a number of what I thought were important and impactful violations, of both common ethics and of actual rule violations for lawyers.

I had no idea why the ARDC would leave out some of the things that I had complained about, and why they would not charge him with other things that they knew were violations of rules which a lawyer is bound by oath to follow. I figured, "They know what they're doing. It's all up to them." Of course, I trusted they were pursuing disbarment in the ways they knew to be most effective.

42
Patience, My Boy, Patience

The next thing I wanted to do was ask the ARDC if they would help me by validating to the USPTO the facts of what Pippenger had done concerning my patent application for the Notification System ("Localized Message System"). In the meantime, I turned to Les Wilson of the Cardinal Law Group in Evanston to resubmit my patent application for the Notification System, including all of the claims this time. Les Wilson is a premier guy and a superb patent attorney, in my estimation. That is an opinion that would quickly be validated by the USPTO.

I had given the ARDC this information, but they did not incorporate it into an accusation against Pippenger for this particular infraction. The ARDC said simply that, "He filed my patent application." They said they were not able to help me get any date reinstated with the patent office. "You may wish to consult with an attorney of you [sic] choice to discuss any legal options available to you."

Pippenger had submitted only one of the nineteen claims I was making for the approval of a patent. He sabotaged my patent application with his forgery when he submitted it, in order to validate his claim to the ARDC that I would never receive a patent for this idea.

It was left to me, then, to pay the USPTO something over $2700 to get the October 9, 2008, date reinstated. Pippenger's seventeen-month delay caused this fine. Add to this the $4000 I paid him for the application that he never submitted, and this guy is starting to cost me big bucks. He's costing me money in other ways, too, as in measures I might need to take to better protect myself from an unpredictable, seemingly malicious person. My losses were not all monies paid directly to Pippenger.

With the exception of the opening flurry of activity, the ARDC moved at a barely discernible pace; I would describe it as, "about every few months we do something new that you didn't really expect."

On September 19, 2012, the ARDC served Pippenger the Notice of Complaint at the Miller, Matthias & Hull offices.

On September 28th, Pippenger decided the situation was serious enough to warrant legal representation before the ARDC, so he hired Mitchell Ex, a former ARDC employee.

This seemed pretty much on par with how things work in Chicago. We at least have moved beyond the Al Capone era, but the City of Chicago would come to a standstill if cronyism were abruptly halted.

So, it's Pippenger and Ex. Stay tuned.

The ARDC then requested all medical records of Pippenger's from the North Shore University Health System, North Shore Medical Group on October 3rd. My guess would be that the ARDC was concerned about something more than his physical well-being.

Mr. Ex promptly requested, and of course was granted, additional time to respond on behalf of his client--from October 10th until November 7th.

On October 15th, the ARDC subpoenaed records from Leydig, Voit & Mayer and lo and behold, what should appear? A Pippenger proof!

Actually, what appeared was his "proof" of a letter addressed to me, which was a part of his computer records at his former firm:

"September 24, 2011

"Dear Wendell,

"Please review the attached (Folding Cart) Action and let me know how you want to move forward. Just call or stop by when you want to discuss.

Very truly yours,

LEYDIG, VOIT & MAYER, LTD.

By: Phillip M. Pippenger"

This was Pippenger's "proof" that he sent the letter to me, which he never did. However, the ARDC chose to accept this "proof," even though I provided an e-mail from him in which he stated he had not received the USPTO Action until January 28, 2012. He had written this Leydig letter in September 2011 and had never sent it.

Yet, there it was, on Leydig, Voit & Mayer, LTD. letterhead, proudly listing the names of the partners of the firm.

Little did I know or suspect how much he had planned ahead. Far ahead. How could I?

On October 12th, the ARDC notified Pippenger's lawyer that Wendell Thomas and Michael Thomas would be called as witnesses for the ARDC prosecution in the Pippenger case if he elected to have a hearing.

On November 5th, Mitchell Ex responded to the ARDC complaint by denying the allegations made in Counts I - III. On Pippenger's behalf, Mitchell Ex requested a hearing.

Added to this, which I found amusing, were the names of two people who would testify in Pippenger's behalf, "regarding his reputation for honesty and integrity." These must have been very close friends of Pippenger's, except that he had previously told me I was his only friend. Where did he find these people? Were they out there for hire?

The next action by the ARDC came on March 21, 2013, when, because of Pippenger's alleged previous behavior, the ARDC hired Dr. Stephen Dinwiddie from the Department of Psychiatry and Behavioral Sciences at Northwestern Memorial Hospital in Chicago. Dr. Dinwiddie is a registered Forensic

Psychiatrist which, of course, sets him apart from a regular psychiatrist. The ARDC stated that, "Opinion witness (Dinwiddie) evaluated Pippenger and prepared a report regarding Pippenger's psychiatric diagnosis and its connection to Pippenger's misconduct."

Apparently, the ARDC deemed Pippenger's behavior toward me as highly unusual, as it is not by any means the norm in their procedures to have an attorney evaluated by a forensic psychiatrist.

After reading this information from the ARDC that night, I checked my doors before going to bed to be certain they were dead-bolted. What in the hell was I really dealing with?

On April 4th, the ARDC ordered that Dr. Stephen Dinwiddie be deposed on or before June 1st.

Also on April 4th, the ARDC ordered that information to be used in the forthcoming hearing be exchanged from one side to the other by June 4th.

On May 21st, the Illinois Supreme Court, representing, "The People of The State of Illinois," subpoenaed Pippenger's medical records from the North Shore University Health System and the North Shore Medical Group for a second time.

On June 26th, Mitchell Ex filed a Supplemental Disclosure of Witnesses with the ARDC, stating that, in addition to the two character witnesses, Pippenger intended to present testimony from his therapist.

The therapist's name was Dr. Aaron Malina, Ph.D., ABPP. (ABPP stands for American Board of Professional Psychology.)

Dr. Malina would be an opinion witness, like Dr. Dinwiddie, according to ARDC public records:

"Opinion witness will offer testimony concerning the causal relationship between Pippenger's diagnosed depressive disorder and his actions as alleged in the Administrator's Complaint herein. Testimony is based

189

upon Pippenger's medical treatment history, medical testing, and the review of Administrator's opinion witness report. Witness's curriculum vitae is attached hereto.

"Respondent reserves the right to reasonably supplement or amend this list if he becomes aware of the identity of others having knowledge of facts relating to the matter.

Respectfully Submitted,
Phillip McKinney Pippenger
By: Mitchell C. Ex"

Frankly, I don't understand how a "diagnosed depressive disorder" could have anything to do with Pippenger's actions against me.

And curriculum vitae? What is that? I looked it up and found it is an overview of someone's credentials, experience, and published work in their field. As described, it is a term usually used in conjunction with an individual's search for employment.

Dr. Malina was not "looking for work" with the ARDC, but was, of course, just offering his credentials. It appeared to me that even though Dr. Malina had a long and possibly impressive list of publications to which he had contributed, Dr. Dinwiddie still had the inside track on psychiatric expertise.

Finally, on August 1st, the ARDC announced that the hearing for the case against Pippenger was set for November 15th at 9:30 a.m. at the ARDC offices in Chicago.

It had taken an incredibly long time for this to unfold. It was now nearing eighteen months since the time I filed my letter of complaint.

My mind was in overdrive during this waiting period. I checked the computer on the ARDC site almost daily. I had tunnel vision. It is safe to say, in my case, "You can't teach an old dog new tricks," i.e., I stayed with my obsession to get justice.

That's where I was as we headed for the November 2013 hearing. I received a letter from Meriel Coleman, advising me to be prepared to be a witness at the hearing and that there was a good possibility that Michael would also be required to testify. I called Michael and he said, "Yes," he would set the time aside to be available. I got back to Ms. Coleman with the news that I would be at the hearing, that we would both be there if need be.

It was at this point that Ms. Coleman punctured another one of my assumptions.

I had been figuring a lawyer who had intentionally done all of the myriad of things that Pippenger had done to me would not ever be deemed fit to continue in the legal profession. My assumption all along was that certainly the ARDC, which existed to protect the public, of which I was a part, would zealously guard their rules and ethical guidelines, allowing only those who proved fit, or who had at least normal or average levels of integrity and honesty, to be allowed to practice law.

Even though the ARDC had elected to charge Pippenger with only some of his transgressions against me, I still felt assured he would be disbarred. That's what the ARDC was there for, they had the responsibility to protect the public. They functioned under the direct oversight of Illinois' Supreme Court. They're not, I thought, going to keep this guy in business as a lawyer. They couldn't do that.

Except, at this point, when I mentioned to Meriel Coleman in conversation, more as a casual inquiry than a pointed question, "At the hearing in mid-November, he'll probably be disbarred, right? How does that work?"

When Ms. Coleman stopped laughing, she said, "No, no. He's not going to be disbarred. That's for serious violations."

"What could be more serious than what he's tried to do to me?" I thought.

It was an ever-so-brief conversation that turned my thinking upside down and gave me a new perspective, which has been validated a few times since then. My new realization was that the ARDC is there to protect the lawyers, not the public. Oh yes, it is true that occasionally a lawyer gets disbarred, but that is usually when they have stolen large sums of money from their client or their client's trust fund or estate, in other words, from a "big fish," a fish too big to ignore.

But for a lawyer to try to destroy someone's very potential livelihood, as in my case, then that's pretty much acceptable.

In the meantime, mini-me jauntily cocked his head while on my shoulder and with a smile he said, *"Destroying a person like you, that's okay. Now, if you had a pot full of money and he stole that, it would be different. But trying to wreck someone as a person? No, we're pretty much cool with that."*

So, the imposing marble columns at the ARDC offices, the plush carpeting, the big round plaque on the wall that says, "Supreme Court of the State of Illinois": It's really just a show—window dressing.

Justice was not going to be served. And justice was all I was interested in.

Then another exception arose. On November 1, 2013, Pippenger's attorney Mitchel Ex requested a postponement owing to the fact that he had had a knee replacement. The healing process was long and arduous and would not allow him to devote the required attention or do an adequate job defending Pippenger.

Of course, as should be the case, the request for postponement was allowed.

The ARDC held a preconference hearing on November 15, 2013, and determined that with the holiday season coming up and the New Year around the corner after that, the best time to have the hearing would be Tuesday, January 28, 2014, at 9:30 a.m.

It was an ironic choice. January 28th was the two-year anniversary of Pippenger's fictional account of being "scammed by the Clerk of the Circuit Court of Cook County, Illinois," and the sequel of "meeting with the judge who was an imposter but was somehow in the judge's chambers."

Just not in the judge's robes…

43
Realization Flips Anticipation

The holiday season was an emotional boost, and it helped me to get through the dreary, dark, shortened days—Halloween, Thanksgiving, Hanukah, Winter Solstice, Christmas, New Year's Eve, and New Year's Day. As each day passed, the January 28, 2014, ARDC hearing date drew closer.

My disappointment in the seriousness of the ARDC disciplinary process still festered, but what the hell, sometimes you can't fight city hall.

I was prepared to testify. Michael would testify. Pippenger would testify. His wife, Hilleory, would testify with whatever he told her to say. He would have either "character" witnesses--or "caricature" witnesses-- to testify. It would be an interesting faceoff; only two people, Michael and I, would likely be telling the truth, unless Phillip's wife turned on him, which was not to be expected.

The countdown was underway when, on January 16, 2014, the Hearing Board, which oversees the whole procedure, filed a First Amended Complaint. All they did was to alter some of the wording and eliminate a couple of sentences from the original complaint against Pippenger.

Then came a surprise. Meriel Coleman called me on the Thursday before the Tuesday hearing and told me Pippenger had requested "Discipline on Consent."

After almost two years of asserting his innocence, Pippenger decided to cave and said, "Okay, everything you have said is true. I have done it all. Not only have I done all that

194

you've said, but I will swear an oath that I have done it all and sign an affidavit."

All of my ruminations about how he might go about trying to prove his innocence drifted away like a puff of smoke. --No forged e-mails to prove he only followed what we had agreed upon? No spliced-together phone call tape-recordings to "prove" I had said something I had not? No forged letters, other than the never-sent Leydig, Voit & Mayer specimen, to prove I knew of this or that, or that I had written this or that. "And here it is in black and white!"

Pippenger had once told me how, when he got someone in a room with a tape recorder or a court reporter and they were giving a deposition, he would keep them there for hours and hammer away with questions until they would break, which they always did, and he would win. When he told me this "deposition procedure" that he used, he got that same cat-killing-the-birds glint in his eye. I had been looking forward to a grilling from this Goliath from next door, because what I had in my pouch for ammunition was the truth.

The ARDC approved Pippenger's request for Discipline on Consent and reiterated the Hearing would still take place on January 28th--as a formality--with nothing contested. I planned on attending, and I did.

Since Pippenger had requested Discipline on Consent, and since it was approved by the ARDC Hearing Board, he was required to sign an Affidavit to that effect.

Pippenger's Affidavit as to Discipline on Consent read:

"Phillip McKinney Pippenger, being first duly sworn, does state as follows:

1. "That I have read the Administrator's Petition to Impose Discipline on Consent (the 'Petition'), to which this affidavit is attached.
2. "That the assertions contained in the Petition are true and complete.

3. "That I join in the Petition freely and voluntarily.

4. "That I understand the nature and consequences of the Petition."

The Petition was then signed by Pippenger and witnessed by his attorney, Mitchell Ex, who acted as Notary Public.

Pippenger was actually dressed in a suit at the hearing. His shirt was buttoned, tucked in, and he also wore a tie. His trousers had a belt even.

Mark L. Karasik was the chairman of the Hearing Panel.

It came out at the Hearing that Pippenger had corrected some of the lies that he had originally told the ARDC, after seeing my response to his original letter, which was replete with falsehoods. I was not aware of the fact that he had ever acknowledged any truths. The ARDC kept that information under wraps.

A number of days after the conclusion of the Hearing the ARDC files a "Petition to Impose Discipline on Consent Pursuant to Supreme Court Rule 762(b)," with the Supreme Court of the State of Illinois. In this petition the ARDC lists any "Mitigating Factors." In other words, the ARDC lists reasons to go easy on this poor guy as though he is the one who has been put-upon. The ARDC said, "In mitigation, Respondent has not previously been disciplined in 15 years of practice. While Respondent's initial response to the Administrator was not candid, Respondent later acknowledged the inaccurate information during the investigative process and has expressed his regret for his misconduct."

So, the ARDC reasons that Pippenger should have sincere compassion because he has not been found guilty of rule violations in the past. Imagine that! Additional sincere compassion should be shown because while he tried like hell to pull the wool over the eyes of the ARDC, alas, he failed. Once

196

the ARDC had all the proof of his lies, Pippenger then said he had lied and said he was sorry for lying.

Of course I remember that the ARDC let him off the hook completely until I made a phone call to them explaining that I had never received an opportunity to respond to his lies because "somehow" my mail was missing. Was Pippenger sorry he lied or was he sorry he got caught? The ARDC didn't say.

And just imagine how wonderful a lawyer he must be and what character he must have to go fifteen years without once having been previously disciplined!

Ms. Coleman, on behalf of the ARDC, and in her efforts to protect the public, gently requested a two-month suspension from the practice of law for Pippenger's acts done against me.

The ARDC would not use any word that could be used in court of law against one of their own, and who was a dues-paying member. The ARDC used words like "redacted," or "altered," or "changed." Instead of saying that Pippenger ended up with $4000 in his bank account for submitting an unpatentable application in my behalf, the ARDC simply glossed over that part entirely never acknowledging anything. In my opinion, it was far beyond the scope of the ARDC to describe what happened accurately.

The ARDC was exceedingly careful not to call a spade a spade. In other words, the ARDC did not use any word that accurately described what Pippenger did to me if that word could later be used as evidence against him in a court case.

I suspect that if the ARDC were asked to describe a murder with a firearm by one of their member's (Mr. John Doe) they might say something like, "Mr. John Doe was thought to be in the area when an object from somewhere approached the other person."

Mr. Ex was asked by the Chairman if Pippenger had done any pro bono work.

Mr. Ex was not able to mention any specific instances of pro bono work but said Pippenger was active in Boy Scouts, i.e., he accompanied his son to Boy Scout meetings. So, they stretched things a little here and there.

The next thing Mr. Ex said caused me to perk up: "As you see in the petition to impose discipline on consent, (Pippenger) has expressed his regret and remorse for what happened that brought him here today. He hopes to put this behind him. I have all confidence that he will. This was an aberrant type of situation."

I thought, "*An aberrant type of situation?*" I sat there, writhing within, wanting to scream, "*Aberrant? Explain what you're saying!*" As I sat, I realized that his lawyer was telling me, without intending to, that Pippenger *had* targeted me, which meant what? "*He had set out to destroy me from the start? He doesn't do this to other clients? He singled me out as a target? What kind of a person am I really dealing with?*"

Chairman Karasik saw me sitting in the back row of the small hearing room and addressed a question to me:

"Mr. Thomas, you're the originating or the complaining witness in the case?

Me: Yes, I am.

Chairman Karasik: Are you satisfied with the result that's been reached here?

Me: The results are, I think, suggested to be a 60 day –

Chairman Karasik: Suspension from the practice of law.

Me: There were questions that I had about what I had originally presented as information that I didn't think was necessarily prosecuted, but the ARDC functions the way they function, and the results are what they are.

Chairman Karasik: Well, I can tell you I have been appointed by the Supreme Court to this Commission for over 25 years, and I know they thoroughly investigate every aspect of every complaint so I want to let you know from my side, having seen it, that they've looked into whatever you've raised and you're entitled to raise. I appreciate your comments, and I know it's difficult to come down on a day like this.

Me: What you are saying is what I hold in trust. I appreciate the work that the ARDC does, and I'm from the outside and I don't know what goes on in investigating everything. In my ignorance, I stand where I am.

Chairman Karasik: No, I understand."

After a few more insignificant exchanges, Ms. Parks, who was a member of the Hearing Panel, addressed me:

Ms. Parks: "And I'm the other non-attorney in the room. I'm the lay panel member, and I've been on the panel for 12 years or so. I would just echo what the Chair said. I had little knowledge of what happened. I didn't know the ARDC existed when I was appointed, which should give you a lot of confidence right there, but I've learned a lot."

***

I tried, and was able, to keep from laughing aloud.

***

She continued:

Ms. Parks: "I would agree that based on what is brought before them, what I can see as a lay person, they take very seriously and do the work to make sure the public is protected."

***

It went from a rather open acknowledgment of Pippenger's psyche to an almost Abbott-and-Costello "Who's on first" comedy routine, all under the guise of protecting the public. I was beginning to wish I were a member of whatever public was being talked about and protected.

There was a brief recess from the proceedings so that the panel members could meet in private.

When they reemerged, Chairman Karasik spoke. He suggested that Pippenger do some pro bono work. He also said that the panel was okay with accepting a sixty-day suspension, but they would also like to have Pippenger watch a two or three hour video in the ARDC offices--on "Professionalism."

Pippenger readily agreed that that was a good idea. In closing, Chairman Karasik spoke personally to Pippenger:

Chairman Karasik: "All right. If you'll amend the petition in any form you need to do to incorporate that additional condition (the view of the video), it's a good thing to do, Mr. Pippenger. We are not trying to be harsh, but you will actually learn something, and it will refresh you."

***

Once again, I was being enlightened, albeit unintentionally, by Chairman Karasik. As he said, "We are not trying to be harsh," he did so in a gentle tone, as one might use when talking with a small child who might not comprehend, or a person who had some type of disorder which might make understanding difficult.

The sledge came down slowly but heavily. I quickly gathered that Mr. Ex and Chairman Karasik must be drawing from Dr. Stephen Dinwiddie's psychiatric evaluation of Pippenger. A flood of information had been released, but because there was no hearing and Dr. Dinwiddie's testimony was not needed, it remained under lock and key, released only to a select few.

I was not one of them.

A few months later, when I retrieved the public records from the ARDC, there was a page that listed costs to the ARDC because of Pippenger's actions. One of the costs listed was Dr. Dinwiddie's fee. His charges to the ARDC were $3587.50. The many hours the forensic psychiatrist spent with Pippenger resulted in a very interesting analysis—I'm pretty certain. That was something that I'd like to see for my own protection.

Pippenger left before I did, and as he passed, for show I'm sure, he placed a hand on my shoulder and said, "I'm sorry," with all the feigned sincerity he could muster. I knew no one was home, so I didn't respond.

44
Negotiating With the Wind

Back in August 2013, as the ARDC hearing date approached, I had an epiphany: If I could get Pippenger in front of a civil jury, I would have a compelling case. Here's a guy who has done all of this insane stuff to me for no reason that I can discern. He's done it to a guy with terminal cancer, who he called his best friend, from whom he borrowed money, and with whom he has shared information that he wouldn't even share with his wife. He's done these things to an old man who has little hair, wears glasses and hearing aids, had multiple surgeries; two hip replacements, and a stem cell transplant among others.

I could be my own good lawyer, and I could probably make a sympathetic and innocent hero out of myself. Not that I've done anything heroic, but that's how it's done in the movies. Why not do it in real life? After all, Pippenger would have some kind of liability insurance, as all lawyers probably do.

What the hell. A jury might award me a million, maybe a million and a half for what this guy has done. I might not be able to cry in court, but I thought I could act old and emotionally beat up.

When I began to research the idea, I soon stumbled across the knowledge that since the work Pippenger was supposed to have done for me was actually for the family corporation, I would have to use a lawyer. There is a federal law (which I believe is 28 U.S.C. Sec. 1654) that requires corporations to have representation by members of the bar rather than act as pro se litigants. This includes a family corporation.

Problem solved. I would just get a lawyer. I imagined there would be any number of lawyers salivating to get a shot at my case.

After speaking to the second law firm on my list, another stumbling block arose. In Illinois, lawyers cannot be sued for any punitive damages.

After my one-day flirtation with a daydream, reality set in again. This time because of the protection lawyers have against punitive damages, I could not find a firm to take my case. There just wasn't enough money involved. I had spoken with six or eight different firms and had left a couple of voice messages, but I couldn't get any help.

Then, I got a return call from one of the messages left, and it was Elliot Schiff, a top-notch malpractice lawyer. In fact, it was ironic that Elliot called back because I had given up on that happening, and he had been my first choice. Right off the bat, I thanked him for the call-back and told him that no one was interested in my case because there was no real money involved.

Elliot cajoled me into beginning my "Pippenger story." He asked me questions, kept me talking, and eventually said, "You know what, I don't care if there's no money in this. I'm going to take it. This is all wrong. I'm going to help you with this."

I said to Elliot that I thought it might be a good thing for Pippenger to settle this before the ARDC hearing, so that he could get some sympathy from the Hearing Board. Elliot concurred. At that time, Pippenger probably knew, through his lawyer, the former ARDC employee, that nothing serious was going to come of anything that was charged against him, maybe a little time off, but no disbarment for trying to destroy a client and deprive him of potential success.

On September 20, 2013, Elliot sent a letter to the head partners at Leydig, Voit & Mayer, Ltd, and Miller, Matthias & Hull, telling them that he had been retained by me to pursue a remedy for what Pippenger had done in a number of situations, including professional negligence and fraud. In the letter, Elliot re-capped Pippenger's major violations, gleaned from the ARDC files published on its website.

The months passed, with an occasional email between Pippenger and Elliot.

At the ARDC hearing on January 28, 2014, Pippenger was suspended from the practice of law for sixty days. The effective dates of his suspension were from April 4 through June 3, 2014.

In February and March, the negotiations for me to get my money back had picked up steam, with a high volume of Internet communications. Elliot had suggested that he thought we might be able to recover somewhere between 30 to 60 thousand dollars. The total of the monies that Pippenger had cost me was actually $39,798.66. The arrangement I had with Elliot was that he would get 33 percent of the money received, and that was certainly fair enough for me.

The long and the short of the negotiations were as follows. I started out asking for $50,000, and Pippenger countered with $20,000, I believe. Elliot suggested that I go to $35,000, as he expected Pippenger might meet that amount, which he did. This meant that I would end up with a little over $23,000. I thought about it and decided to make this kind of peace and be done with it. With all that I felt I'd been through and feeling so tired from the constant emotional drain, it seemed worth the tradeoff. I would be giving up around $17,000, but at least it would all be over. Ah, relief, salvation.

Pippenger would write a contract, and we could then finish the whole thing off. He had asked, because he did not have $35,000, if paying on a monthly basis would be acceptable.

I responded, "Of course."

So, Pippenger wrote the contract, and Elliot forwarded it to me. When I read it over, I thought, "What the hell is this idiot trying to do?"

In the contract, Pippenger wrote something like, "Thomas and his extended family may not disparage my name or say anything negative about me. If they do, Thomas will immediately owe me $500,000." While this is not exact, it is the essence of what the contract said.

Elliot struck the paragraph, and I sent him an email thanking him.

Pippenger responded that he really didn't want a nickel of my money.

As per his word, the next contract he wrote, he changed some wording and also changed the $500,000 to a measly $72,000. When he did this, which I once again rejected, I decided that I would accept nothing less than the full amount of money that he had cost me, which would include the fee for Elliot.

Something was definitely wrong with this guy. Of course, I was not going to get on any hook for any money to him. Smart might not be my strongest point, but neither is completely stupid.

These negotiations were taking place during the first part of Pippenger's supposed suspension. They were not going forward, but they were going on. Pippenger was actually the only one of the three of us who really knew what was going on, and what the method of his madness was.

It was one contract after the other, in none of which could we find anything acceptable, and I became aware around the beginning of May that Pippenger had no intention of settling anything. I realized that he never had, and I put a deadline on reaching an agreement of May 15, 2014, at 12:00 noon.

On May 5, 2014, I inserted the dollar amounts into the contract that Pippenger had written. My insertion brought the total payments for the following 40 months up to about $60,000. This amount took me to break-even for what Pippenger had cost me, and it took into account the money for Elliot Schiff.

Pippenger responded on May 8th, saying, in part:

"In overview, the edits essentially reduce the agreement to one that requests that Pippenger pay $50k to keep Thomas from filing 'wrongful' lawsuits. As you know, such a request, especially given the amount requested, is a Class 1 felony in this state under IDD 1961 and others. To be very clear, I did not solicit the request, could not have anticipated the request, and am in no way involved in the drafting or transmission of that request."

I didn't know what I had done wrong, but Pippenger is a lawyer, so I emailed the following to Elliot:

"Hi Elliot,

"Please forward the attachment to Pippenger. I deleted the paragraph he wanted deleted. I deleted the one he said was useless. I made a couple of other minor changes. I also went back to his dollar amount not realizing at the time I did it that I was breaking some law or another. I'm glad he warned me.

"If he wants to change the dollar amount he will have to do so on his own. Or, he can just send back the original contract that he wrote. I don't care much what he does. This all ends Thursday at noon.

Thanks, Wendell"

The next day, Friday, I grew curious as to what I could possibly have done wrong. I thought that when a contract was negotiated, a party inserted what it was that they would accept. I called the State of Illinois Legislative line for assistance and was connected to a woman who steered me to the site that contained all of the laws of the state. She said that I might find my answer there.

I spent about two hours searching the Illinois statutes and found nothing that could help me in the "Felony" section. Then I hit upon a bright idea, which was to ask Elliot. I sent him the following email:

"Elliot,

"Do you happen to know what Class 1 felony Pippenger is referring to? I've looked and can't find a thing. Obviously I don't know where to look.

"Would you know a number of the law or something like that so I could access it?

Thanks,

Wendell"

Elliot soon responded with the following:

"This claim is ridiculous. There is no felony, period!!!!!!!!!!!!!!!"

The fourteen exclamation marks were Elliot's.

I believe that is the last time I responded to anything from Pippenger. Over that weekend, I realized that the interest I had lost from not having the money in the mutual fund account from which it was withdrawn was additional money that Pippenger had cost me. I sent Elliot one last amount to pass on to the other side.

I say the other side because Pippenger had now hired a lawyer. Perhaps he realized he had gone overboard with his accusation of "a Class 1 Felony." The lawyer's name was Mathew Henderson, a partner, or a senior partner, at what I would describe as a third-tier law firm in Chicago.

I wondered who had caught whom while bottom-fishing.

Neither Pippenger nor his newly hired lawyer reinserted the amount of $60,000 into the negotiations. They held at the $30,000 or $35,000 level.

The negotiations wound down, and the deadline passed without further incident.

Along with the failed negotiations, I had noticed that Pippenger's kids had stopped nodding or saying, "Hello," when they saw me. I started getting blank stares. When I would throw a soccer ball back over the fence to their yard, they wouldn't even acknowledge the gesture with a wave or a, "Thanks." Along with this, Hilleory no longer acknowledged me, although I had continued to treat all of them as "the innocents they are."

One morning, as I was in my front yard next to the public sidewalk, I saw some kind of a small, dead animal laying in my grass. At this moment, Elias, Pippenger's second oldest son, came out of his house with a friend. As they were passing, I said, "Hey, you guys, look at this." I pointed to the animal. They stood for a moment, about eight feet away. I said, "I'm serious. Look at this thing. What do you think it is?" I actually didn't know.

Elias' friend came over and looked, as did Elias. "Maybe a squirrel?" said his friend.

It struck me that he was right. I had never seen nor thought about a dead baby squirrel before, and I didn't realize it would have a disproportionately enlarged head and a hairless body. Its legs looked like arms, and its claws, of the future, looked like small hands. Grotesque looking, I thought, like a baby monkey.

Anyway, throughout this twenty or thirty second exchange, I became aware of the isolation that Elias had put himself in, and I wondered what was going on. Was he now mad at me also?

A couple of weeks after that, I happened to look out my den window, facing the street, and I saw that Hilleory's hired landscaper had cut down some of my prairie plants on the two foot wide shared strip of dirt that separates their dead-end driveway from my brick sidewalk. He had replaced my plants with something new and very different. I went outside, as I saw her there, and I said, "Hilleory, you've cut down my prairie plants."

She said, "No, I didn't. My landscaper did. And if you don't like it you can call the city." I hadn't seen such a look of standoffish anger or heard that tone of voice from Hilleory before.

What was wrong with her? I looked at her, baffled by this degree of aggression, but I kept my mouth shut. This was not something I would call the city about. In a case like this, a couple of neighbors would typically exchange a sentence or two in an attempt to resolve the problem. But as I could see this wasn't her current mode, I let it go.

Little did I know how far astray she'd already been led.

45

The ARDC Chooses Sides

What Pippenger had done in our "negotiation" was deceptive and misleading. There was never any good-faith attempt on his part to finalize any agreement. It was all a come-on. I had been duped into thinking we were negotiating, until I realized he had no intention of fulfilling anything, other than winning some game in which he was the only participant. Was he having fun? Did he have fun? Probably, because he was at work on a much bigger twist that I would find out about later.

After a few weeks, I decided to turn Pippenger in to the ARDC again, not only for his false felony claim in order to better leverage himself in a negotiation but also to ask the ARDC to revisit some of the things they had neglected to charge Pippenger with from the first complaint.

On June 21, 2014, I sent my letter of complaint to the ARDC. In that letter, I told the ARDC, "I will continue to pursue justice at any level that I can. I will not ever be treated by an attorney or anyone else the way I have been treated by Mr. Pippenger without making the attempt to stand up for my inherent rights as a human being as I seek justice."

I wrote the ARDC, telling them that I had occasion to revisit the complaint I had originally filed and found that they had omitted "some things" in the charges they eventually made against Mr. Pippenger.

I told them what they had omitted, and I included in parentheses the reasons why Pippenger might have done what he did:

"Forgery: Mr. Pippenger forged a United States Patent and Trademark Office receipt. On January 25, 2012, at 22:51:09, Mr. Pippenger sent me an email stating, 'Hey Wendell, just wanted to scoop up a few of the word drafts before I sent, here are the patent docs attached.' The 'patent docs attached,' included the counterfeit electronic receipt sent by Mr. Pippenger. The counterfeit receipt was sent to me 15 minutes and 37 seconds after he had filed the patent application that same night at 22:35:32.

"On the receipt that Mr. Pippenger sent me, he committed the following acts of, Forgery:

"He forged the receipt date. The USPTO Receipt date was: 25-Jan-2012.

"The forged Receipt Date that Mr. Pippenger sent me was shown as: 'Verified.' On January 28, 2012 when I asked him what 'Verified' meant, he said that it meant it was attached to my previous and rejected application date of October 9, 2008. This is untrue.

"(Mr. Pippenger did not want me to see the actual Receipt Date. He wanted me to continue to believe that he had filed the patent application on September 15, 2010.)

"He removed his email address. The removal of his email address was a forgery. Had he filed the patent application on September 15, 2010, (as he had claimed to me from that date forward), his email address would have been the email address he used in all of our correspondence when he was at the firm of Leydig, Voit & Mayer Ltd.

"(Mr. Pippenger did not want me to see the email address he used when he actually submitted the patent application. He removed his email address from the USPTO Electronic Acknowledgment Receipt.)

211

"He forged the Time Stamp. The Time Stamp from the USPTO was 22:35:32, which is 10:35 PM on our 12 hour clock. The Time Stamp that he showed was 13:35:32 which is 1:35 PM on our 12 hour clock.

"(Mr. Pippenger did not want me to see the actual Time Stamp. He did not want a Time Stamp to be shown at 10:35PM.)

"On Thursday, September 16, 2010, at 8:20PM, as I was about to return from a trip to California, I emailed Mr. Pippenger, saying, '...I'm thinking that our patent app went in on Wed.'

"(Eight minutes later, at 8:28PM, Mr. Pippenger replied, '...yes indeed, you are now the proud applicant/inventor with the USPTO....' Mr. Pippenger wanted me to continue to believe that the patent application had been submitted during normal business hours on September 15, 2010 at 1:35PM.)

"He removed the word, 'no,' on the Submitted with Payment line. The actual USPTO receipt had the word, 'no,' printed adjacent on the line that reads, 'Submitted with Payment.' Mr. Pippenger's removal of this word constitutes forgery.

"(Mr. Pippenger did not want me to see the word, 'no,' printed on the, 'Submitted with Payment' line. Patent applications are abandoned by the USPTO if payment is not made within 5 months along with late payment fees. Since the receipt he was presenting to me was ostensibly from 16 months prior, he would not want me to see that the patent application would have automatically been abandoned.)"

I pointed out to the ARDC that they had omitted from my complaint against Mr. Pippenger on April 2, 2012, the fact that he committed:

"Sabotage: I am presenting the following facts regarding the submission of the patent application for the Localized Message System.

"Mr. Pippenger's submission of the patent application on January 25, 2012, (Application Number: 13358505), was an absolute SABOTAGE of the application that we had previously agreed upon submitting in September of 2010. He copied the previously agreed upon application verbatim until he came to the, 'CLAIMS,' section of the application. He then copied only the first of seventeen (17) claims. So, as he was submitting the patent application 15 months late, he then decided to make sure I would never get the patent anyway!

"He submitted the first of the seventeen claims we had agreed upon in verbatim and omitted the next sixteen (16) agreed upon claims. Omitted!

"After the first claim, he wrote six more which he made up and that were irrelevant, unimportant, abbreviated, and totally unacceptable, for a total of seven (7). Mr. Pippenger absolutely and unequivocally sabotaged my patent application."

I went on with my complaint, explaining that the information to follow was new information and should be considered a new complaint. My new complaint involved "False Accusations," which comes under the ARDC Rules of Misconduct.

I explained Pippenger's false accusation against me for ostensibly committing a Class 1 felony. I gave some background of the failed "negotiations." I claimed that Pippenger had quite clearly committed a violation of the Illinois Rules of Professional Conduct. To be more precise, I cited the violation of Rule 8.4: Misconduct (g).

Rule 8.4: Misconduct (g) reads as follows: "It is professional misconduct for a lawyer to: (g) present, participate in presenting, or threaten to present criminal or professional disciplinary charges to obtain an advantage in a civil matter."

"Finally," I said in my letter, "I believe his false accusation of me having committed a Class 1 Felony in our agreement negotiation definitely contributed to keeping anything from getting settled... I think that the false accusation directed at me falls under Rule 8.4: Misconduct (g)."

Well, Pippenger once again got the hired hand, Mitchell Ex, the former ARDC employee, to come to his rescue. Mr. Ex performed very well, with the full support of the ARDC, and my complaint was put asunder.

An American Bar Association publication discussed: "What constitutes a threat? If it is a threat, was it made solely to gain an advantage in a civil matter? New York State Bar Association Opinion 772 (2003) addressed these issues... the opinion summarized state bar ethics opinions and case law on the subject. ... Some ethics opinions and court decisions interpret the mere allusion to a criminal prosecution... as a veiled threat to present criminal charges to a prosecutor."

But, what the hell, this is Illinois, and the guy representing Pippenger used to work for the organization, right?

Mr. Ex, the former ARDC employee presented his "information" and, alas, the "integrity" of the ARDC dictated that they let Pippenger off the hook yet again. The ARDC allowed the misrepresentations of information presented by Mr. Ex and Pippenger to stand in good stead and Pippenger was able to remain unscathed.

In his final paragraph of misinformation, Mr. Ex admonished the ARDC, stating, "It is now time for the Commission to bring this matter to a close."

The ARDC acquiesced in Mr. Ex's admonishment and immediately sent me a letter telling me, in a convoluted way, that they had discretion and that Pippenger had not done what he had done.

And you, Mr. Thomas, your bus will arrive shortly. Please be under it.

The ARDC had previously told me, when I had questioned the minimal punishment they were meting out to Pippenger, that I could rest assured that the next time Pippenger violated a rule, they would really and truly punish him, come down on him like a hammer. Although, in this instance, they must have felt obliged to listen to the wise, and what I interpreted as the sometimes false words of Mr. Ex, their former teammate.

And me?

"I am asking the ARDC to acknowledge the evidence that I presented and am presenting. I request the Attorney Registration and Disciplinary Commission under the Illinois Supreme Court to acknowledge the truth that Mr. Pippenger FORGED the United States Patent and Trademark Office Electronic Acknowledgement Receipt and, in addition, that he SABOTAGED Patent Application 13359505. My request is simple. I want the truth. Justice."

My request was denied by the agency that protects the public against lawyers like Pippenger.

The ARDC did try to add a bit of humor to the situation in its final letter of November 19, 2014, wherein they stated in their final two paragraphs:

"Assuming Mr. Pipperger's [sic] views about your additions to the settlement agreement were incorrect that, alone, is not a sufficient basis to warrant formal disciplinary proceedings. We also considered that there was insufficient evidence to prove that Mr. Pippenger used a threat of a criminal prosecution against to [sic] you [sic] gain an advantage in the negotiations. You were represented by counsel during the settlement

215

negotiations and he did not view Mr. Pippenger's comments as a threat.

"While we understand that you disagree with our decision, our file in this matter will remain closed in this matter."

What's farcical is that the violation of the rule is not whether or not you "intend" to take anyone to court with your false accusation. The violation is the act of making the accusation in the first place.

Of course, Elliot Schiff did not view Pippenger's comments as a threat because at the time it happened, Elliot said in his email to me: "This claim is ridiculous. There is no felony, period!!!!!!!!!!!!!!!!"

What could Pippenger take me to court about if he "intended" to? A cloud or mirage of his own making?

I laughed for a while, mostly in frustration, hiding my anger, and then put on a coat and scarf, as I stood out in the cold, alone.

46
A Big Leap to Nowhere

In mid-October, I'd finished another good breakfast at the Golden Olympic Restaurant where I go periodically with my friend Teddy. Or if you met him more recently, you might know him as Ted, or even Theodore. But since I've known him for more than sixty years, he's still "Teddy" to me. And his younger brother, who's my age, is still Demo.

You want to know something about Evanston? Evanston Township High School? Downtown Evanston? The south end, the north end, Nichols, Haven, or whatever other school you wonder about? Or politics? You want to know about the city council? Hey, whaddya wanna know? Teddy's the man to ask.

We get together about twice a year for a breakfast at the Olympic, and the last few years, I've tried to beat him to the punch and pay the waitress for our breakfast even before we sit down. Teddy eats there every morning and speaks Greek with all of the owners, so I'm usually in over my head in as far as doing anything on my own in that environment. But on occasion, I get to win.

Anyway, when I went outside after our breakfast this particular morning, the Northwestern University bus had just pulled up to a stop. Off the bus and stepping lively came another friend of mine, who is about fifteen years younger than me. He's one of those people blessed with a look of eternal youth. And he's a law professor.

We greet each other and shake hands with "the grip," let go and smile. As is his custom, he immediately inquires as to how I am and what I'm up to and how is life. It doesn't take much, I admit, for me to get started on Pippenger.

I spewed out my latest, which I've become pretty adept at doing.

He dug into it a bit, and I gave him some particulars.

He said, "These things could be reported to the police."

I'd never thought in those terms before. I just knew they were wrong.

"You can go to the police with this, and they should charge him," he said. "That's what it sounds like to me."

As we parted, he called over his shoulder with a smile, "Go for it, Wendell. Really!"

That was enough to make me think for a day or two before I decided to act on what was said.

And act I did.

I made an appointment and went to the Evanston Police Department and spoke with a couple of detectives. We sat at a long table in a conference room, with them on one side and me on the other. They were paying attention, and I laid out the whole story.

Occasionally, one or the other of them would ask a question. I had all of the information in duplicate, so that we could talk and literally be on the same page.

After about an hour, I noticed a binder on their side of the table. I said, "What is that? Is that a file on somebody?"

The detective, who apparently had brought the binder into the room, said, "Yeah, it's a file. We have a lot of files."

My mind clicked a notch or two further. I didn't think they would bring a file into our meeting that was about someone else when they're meeting with me.

The folder was about a half-inch thick.

"Is that a file on me?" I asked.

"Yeah, actually it is. This is a file on some things about you," he said.

Right away, I figured the folder must be from the reports that Geri Shapiro from across the street had filed against me when I used to take down her iridescent pink and orange signs that she used to plaster all over the neighborhood in violation to my senses and a city ordinance which stipulates that only two signs are allowed and they must be on private property. She was violating the ordinance, and then she filed complaints against me. She must know something I don't.

Maybe it was petty on my part. I'll take that rap. It's stuck in my craw for years that she cheated one of my sons when he did yard work for her and then she only paid him half of what they had agreed upon. On the other hand, a number of neighbors who also found the signs to be a blight have thanked me.

It looked like she sure had made a lot of reports.

We kept on with the conversation about Pippenger until, at one point, the detective who was doing most of the talking asked me something about automobile damage.

I told them that one time, the Shapiro woman had gone down to Michael and Lene's house and rang the doorbell. Lene had answered. Ms. Shapiro had wondered to Lene if perhaps I had stuck twigs in the door lock of her car door.

Lene had told Ms. Shapiro, "No, that's not the way Wendell does things, to you or anyone."

Maybe Geri Shapiro filed a complaint about that. I don't know. Actually, I've never done anything to anyone's car.

Anyway, the detective asked me something about the Pippengers' car and I said that at one point, the car they park in the driveway had a flat tire.

I told them that it was flat at the same time that somebody had gone down our street and punctured about fifteen or twenty tires in one night. I told the detectives that I was glad to see that the Pippengers didn't get left out. This episode in the neighborhood happened the previous spring, sometime in April or May, if I remembered correctly.

The quieter of the two detectives said, "Well, that's an honest answer."

I didn't connect any dots.

We continued to talk about forgery, sabotage and the various frauds that Pippenger had done, and after an hour and a half or so, we called it a day. The lead detective said that, given the information I had presented, he would interview Pippenger, and then he would get back to me. He said it would probably be four or five days before he called me.

All of the claims of crimes to the Evanston Police Department that I had made about Pippenger's actions towards me were taken from: U.S. Department of Justice; Federal Bureau of Investigation; Criminal Justice Information Services (CJIS) Division. The definitions are in the "GLOSSARY" following the article titled: "The Measurement of White-Collar Crime Using Uniform Crime Reporting (UCR) Data," by Cynthia Barnett.

The definitions are:

Embezzlement: The unlawful misappropriation by an offender to his/her own use or purpose of money, property, or some other thing of value entrusted to his/her care, custody, or control.

Counterfeiting/Forgery: The altering, copying, or imitation of something, without authority or right, with the intent to deceive or defraud by passing the copy of thing altered or imitated as that which is original or genuine; or the selling, buying, or possession of an altered, copied, or imitated thing with the intent to deceive or defraud.

Fraud Offenses: The intentional perversion of the truth for the purpose of inducing another person or other entity in reliance upon it to part with some thing of value or to surrender a legal right.

False   Pretenses/Swindle/Confidence   Game;   The intentional misrepresentation of existing fact or condition, or the use of some other deceptive scheme or device, to obtain money, goods or other things of value.

Wire Fraud; The use of an electric or electronic communications facility to intentionally transmit a false and/or deceptive message in furtherance of a fraudulent activity.

When the detective from the Evanston Police Department called about five days later, he said that they were charging Pippenger with forgery and that the charge would have to be turned in to the Cook County State's Attorney. He said that this was one of those situations in which you could flip a coin as to whether or not the State's Attorney would choose to prosecute him. He expected to get an answer back from the State's Attorney's office in four or five days.

When he called after about another five days, he said, "I told you it was about a fifty-fifty chance on prosecution, and they have elected not to. Sorry about that." I must have called, "Heads," and here it turned out to be, "Tails."

I didn't seem to be getting any breaks. Not only had the Evanston Police Department quit on me, so had my computer. It had started flipping to different websites when I hadn't even touched any keys. Sometimes my computer had locked me out.

Damnit, another couple of failures. I've found though, good, bad, or indifferent, that if I feel that someone is out to destroy me--and this is the first time it has ever happened--I don't quit defending myself.

I was disillusioned. I knew the detective had to cover himself in case the State's Attorney elected not to prosecute Pippenger. That's why he gave me the "fifty-fifty" on chances. Yet, somehow, I have always believed that justice will prevail. I had to believe it. I believe in our society. Our country. My community. You just can't do to someone what Pippenger did to me. If you could get away with this stuff, society would cease to function. It would be a free-for-all. It would be a matter of last one standing gets all.

A few days later, I had a thought. I knew a top-notch guy who was a police chief in a neighboring town. I thought it might be a good thing to talk to him and see if he might have any ideas.

I met him at his office. He was generous and gave me about forty-five minutes. It was enough time for me to get the story over to him, and he took it all in.

He sat for a minute and then said, "I think what you should do is go to the State's Attorney's office and see if you can speak with someone. You are a citizen, and you're entitled to know why their office has decided not to prosecute."

It seemed like a fairly simple approach and something that I could try. It was sound advice, I thought.

When I called the State's Attorney's office, I found out they didn't see people by appointment, but if I wished, I could just come to the office to speak with someone.

"Okay," I thought. "I'll write a letter along with all of the information that I'll take out there. I'll take the binders. Goddamnit. I'll beg if I have to." And so in my way, I did beg. I don't usually promote myself in anything that I do, but at this point, I felt that I'd run out of options. I wanted some attention from someone who would acknowledge the truth.

In the letter, I gave a short introduction about Pippenger and in general what he had done. I continued, and this time I played the sympathy card. Following are some excerpts from the letter to illustrate my attempt at being persuasive:

"...In addition, I am an elderly, terminal cancer patient. I have been both elderly and a terminal cancer patient throughout the time during which Pippenger has executed his criminal offenses. I am aware that the Cook County State's Attorney is an advocate of the elderly and I now seek that advocacy.

"For someone with the makeup and nature of Pippenger, the fact that I am an elderly, trusting, electronically-ignorant, and a terminal cancer patient was a perfect fit. There was a good chance that I would die before I even discovered the many-many things he intentionally did to destroy my ideas and cause me to be short-changed. Or, maybe he thought my easy going and trusting manner along with my electronic ignorance about anything"high-tech" was all he needed.

"...In my own behalf I would like to say that I have been a law-abiding citizen. I, like most people, have done the things that I consider good and positive for my family, my community, and my country.

"I am an army veteran.

"I have been the sponsor for the past 24 years of an annual scholarship given at Evanston Township High School.

"I was given a City of Evanston Citizen Award for being the sole and instrumental person in the arrest and successful prosecution of a criminal who was given an 18 year sentence in the penitentiary and who the judge called, 'A menace to society.'

"I have done years of volunteer work at the Cook County Forest Preserve system.

"There is much more I could say in my attempt to get positive attention and results from the Cook County State's Attorney office.

"...I want it known that I am not trying to use the system for personal advantage.

"...I would guess that I am (or was) his only elderly client. Are the people at Microsoft or

Caterpillar too clever to be duped? Why did he pick on me? I am not as bright as his counterparts, it's true. My mind makes me forgetful and I can't always connect the dots.

"What pleasure would someone get out of duping someone like me for more than two years?

"Or are there other very real possibilities? Did Pippenger fail to file the lawsuit against Vokal because he had taken a payment from Vokal sometime between September 2010 and the end of January 2011?

"Did Pippenger not file the authentic Localized Message System patent application because he was actually going to either give it or sell it (using a different title/name) to a relative or someone else? Was his plan going to be to steal the patent idea?

"I know that the Cook County State's Attorney protects people like me and prosecutes people like Pippenger. I expect this to be the case. I expect this to be the case even though he is a lawyer. I don't think he is better at what he does than the Cook County State's Attorney is at what they do…"

***

I met with the top man in the Cook County State's Attorney Office, and he listened, responded, and said that he would look over what I had presented in the three binders.

The definitions I used in the accusations I made to the Cook County State's Attorney were taken from the U.S. Department of Justice, Federal Bureau of Investigation. Once again it was the same source for definitions that I used with the Evanston Police Department.

I claimed, and gave the evidence of: 1 charge of embezzlement, 11 charges of fraud or wire fraud, 1 charge of attempted bribery, and 2 charges of forgery.

The letter to the Cook County State's Attorney was dated December 3, 2014.

After the meeting, I fell into thoughtful mode. First of all, the head of the office with whom I met struck me as personable, attentive, and trustworthy. He looked me in the eye as we spoke. He said I could get back to him in a week.

The only thing that I wondered about was a comment he had made sometime during our talk. I heard it, but I had continued plowing ahead with my agenda. That evening, it came back to me.

"There might be more to this." he had said.

47
Full Strength Kafka

In the mid-afternoon on December 10, 2014, I went to the northwest side of Chicago to wander around a store that has all kinds of stuff I don't really need, much of which is mind-bending. The store is called American Science and Surplus, and I probably go there two times a year. I like to look and to daydream. I am usually able to get some things for both me and my seven-year-old grandson.

I got home at about 3:30 p.m., and shortly thereafter, the doorbell rang.

There stood a woman dressed in dark clothing. A few weeks earlier, I had changed from using my screen door to using my winter storm door, which is not that easy to hear through, particularly if I'm not wearing my hearing aids.

I opened the door and said, "Hi, how are you?"

She asked, "Are you Wendell Thomas?"

I said, "Yes, I am."

With that, the woman, who I guessed was in her late forties, began her rote recitation. She spoke very quickly.

I was picking up some important words here and there, but also missing a lot because of her rapid-fire monotone.

She hadn't finished talking, but I had picked up on a few of the words: "subpoena," and "Pippenger," and "court."

I opened the door further and interrupted her. "Would you like to come in? Would you like a coffee?"

"No," she said and went on with her spiel.

I said, "Oh, Pippenger." I pointed over her head at the house next door, "He lives right there. He got suspended from his law practice for what he did against me. So what's this about?"

"You've been served. It's a subpoena," she said.

"Do you want me to sign something?" I asked.

"No, these are yours," she said, and handed me a packet of papers. She turned and left as she added, "Have a good day," but her smile was cold and distant.

A subpoena? Is this a TV show? Was she a cop?

I went and looked out of the den window and saw her get into a car with big bold lettering on the door panels, "Cook County Sheriff's Police."

"So this is what they do," I thought, as I started scanning the papers she had handed to me.

"What the hell?" The top page said, "Summons/Stalking No Contact Order. Phillip Pippenger versus Wendell A. Thomas"

"What the hell is this about for chrissake? Contact? I haven't even talked to the bastard since 2012. Not one word." I folded the page over. The second page was more of the same stuff. Court stuff, with his name versus my name. I turned to the next page.

It said, "Case No. 14OP20397," with some kind of an official stamp in the upper right corner. To the left of the number, it said, "Phillip Pippenger (Petitioner) versus Wendell A. Thomas (Respondent). Now comes the Petitioner Phillip Pippenger," and I stopped reading and looked below on the sheet.

My name was there again: "Wendell A. Thomas; 547 Judson Avenue; Evanston, IL 60202; Tall, Very Trim, Grey Hair, Glasses… Retired I believe." And then, "Phillip Pippenger, Hilleory (Wife), Alexandra (Daughter, 16), Jeremy (14), Elias (11), Asa (5)."

Below this information was more. It was printed by hand and not easy to read. I began reading it and it began to seem like a practical joke or something. I mean, "What is all this? What's going on? What is this shit?"

***

The actuality of what the guy had written on the bottom six lines, and three more lines of his own making, and then up the long side of the paper, squeezing it all in, was:

"First Incident Date: Approx 1 yr ago to present... Location: Our House (543) Judson... Description: I have ordered all Police reports to get exact dates. Incidents are: Came on property, loosened wifes [sic] Lugnuts [sic], Keyed wife's car [sic], Keyed my car [sic], tampered with my wheels (super glue in valves), vented full tank of propane in back yard (House Across street was destroyed in same manner) [sic], Hid in yard at night to approach children (my 5 yo) & then ran when I saw Him & chased Him [sic], ATTempted to Lure Pre-TEEN- Boys Into His overgrown yard to "See A DEAD BODY", (ANIMAL?) [sic] BRAGS About BLACKmarket Glock 9mm, I witnessed the Gun [sic], & He ALSO BRAGGED To NEIGHBOR And Described what he would do with this to me [sic]. Many other Incidents. He is unbalanced & DANGEROUS & HIS FAMILY Lives Close But Doesn't Help [sic]."

***

I turned to the final of four pages without reading the fine print, because I could see that more was handwritten, and that's what I honed in on. He wrote:

"PRETENDS TO BE FBI AGENT W/FBI SIGN IN WINDOW. ATTEMPTED $70K EXTORTION (IN WRITING. POLICE REPORTS for MANY INCIDENTS, & OTHers were DESCRIBED TO DETECTIVES AS PART of WHOLE THreat ISSue [sic]."

228

It was more than I could take in. It was too insane to take in. It wasn't frightening. I just didn't know if something had happened that I didn't know about.

And then the realization.

Holy shit! He's got me luring pre-teen boys into my yard? He's got me in his backyard at night to approach his children, with a special parenthesis to highlight his five-year-old? The dirty scum bastard! He's trying to make me out to be a pedophile who's trying to light his house on fire!

The next day, after my yogurt and banana, I looked at the papers from the court.

On the front page, I saw that it said I was to report to Courtroom 106 at 5600 Old Orchard Rd. in Skokie, Illinois. I was to be there on December 18, 2014, at 1:30 p.m. This was too stupid. This was insulting.

Later in the morning, after I had decided to hell with all this crap, I called a friend. As we talked, I told him about getting this stupid court summons from my next door neighbor. It's the same guy who's done all the crazy shit to me and now he's filed something in court. "In fact, this is so much bullshit that I'm not even gonna respond," I told him.

"Whoa! Hold on, man," he said. "Do you know, and I'm serious, I know about this stuff, and, if you don't show up, they'll find you guilty... automatically. You don't want that on your record. You have to show up. You really don't want this on your record."

This was unwelcome news.

He continued, "It might all be just more of his bullshit, but you have to show up. You don't have a choice. You don't want a record. This is serious stuff."

Oh.

So here I was, a week from when I was supposed to go to court about Pippenger's insane fabrications.

I called all of my sons and told them about the summons and that I would have to go to court. I told them about my original inclination to blow the whole thing off.

They all said, "Dad, you have to get a lawyer. You have to go, and you have to have a lawyer with you."

This was making less sense all the time.

I told Michael that I didn't even know a lawyer who would do this kind of stuff, and he immediately suggested his friend Bill Luby.

Well, I've known Bill and Janice Luby for years. Michael did a semester in Rome through the Loyola extension program, and Bill was a classmate who became a close friend and has remained such. "Yeah," I thought, "Bill would be a good choice."

Michael gave me Bill's number. I called him, and we talked. I gave him the background on Pippenger and me. He asked me to fax him the summons, which I did from Michael's fax machine.

It was getting late in the day and I thought I'd send an email to Bill to check about the fax, but I couldn't get my damned computer to work. A quick flash kept appearing on the screen with "new wireless connection" or something similar that was printed for a split second. I had to give up trying to send my email.

The next day, I spoke with Bill again. He had received the fax, and he asked me if I had done any of these things.

"Of course not," I said. I still remembered the date that I gave the house keys back to Hilleory. "I haven't set foot on their property since June 7, 2012. This guy's being a bastard, that's all. He's trying to get back at me because he got suspended from his law practice."

The idea had entered my mind by this time that there must be something that Pippenger was trying to get for himself. What made the most sense to me was that if he could do this to me, he could go back to the ARDC and show them that he had had to try to cope with this guy next door who was doing all of this stuff to him. So, I reasoned, he would tell the ARDC that he was only trying to defend himself, and maybe they would feel sorry for him and then expunge his record.

That was the only thing I could come up with.

As each day went by in that slow, dark, and dreary winter way, I was getting more anxious about the court hearing set for the coming Thursday.

I was luring young boys? I was approaching a five-year-old at night? Holy shit! He's describing a pedophile!

Pippenger had been acting weirder than usual since shortly after the time I had filed the criminal complaint against him with the Evanston Police Department. Or rather, since about the time that he would have received notice from the police that the Cook County State's Attorney was not going to prosecute the charges I had filed.

He'd come home from driving his kids to school and I'd be sitting in my den reading. He would look in at me and stare. Then he would sometimes get his phone out and pretend to be taking photos or videos of me while I sat. I found that behavior odd, and since I was going to court in a couple of days, I thought I should do something to protect myself by letting Bill Luby know what was going on.

I sent Bill an email on December 16, 2014, at a little past 10 o'clock in the evening, telling him of Pippenger's behavior. It was two days before our scheduled hearing of December 18th and for the most part this is what I wrote:

"Hi Bill,

"I am sending this to put it in the record about Pippenger's behavior.

"In the morning when I get up I take a thyroid medication and cannot eat for 1 hour minimum.

"For the hour (which sometimes becomes longer) I sit in my den to read and watch Judson Avenue awaken and unfold it's [sic] day. My front two den windows are each 5x5 (feet) and next to each other.

"One of the more regular occurrences is that Phillip Pippenger drives his kids to school. As of about a month ago, when he returns he often looks at me and gives me his version of what I would guess is a "stare-down." Since the driveway (that dead ends) is next to my property, I would estimate that Pippenger is about 15 to 20 feet away.

"More recently (in the past couple of weeks), he has either been (or pretending to be) photographing me or making a video of me with his smartphone.

"This morning he did a video (or pretend video) as he was about to begin the school run.

"The reason I'm mentioning this, Bill, is because I care what he does if it might later affect me. I am not going to try to film him or take photos of him as he tries doing whatever he's doing. With today's ways of photo shop (photoshop?) I don't want his photos (or videos) to make me appear to be anywhere besides my den, in the morning, reading, looking out the window and minding my own business.

"Pippenger is unfettered and unlimited to anything he might do and I wanted you to be aware of this situation.

"As an aside... The aggressive "stare downs" from him did not begin happening until after the Evanston Police had charged him with forgery and the State's Attorney's Office had declined to prosecute. I suspect he now once again thinks that he doesn't' have to subscribe to any of our normal mores.

"See you Thursday.

Thanks, Wendell"

Bill responded the next morning, at a little past eight o'clock:

"Got it."

What I've noticed about lawyers is that sometimes they get right to the point. No mincing or bobbing and weaving.

48
At Court

My son Peter rode out to the Skokie courthouse on the Thursday of the hearing. I wore a sport coat, as I don't actually have a suit that fits. My weight ballooned after my chemo, and I never have gone back down to where I was when I was somewhat more fit. As in fifteen extra pounds or so.

We were to meet Bill in the eating area of the courthouse, where an array of vending machines stocked almost everything I wouldn't want. Peter and I found a table next to the row of windows lining the south side of the room. There were a few birds flying here and there and people leaving the building. I got a bottle of water from one of the machines and we talked about nothing in particular, as each of us regularly looked around for Bill. We were supposed to meet him at about 12:45 p.m., which would give us 45 minutes to talk strategy and hear what Bill had to say. Bill got there at about 1:00 p.m., and by that time, I was just relieved to see that I hadn't been abandoned. I wasn't sweating but was quite uncomfortable. It wasn't a place where you see much laughter, except from the occasional group of Cook County Court employees on lunch break.

Most of the people in the building were either Sheriff's Police, lawyers, or people like myself, who didn't want to be there because they were going to be put on the block. If they were lucky, their family or friends showed up to support them. The atmosphere in the courthouse is somber. The building itself is well-enough lit, but at the same time it seems dreary and grey. It's a clean building, but feels dirty. It's hard to tell if you might be looking at a plainclothes detective, an undercover agent with tattoos, a gangster, a gang member, a john, a pimp, a prostitute, a felon, an abuser, a dealer, an alcoholic driver, or someone who just might be falsely accused. Who knows? It's a rough place, tough on the mind, and filled with sorrowful lives.

Not my cup of tea.

Bill explained some of the things that would happen procedurally, and I tried to pay attention, hearing it all, taking it in, then immediately forgetting what had been said and the sequence of things.

Bill stressed to me that I would answer questions with a "yes" or a "no." I was not to elaborate on anything unless Bill was the one questioning me--none of my natural inclination to provide background or tell a story. I was to remain stoic: no expressions of exasperation, frowns, humor, or shock. I was not to try to get the judge's attention or shrug my shoulders or convey anything to the judge through body language, should the judge happen to look my way. A whole bunch of ways to behave by doing nothing. Less said the better.

Michael showed up, and he and Bill had some smiles together and some reminisces about their days in Rome and about their kids and how everyone's doing. I watched the interaction and could pick up a word here and there, but I knew it was all just a nervous-cover for my dilemma.

Then it was time to go to the courtroom. "Yes." "No."

We walked down the wide corridor to Courtroom 106. The sign on the door said, "In Recess." We stood in the hallway, and I sat on one of the benches. Bill asked me how I was doing, and I said, "Okay, I guess."

"Don't worry. Everything's going to be okay," he said.

Then, down the hall a short way, I saw the Pippengers, some guy that I took to be their lawyer, and another neighbor. I wondered what the neighbor was doing there. I pointed out the Pippengers to Bill, and he recognized the opposing attorney, saying, "It's Scott Gordon. He's an okay guy. He's alright."

One of the Sheriff's Police came to the court door from the inside and unlocked it. A number of other people were waiting—most were there before us—so we waited while they entered. Then Bill opened the door and we went in.

In the courtroom, the forward-most benches were for lawyers and police only.

Peter and Michael sat with me. Bill, in between going over to talk with Scott Gordon and filling out some paperwork near the judge's bench, would come back over to say a few words and then drift off again.

He came back over at one point and said, "There won't be a hearing for you today. There are police reports involved, and I haven't seen them, and they supposedly have some other evidence that we don't have or haven't been given. We'll put the hearing off until we have all the information we need."

He and Scott Gordon went off into an anteroom, to the side of the courtroom.

The neighbor who had accompanied the Pippengers came over to say hello to Michael, Peter, and me. Lightheartedly, I said to him, "I'm surprised to see you. If I knew you were available, I'd have asked you to come for me."

He said back to me, with seriousness, "Well, when you have youngsters, you can't be too careful."

What the hell's he talking about? But I didn't forget it.

Court was called to order, and we all stood, as instructed, while the judge entered the room and took her seat on the bench. Her name was Callie Lynn Baird.

There were two quick hearings, in which the people involved went up to two podiums in front of the bench and raised their hands, swearing to tell the truth. The podium on the left was for the Plaintiff, and the one on the right was for the Respondent.

The third hearing brought me into the realm of my reality.

Three people went up to the podiums. Two stood on the left, and one man stood at the right-side podium. The men on the left were younger by many years than the older man on the right, who was probably in his seventies, with only wisps of hair. The young man on the left had a lawyer who spoke for him. I could only pick up a word or two here and there of what was being said by each of them. The gist of their hearing was that the young man on the left, along with his lawyer, was attempting to get a stalking/no contact order against the older man, apparently the same thing Pippenger was trying to do to me.

They talked for less than five minutes, and then Judge Baird spoke. "I am allowing the no contact order."

She looked at the Respondent.

"Do you understand what this means, Mr. Blotting? This means that you may not step on Mr. Roberts' property. You may not speak to him or his family as listed in the complaint. You may not touch any of his property which includes his vehicles. You may not do any uncivil thing to Mr. Roberts. You may not touch him. Do you understand what I am saying, Mr. Blotting?"

Mr. Blotting said something that I took as a positive response to Judge Baird's comments.

Judge Baird continued. "If you violate any part of this order, Mr. Blotting, it means that you will then be a felon. You will go to jail. Do you understand that?"

Mr. Blotting affirmed, once again, and the hearing was over.

I was drained. I was empty. This is what Pippenger had in mind for me. If he could get the order against me, he would then come back to court with more of his lies and for which I would once again be found guilty and I would then go to jail!

I was screwed.

We went to the podium. Bill and I stood on the right, and both Pippengers along with Scott Gordon stood at the podium on the left.

Bill immediately asked that the judge issue a postponement for the hearing because he had not been given the police reports that were a part of the evidence, and it would not be ethical to try to defend his client without all the evidence.

Scott Gordon said, "I can email them to you."

And then Pippenger opened his mouth, saying, "Your honor may I say something?"

Bill responded immediately with, "I object your honor. We are not in the hearing. There has been no swearing in, and it is out of order for him to say anything."

Judge Baird said, "Yes," looking at Bill. She then added, while looking at Pippenger, "Hold off on anything that you want to say until we are in the hearing."

Pippenger didn't care that the Judge had made this statement. He screamed out, "Your honor, this man is stalking my children every day, and he has a gun!"

I flinched and moved half a step backwards and then realized that Bill had given me a sideways glance, so I moved forward quickly to where I was.

Judge Baird said to Pippenger, "You are out of order." And she then looked sternly at Scott Gordon.

The lawyers and Judge Baird then talked about when to have the hearing and decided that January 8, 2015, would be the day.

When we left, I had to pay a fee at the Clerk of Cook County Circuit Court, for whatever the reason. Bill was with us, and he said that he'd seen guys like Pippenger before and that they were their own worst enemy. He didn't think that Judge Baird would forget his outburst.

He said my step back wasn't a tragedy but that it would be better to just remain conscious of that kind of behavior in the future and avoid it.

In parting, he offered, "Janice and I are heading out to the west coast for the holidays, and we'll be back on January 4th.

We'll have plenty of time to talk. And I'll tell you what I tell my other clients in this kind of situation. I guarantee you that none of them heed my advice, but here it is anyway. Put this whole thing out of your mind until January 8th. Don't even think about it."

"And, oh! One last thing," Bill said. "You know and I know that you're not doing anything wrong sitting in your den and reading, but, and it's only my opinion, I really think you should stay out of the den until we're all finished with the hearing. It's up to you and of course you'll do as you choose, but I would encourage you to stay out of that room."

We said good-byes and wished happy holidays to each other.

Michael went his way, and I drove Peter home, but I don't remember doing it. I stayed in "phased-out" mode the rest of the afternoon.

49

The Torture Interim

So there I was, in limbo again, with no hearing until January 8, 2015. That was a relief of sorts, though his attorney had all the alleged police reports and we had nothing. The next day, I went up to the Evanston Police Department to get the reports, only to find that I was not allowed to have them. I had to go to the City Clerk's Office at the civic center and apply to get the reports through the Freedom of Information Act. One thing or another happened with the Christmas holiday, and due possibly to my negligence, or avoidance, my application for the information did not get registered with the City of Evanston until December 30, 2014.

For the most part, I was heeding Bill's advice about staying out of the den. At least I was taking the precaution that if I was in that room, I stayed out of view, more or less hidden on the couch, and never near the window, as I read.

I thought back to the day of the last hearing on December 18th. That day, I was sitting in my chair near the den window as I read. It was probably a couple of hours before I had to leave for the courthouse. I looked up and saw an Evanston Police Department car pull up and park directly across the street. From the car came a uniformed officer. His uniform was a deep, dark blue. He wore a black knit wool skullcap. He began walking from his car toward the Pippengers' front porch, and as he did so, periodically, without turning his head in the slightest, looked toward me with a sideways glance. When he did this, I could clearly see that he was looking at me. He did this sideways glance three or four times as he approached their porch. I watched him, while my book rested on my lap.

He was probably in their house for twenty minutes, and I did not see him come out. I was still with my book. When I looked up, I saw the police car pulling away down Judson Avenue. I wondered if he looked my way as he went back to his car.

I didn't like this whole deal. Something was up, and I didn't know what.

Something stunk much worse with Pippenger's pedophile insinuations.

I fantasized that the Pippengers wanted the police officer to make a statement about how frightening I looked, or how I was doing something wrong. I'm pretty sure the police officer didn't because there was never any mention of his visit at the hearing.

I felt imprisoned, though. My own lawyer had advised me to stay out of my own den. What had I done wrong? How could reading in the den have anything to do with anything?

It was Pippenger who was the kook. He was out there in the driveway, or sitting in his car taking pictures with his camera, or pretending to. He would stare at me and then laugh sometimes.

The whole thing was getting too sick for me. I was being accused of stuff I'd *never* done by a guy who had been suspended from his law practice for stuff he *had* done, and now he was taking me to court. What kind of backwards world are we living in?

Senseless days and mind-wandering nights. My access to my own home was limited. Claustrophobia began to set in.

Before Christmas came, feeling the need to expand within my home, I raised the blinds in my living room on the south side of the house. I had closed the blinds on those two windows since the Pippengers had moved in. Also, years ago, I had put a translucent covering over another living room window that sits about twelve feet high on the same side of the house. I had covered the high window to give me some privacy from eyes that used to look down into my living room from one of their upstairs bedrooms. His eyes or her eyes, it didn't matter. I didn't like it, but I didn't want to confront them because I think people are often just curious. I'd become so used to the translucent sheet, I'd forgotten it was there.

Directly opposite one of the windows with the blinds is their large, mullioned window which at that time had no window covering. After all, why bother with a window covering if your neighbor always keeps his blinds closed? Well, that changed with a pull of the cord on each window.

Let there be light!

I felt like I was making some space and letting in some light. It wasn't as dark as before. Of course, the inside of their home became visible, but that wasn't my problem. They could put up curtains or blinds, like I had.

Since I was staying out of the den, the living room became my room of choice. The fireplace helps to heat my home with warm air blown off the top surface of the steel plate, which is one side of the steel box that the fireplace sits in, with a sealed window in the front. I have no mantel.

Hanging on the wall above the fireplace are six different three-dimensional faces I made using copper wire and mounting them on sheets of Plexiglas for stability. Each face dangles on a fishing line that is about a foot away from the wall and tied to a Plexiglas "arm" which extends from the wall. I have two spotlights that cast shadows of the faces against the wall. The faces are well-balanced so that as air moves through the living room, they rotate, creating illusions of faces and oddly shaped shadows on the wall. In the winter months, I often have one or the other of the spotlights on so I can observe the shadows and the constantly changing forms of the faces.

Still, while I was trying to feel less constricted, I didn't like the whole deal.

It was oppressive. Thoughts of the upcoming hearing stirred in my head like squirrels in an attic.

I still hadn't seen the police reports, and I had no idea what they might say. And the judge, what would she think? I mean, all I could do is tell the truth. He had manufactured all of his stories about me being in his yard and maybe trying to burn his house down and damaging his cars and telling people I was going to shoot him. What if the judge believed any of it? How could I prove that I did none of it? Then he yells at the judge that I'm stalking his children!

This isn't good. They've got my feet in buckets of cement and are about to pitch me into the bay.

Every day, the same questions. Every day, I knew there was the chance the judge would believe just one thing. This wasn't fair. Not at all.

What if he said I beamed down from the moon? How could I prove I didn't? I didn't, and that's all I can say. What if she doesn't believe me? Since I never did anything, there's nothing he can prove. But... what if she believes his crap anyway?

I'm really in trouble.

I once knew a woman who would always go shopping for a new hat whenever she was feeling distressed. She said it really worked and always made her feel better.

That's all fine but I've never been much of a hat person. The only hat I wear is a wool beret in the winter. It keeps part of my head warm. Simple.

On the other hand, as I used to own a café and drink espresso and have cappuccinos whenever I felt like it, and since I really do miss that part of my life, and since I can't afford it, and since I'm probably going to end up in jail, somehow, as a part of this nightmare, I decide I'll go buy a cappuccino machine for my home.

On December 30th, I went to the shopping center and spent $653.82 on a Breville Barista Express so that I could enjoy cappuccinos during whatever was left of my disintegrating life.

I thought I would further lighten up my life by emailing a chocolate-loving friend, acclaiming to her the virtues of enjoying cappuccinos along with a piece or two of dark chocolate. Alas, my effing computer was still on the blink. I suddenly tired of everything.

The mental distress was constant. I don't even remember the holidays that year. Finally, the dreaded day of reckoning arrived: January 8, 2015.

50
The Kafka Trial

I made arrangements to meet Bill Luby in the lunch area of the courthouse, and once again, Peter was with me. Bill was going to remind me about how to behave properly in court, mainly answering "yes" or "no," without adding background information and making everything into a story.

As Bill asked me some hypothetical questions, I began answering in my usual way.

"No, no, no," he said. "I want you to answer 'yes,' or I want you to answer 'no,' and neither I nor the judge want more than that."

Peter said, "C'mon, Dad, you've got to pay attention."

We tried again, and I gave a simple "yes" and "no," without the added flavoring and the attendant hazards.

Michael arrived just as it was time to head to Courtroom 106.

When we got to the courtroom, I noticed that the neighbor who had previously been there was absent. I mentioned this to Michael, and he told me that he had given him an article by Michael E. McCabe, Jr., an attorney from the east coast. According to the article, if I had turned Pippenger in to the USPTO instead of the Illinois ARDC, he probably would have been disbarred, rather than have been given a 60-day suspension.

When Michael gave the McCabe article to the neighbor and had a brief conversation with him, it turned out that Pippenger, of course, had neglected to tell the neighbor the truth about the situation, including his suspension. Whoops.

The Pippengers had now enlisted a new neighbor as a replacement. Priscilla MacDougall who lives in the house next door to them on the south, showed up, ready for action.

Michael, Peter, and I sat, waiting for what, we did not know. Bill and Scott, the two attorneys, went into a side room to talk. Bill came out after a few minutes and showed me some photos. I identified whatever I could, as best I could. It was a shock, actually. There were photos of the Pippenger kids undressing, with a bright light that took up the whole picture in another photo. The light was obviously coming from my home. They had photographed the spotlight I use for the art works on the wall above my fireplace. There might have been a photo of me sitting in my den, also, but I don't remember that one. Bill shrugged, as though there was nothing he could do about this now.

I became more uneasy and felt my chances of justice diminishing.

Who takes photos of their kids undressing and brings them to court? What kind of evidence is this?

Then I understood; it's Pippenger's attempt to support his undeclared pedophile insinuation or claim.

When Bill and Scott came back in the courtroom, everything was ready for the hearing. Bill had been given the police reports somewhere along the way, and I had retrieved mine from the City of Evanston just two days before the hearing. I read them, but I didn't study or memorize anything in them. That would come later.

We were all sworn in. It was the Pippengers, Michael, and I. Mrs. Pippenger and Michael were asked to go out of the courtroom and wait in the corridor to be called.

Scott Gordon asked if Priscilla MacDougall, being a lawyer, could sit up close, in the jury box, because of her hearing difficulties. Judge Baird approved.

246

Scott Gordon made an opening statement. I believe attorneys are inclined to accept at face value the things their clients tell them. That's unfortunate when you have clients like the Pippengers. Some of the lies that Scott Gordon inadvertently told were: How the respondent (which was me) harassed the Pippengers. How I interfered with their general lifestyle. How his wife will offer eyewitness testimony to some of the events.

The truth is I never harrassed the Pippengers. I never interfered with their general lifestyle. There was never anything that Mrs. Pippenger could offer eyewitness testimony to because I had never done anything to the Pippengers.

Bill then made his opening statement, saying that Pippenger would have no proof of any allegation he was making and that what he was doing was an obvious attempt at retaliation for having been suspended by the ARDC for what he had previously done against me.

Pippenger was his own first witness, and right off the bat, he perjured himself by claiming that he was currently working as a patent attorney. The fact, which I did not discover until a month later, is that he was still suspended by the USPTO. He was suspended from July 15, 2014, to May 8, 2015, by the USPTO.

And then... The following is taken from the court transcript:

"Scott Gordon (Gordon): Why did you come to the Court to ask for the Court's protection?

Pippenger: Well, there were a series of incidents that were escalating and had been getting – some had been dangerous, but getting more dangerous.

Gordon: And based on that, could you tell us the most recent incident that you can describe?

Pippenger: Prior to filing the petition?

Gordon: Yes

Pippenger: It was the respondent in my backyard.

247

Gordon: Could I interrupt you? Could you tell us what time, what date we're speaking of, what time?

Pippenger: I tracked it on the –but I think it was November 4.

Gordon: November 4 of 2014?

Pippenger: Of 2014.

Gordon: Could you tell us what occurred?

***

As Pippenger prepared to speak, he began to look at me, directly at me and not at anything or anyone else. I held his stare.

As he proceeded, his face transformed into an expression of pleasure and satisfaction. He seemed close to smiling, and the look in his eyes, as he squinted slightly, resembled joy. *He was relishing this moment.* He continued to stare at me. *It was his cat-killing-the–birds face.*

Sometimes a cat will play with a cornered mouse and I imagined that I was the mouse on the floor in the corner of his basement and he was the cat. He would take his time, swatting, batting, wearing me down, and then pluck an eye, as his prey becomes comatose or goes into shock.

This is making me queasy, wanting to counter, yet I don't want to make things worse. I can't yell out in court, while he's wallowing in his trough of lies. I have to sit passively. My instructions have been to sit passively and not show emotion and I'm trying like hell to do just that.

In addition to not yelling out in court, it would also be frowned upon if I were to laugh. What was there to laugh about? Well, the Pippengers' support team of one, Priscilla MacDougall, our esteemed neighbor, had chosen this moment to begin her nap.

Priscilla's head bobbed down, and her chin went to her chest. She was out, her thinned hair readily showing her pink scalp. There was no interruption of the courtroom procedures, and, fortunately, there were no snorts or excessively loud

248

snoring. I paid attention to the witness, and only occasionally did I see, in my peripheral vision, a twitch, spasm, or body-shudder of sorts.

***

He continued:

"Pippenger: Yes. I had returned home from Barnes & Noble or some – you know, Dunkin Donuts, I don't know, with the kids. I had just taken Alexandra, the 16-year-old and Elias, the 11-year-old boy. And unfortunately, I park in the alley behind our garage because I have a lot going on in the garage, and I'm always being asked to clean it up by Hilleory, but there's still a lot of projects in there. So I park on the alley. So, for better or worse, you don't really hear me when I come home.

Gordon: Could you tell us what occurred?

Pippenger: So, we opened the garage door, and I went into the garage with the kids and said, 'Why don't you guys go on inside, I'm going to work on a project here and I have several things going on.' So, they opened the door and went out into the yard which is on the way to the back door of our house. And they started screaming. I heard screaming, because 11 year – old Elias screams just as well as Alexandra who's 16. So, I ran to the door which is about five or seven steps away. And Alexandra, the 16 – year old, is running past me this way and Elias, the 11 year – old is running that was which leads to the back door of the house which is kind of on the side. And in the middle is the respondent. And of course, there I am.

Gordon: If I could interrupt you, please. You said there's the respondent. Could you tell us where he was when you said, 'There he is?'

249

Pippenger: There's a large tree in the corner of our yard, there's sort of a fence that divides our back yards; then a large tree kind of in the corner by the house, and he was over there and he was coming my way. But then when I came out, he went the other way, and he ran out. I watched him run down between our houses. My plan was to get into our back door and get everyone safe if he was going to go into the front door.

Gordon: Could I ask you to slow down because there's a court reporter taking down your testimony. Thank you. You can continue.

Pippenger: But he didn't turn in front of our house; he actually turned in front of his own house, which is next door. He doesn't have a front door; he only has side doors on either north and south of his house.

Gordon: So, if I can understand from your testimony, because I'm confused: You're saying he was in your backyard?

Pippenger: Right. In the corner of our yard.

Gordon: And the first time that you saw him in your backyard, could you be more specific as to how you [saw] him and what he was doing?

Pippenger: Well, initially, I came out. I just heard the screaming; I saw the kids and I looked where they were running from. And it's the respondent. He's been behind the tree and he's moving, but then when he sees me he stops and goes very fast. And there's a broken piece of fence in the corner, I found out, that he was using to access the yard.

Gordon: How did you find out that there was a broken piece of fence in the yard?

Pippenger: I watched him run through it.

Gordon: And that was the day that you're speaking of?

Pippenger: Yes.

250

Gordon: When was that?

Pippenger: November 4, I think.

Gordon: And after that you saw him run back, essentially to his house [?]

Pippenger: He ran in the other side and went in. So I watched him just kind of come across and flop down in a chair.

Gordon: Did you or him say anything to each other?

Pippenger: No

Gordon: How did that make you feel?

Pippenger: Very worried. I mean the fact that he–

Gordon: Why?

Pippenger: Because I already knew he had a gun, I knew he had issues. I mean I don't want to – you know, I don't want to say a lot of ancillary things, but I knew there were some things with, you know, other people that had gone on."

***

There was no police report or record of a 9-1-1 call for this alleged situation. That, in and of itself, is pretty incredible. This guy claims I've been doing all of these things to him, and he doesn't report this one to the police? Neither he nor his wife call 9-1-1? What is wrong with these people? If something like he described happened to me, I would have called the police.

Pippenger filed a police report five days after he claimed I had "put super glue in the valves of his tires." Super glue in the valves of your tires is something worth reporting to the police, and yet a person is supposedly in your backyard, at night, who you recognize and chase, and who you think is there to "approach your children," is not worth reporting to the police?

Where are your priorities, folks?

In the four false police reports that Pippenger had filed eight and nine months earlier, he always requested that the police "not talk with Thomas about this."

251

Wait a minute. If you call the police, don't they come out immediately? This would not be a situation where you would say, "But don't talk to him." The police would have talked to me. The police would have talked to the children and you certainly wouldn't want that to happen. Your wife might testify that the children came running into the house, out of breath, and said that someone was in the yard. I believe your wife is either a willing liar, saying that the children came running into the house out of breath after having seen someone in the yard, or she can't distinguish the truth from fiction from her children's mouths. In my opinion, either way, she sure does fail as a parent.

You might try to hide behind the children, but that will all be without them having to do anything. You'll just do your best to present yourself fictitiously as the frightened parent.

Since there was never anybody in your yard, and since you can't even remember where you had been with your children that evening, and since the incident never happened, it would be best not to report it. Of course, once in court, you and your wife can each say the other reported it. But why didn't the police come out and interview you? Why didn't they interview me?

Would it be even remotely likely that you wouldn't have called the police?

Judge Callie Lynn Baird probably has the police reports in front of her. She probably sees that this was never reported.

Do you think she's not familiar with people making false claims? She's in this courtroom every day. She's seen the likes of you and your wife a hundred times. Not just people who lie, but who don't lie well.

Judge Baird probably had the police reports that you filed in front of her or on her computer screen. She probably saw that your testimony in her courtroom about the valves of your propane gas grill having been turned on and left on overnight, was a full six hours off from the police report you filed. The police report said it occurred at 4:00 p.m., and the testimony you gave in court said it was at 10:30 p.m. The police report said your discovery of the turned on valves took place at 2:00 p.m., and your court testimony said that it was at 7:00 a.m.

What world do you live in? Don't you remember the rule about keeping lies straight from, "Lying 101?"

Do you think Judge Baird is going to buy your story of the Evanston Police filing "cut and paste" incident reports that are approved by supervisors? Remember the rule about keeping lies in the realm of reasonable possibilities? You know, "Lying 101," the basic course you took.

That was how his testimony began. It went on and on and on. The number of times he claimed I damaged his cars, coupled later with his wife's claims of damages, came to once every three days from early April until about the third week in May. Sixteen times! And I was never seen doing it. Just call me Houdini.

His wife's testimony was so inconsequential that the judge did not bother to offer any assessment of what she had sworn under oath to be true. Soon into her testimony, when asked about damages or dates of damage to the car, she giggled and said something to the effect that, "Oh, there were so many."

When she was asked about her husband's transgressions against me, when he was my attorney, her response was, "They had their day in court." She didn't seem to have any idea of what he did to me (a) as my lawyer, and (b) as my neighbor. In fact, I don't think she has much grasp of the personality of the person she is married to. At some point, that lack of knowledge begins to look like denial, and her acceptance of the retaliatory things he does becomes complicity. His oversteps become her responsibility also.

And why would he take photos of their children undressing? Did he need the pictures to make his point about the brightness of the light from my window, which I explained previously? My shades were not down; that's my call. What was stopping them from covering their windows? So they could take

253

photos to show in court to support their accusation that this Thomas next door was a pervert. Who's the pervert here? I was in his back yard at night to approach his children? No. His five-year-old? No. I lured preteen boys into my "overgrown yard," to see a "dead body?" No. I did show them the dead baby squirrel; maybe they'll take biology someday. I shine a spotlight into their den so I can watch their children get ready for bed? No.

When Bill Luby cross-examined Pippenger, he made mincemeat out of him. He got Pippenger to acknowledge having mislead me, cheated me, and that he had been suspended for what he had done. Eventually, Bill Luby asked the broken-down Pippenger if he was a liar. Pippenger, having boxed himself in, glanced at Judge Baird, dropped his head and then responded, "Sure."

Scott Gordon then questioned me. He tried in vain to correlate our negotiation attempts of the previous spring with the damage to the Pippengers' vehicles. It seems to have been Pippenger's long-term plan. Putting the periodic roadblocks in the way of our negotiations allowed Pippenger to file false police reports at the same time as the stoppage. I quit the negotiations because I came to realize that he had no intent to settle on anything. Later on, which was now, in court, he would try to use the failed negotiations to explain why I was damaging his automobiles. Perhaps it made sense to Pippenger, and Scott Gordon tried to push in that direction. All I did was tell the truth.

In each of the four false police reports that Pippenger filed, he stipulated that the police were not to interview me about the incidents that he reported.

Pippenger had been planning this hearing for many, many months before he filed his "Emergency Order," for a stalking/no contact judgement against me.

In hindsight, it was probably why his wife showed anger toward me when she was the one who cut down my prairie plants. It was why his kids stopped speaking to me, or even looking at me. Hilleory doesn't have a mind of her own. The kids were probably just following orders. The youngest, Pippenger testified in court, "only knows 'evil Wendell.'" Where did he get that? Not from me.

Hilleory actually testified in the hearing that, "the scratches on the cars weren't from going in or out of the garage." In fact, they have never used their garage for the cars. The garage is used for his motorcycles; his "steeds," as he calls them, and for his other toys.

About 75,000 people live in Evanston, some of whom are vandals. In her testimony, when Hilleory was asked who she thought damaged their vehicles, she laughed and said, "Wendell, of course. Who else would have done it?"

In my opinion, if there was ever any actual keying of their cars, Pippenger had done it himself. It would be a small investment for what I think he hoped would be a great return; the eventual felony conviction of Wendell and possibly a little jail time.

When I testified, I told the truth to every question asked. Michael did the same.

After closing arguments by the lawyers, Judge Baird said:

"I've heard the testimony of the witnesses in this case… Phillip Pippenger himself, as well as his wife, Hilleory Pippenger… Mr. Thomas testified as well as his son, Michael Thomas…

I heard the testimony from the Pippenger's…

Mr. Pippenger was the only witness to the propane gas valves on the grill having been left open all night…

Mr. Pippenger was the only eyewitness to Mr. Thomas allegedly being in the back yard at night…

The additional incidents in May involving the cars… nobody saw Mr. Thomas near the cars…

And in December, that Mr. Thomas had written Voila, on his window...

And that he was, at times, standing in the window when the Pippenger children would go to and from school...

And there were the incidents of the spotlights over Christmas vacation where the petitioner has photos of his home and a light you can see in the photos, what appears to be a shining light...

Then Mr. Thomas testified...

He denied all of the allegations in the incident...

He said he didn't ever threaten the petitioner or his wife or his children...

He didn't damage his car...

He was not in Pippenger's back yard...

And, yes, he had painted Voila on his window... But he has a peace sign on the front of his home, and he as other artistic things around his home and in his backyard and the painting of the Voila was just something that he decided to do...

Mr. Thomas testified, he admitted, 'Yes, I have two spotlights, but no, I did not shine them in the home of Mr. Pippenger.'...

Then we have testimony regarding the professional relationship between Mr. Pippenger and Mr. Thomas...

Mr. Pippenger admits he lied to his client...

That he also falsified documents...

He could not recall a conversation with Mr. Thomas and his son Michael. He did not deny that it occurred, he just said he couldn't recall...

I believe Mr. Thomas and his son testified very credibly and in great detail about the nature of the conversation...

They testified that Mr. Pippenger said that he had had an ex parte conversation with the judge and that he had been scammed because he discovered that it was not a real Judge...

And it's not really disputed that the ARDC found that Mr. Pippenger did engage in this conduct and was suspended for 60 days...

So, with that being the evidence, when I view the incidents that occurred, this is a credibility contest...

I do believe Mr. Thomas and his son...

Mr. Pippenger admitted that he fabricated documents in lying to his client...

I cannot find that Mr. Pippenger is a credible witness...

For all the reasons I just stated, the request for the order of protection is denied."

***

Scott Gordon stood and looked down at his briefcase on the table in front of him, shaking his head, "Not credible," he said, with a tone of both exasperation and disgust. From Mr. Gordon's reaction, it seemed that whatever Pippenger had told him, it did not entail the truth.

I sat where I was, not wanting to move. I've been confronted with a diagnosis of terminal cancer. I've lost people that I dearly loved. I am no stranger to adversity.

But I've never been targeted, put upon, deceived, cheated, destabilized, swindled, and mentally tortured, all by the same person.

No judgment against me. That's fair. That's some justice, at least, although in a just world, it would never have come up. Thanks to Bill for his great work. Thanks for his punching Pippenger's lights out. Thanks Michael, and thanks Peter. This has been rough. I am drained, and I'm suffering, even though I won.

But what's the next salvo gonna be?

51
More Coming

The next night, I went out to dinner with a friend.

My preoccupation with Pippenger took center stage. I felt like a victim. I have read that sometimes one person has the ability through what they do to another person, to get inside their victim's head and dominate their thought processes. I began to imagine that Pippenger's real goal had nothing to do with the hearing we just had, but with hacking my computer.

My "overgrown yard," "luring preteens," "spotlighting his children," and "hiding in his yard" all kicked in. Why's he doing this? What's it about? Really about? Forget the hearing. He didn't care. What's he doing? C'mon, it's something else.

"Oh my God," I said, "I know what he's doing!"

I began to lose touch with reality about the situation. I was breaking down and didn't know it.

"What are you talking about?" my friend asked.

"Pippenger, that son of a bitch, I know what he's doing!" I said again.

She knew the story, as did many friends, from when it began to unfold those years before. She knew from our earlier talk that night all about the court case, how Pippenger got caught up in his own lies, and how their stalwart companion, Priscilla, had fallen asleep. She knew of his pedophilia insinuations.

"What?" she said.

"Oh, no!" I said. "What he's doing is much bigger. Of course he didn't care about the court case. He filled out the forms to try to make me look like a pedophile. That's why he used the words he used, like "approach," "lure" and, "overgrown yard." He's setting me up. He's hacked my computer. That's why it hasn't been working! He's hacked it, and he's loaded it with pornography. Child pornography. That's what he's done. I'm sure of it. He wants me in prison. The hearing was child's play. He wants me in the clink.

"I've got to get to the police first. I've got to get over there. He's probably heading there himself to tell them I have child pornography on my computer and that he's seen me watching it when he watched me through my den windows. This is getting worse!"

My mind was racing like crazy with this new theory of what was going on. Why didn't I see this sooner?

"That doesn't sound right," she said.

"What the hell would she know?" I thought. *"I'm the one up against this guy. I'm the one who knows he'd stop at nothing to get back at me."*

"You have to talk to someone," she said. "You should talk to someone right now."

She said that and reached her hand across the table and laid it on top of mine. She gave my hand a squeeze.

"You have your phone with you, don't you?" she said, raising her eyebrows and squeezing my hand again.

I nodded.

"Use it," she said. "Call one of your sons."

I reached for my phone in my zippered coat pocket and got it out.

Yeah, I thought. I could call Peter or Steve or Michael. They'll help. I'll tell 'em what I know now. Wait. They can't help. Ah, Luby! Bill could help. He could go to the station with me to be sure they didn't put me in the clink right now. He could keep me out of there for now.

I called Bill, and there was no answer so I left a message.

My stomach churned. The food wasn't so good tonight. It had been good before. I'd been there lots of times. There was hummus and pita and wine.

259

Bill called back in ten minutes.

I told him what was going on. He tried to calm me, which I overrode and told him again what I thought Pippenger was doing. Bill wasn't getting it.

Bill said, "Okay, here's the deal. I understand what you're saying, but I'm not getting through to you. You and I, we have to compromise.

"I can't get down to Evanston tonight, so I want you to promise me that you will not go to the police tonight or tomorrow. We can talk over the weekend, and we will do something on Monday. For now, though, neither of us will do anything. Fair enough? We have a deal?"

I couldn't take in everything he said, but he did say that we'd do something on Monday. I was sure I'd heard that. That sounded like it was maybe okay, but what if Pippenger went tonight?

"What if he goes tonight?" I said.

"I promise you that he will not," he said. "So, do we have a deal?"

I said, "Okay. If you're sure. Okay. But on Monday, we have to. Right? This guy's really screwing me over. I really need help with this."

"Okay, we'll talk then," he said, and we hung up.

At least I would be taking care of myself on Monday. Somehow. Hell, I could hang on for two days, I thought. Maybe.

My friend and I finished dinner. I took her home, not staying to visit or linger at her place. I had to get home where it was safe.

At about ten o'clock, Michael called.

When he began to talk, I realized Bill had called him, and I asked him if that were the case. He said, "Yeah, Dad, what's going on, anyway?"

I told him what I had just realized and that I feared Pippenger had hacked my computer and put child porn on it. I told him how it all made sense because of the summons I got with all of the slanted language. He had loaded my computer.

Michael asked me if it made any sense, really, that Pippenger would have this kind of ammunition and would not have used it. If he was trying to get me with this kind of stuff, why would he wait? Why wouldn't he already have turned the information over to the police?

Michael said again that if Pippenger had anything at all that could be used against me he would have used it. He said the judge could see that Pippenger was a liar. "Nobody's gonna believe him from here on out," he said.

Hmm. That kind of made sense. I began to calm down. Yeah, I thought, he's a little right. What's wrong with me, anyway?

Somehow, I got through the next day, Saturday. Pippenger was in my brain with what had happened in court and what he had tried to do.

I could see the joy he had as he surprised me in court with his story about me being in his yard at night. He was evil. He knew no limits. I've known people I don't consider "good." I've known a few who seemed inherently mean. But Pippenger is the first person I've known who targeted to destroy.

Early Saturday evening, and not feeling like being alone, I went to Michael and Lene's. They had gone out for some kind of post-holiday party, but Cecilia and Josie were home. Cecilia was a freshman at Wisconsin, and Josie was a junior at Evanston Township High School. They were still home at seven-thirty, as the younger set doesn't start their social functions until nine-thirty or ten.

We talked a bit, the three of us, and then, somehow, I probably led the conversation into the realm of the hearing from two days before and the jeopardy I was in. When Pippenger's accusations first came to me in the summons, I talked to my family and told them that I hoped, no matter what the outcome of the hearing might be, that my family would truly believe that I had never done any of the things that Pippenger claimed I had.

They all said, of course they knew and that they would believe that no matter what the outcome in court.

I thought of the repercussions to my family if I were found "guilty" in the hearing and had a judgment placed against me. They could know I would not do the things I was accused of doing. They know me as a person.

And yet, if I were found guilty? If I were? Well, of course they would know that I never did any of these crazy things. And yet, they would wonder about it once in a while, somewhere else, deep within.

I was sitting next to Cecilia on the couch in the den, and I put my head on her shoulder. I felt my eye-well fill, and I felt the trickle wind down next to my nose and onto my upper lip. It was salty. A drop, and another. Some poison was let. And then more.

52
Pappy Helps Junior

It was time in Pippenger's life to pull out the big guns. What better way to do that than get help from his father. Two big guys is always better than one single "misunderstood" patent attorney.

A few weeks after the hearing, as was my routine at that time, I punched up Pippenger's name on Google and came up with some interesting and, once again, laughable stuff. It wasn't a one-day deal. The information was posted on the Internet for at least a year.

Somewhere along the line, young Pippenger next door had decided to change his identity.

Here we go with more of the Abbott and Costello routine; "Who's on First?"

Of course, Pippenger wasn't getting paid, and he wasn't doing it for comic relief. This time, for a change I could appreciate, he was aiming at anyone and everyone who might look at his website or Google his name. It wasn't just me he was trying to dupe.

Pippenger has the same name as his father, with the exception that he's Junior, or Jr. His father also happened to be a lawyer. Hmm.

"Hi Pappy, it's me. I need your Avvo password so I can…"

Pappy also happened to be a registered patent attorney who retired his registration in 2013. How fortuitous!

"I really should be able to do something with this…"

"No-no, Pappy, of course I haven't, it was all a misunderstanding…"

Or was it, "Son, I have a great idea! Why don't I give you my Avvo password and then you can…"

Ah, this is getting better. What an opportunity. Pippenger and his father were both registered with Avvo.com, which does ratings of lawyers. Avvo claims to asses most every lawyer in our fair land.

Did his father give him access to his Avvo site, and his secret password information, so that young Pippenger could go in and change things? That's how it's sometimes done on Avvo. There is a secret password, supposedly known only to the person controlling the information. Or did young Pippenger find a way to make the changes on his own? Some Avvo listings do not require a password for entry if the lawyer has not chosen to enhance their profile. Whether or not young Pippenger enlisted the aid of his father doesn't matter. The fact is, he got the job done.

"Thanks Pappy! This is the first time it's ever been such good luck to be named after you."

On the Avvo site, with young Pippenger's name, the photograph of his face was suddenly missing. No photo? Where'd it go? C'mon, let us see who you are.

Avvo had shown young Pippenger as having a rating of 1.7 out of a possible 10. That's not a rating anyone would want others to see, especially accompanied by a photo. Avvo showed young Pippenger to be licensed as a lawyer since 1998, which is correct. There was a warning notice that said:

"Professional Misconduct

"This lawyer was disciplined by a state licensing authority:

"Suspension Until Compliance With Condition(s) issued in IL, 2014 updated on Oct 20, 2014. A suspension until compliance with conditions reflects a determination that the lawyer has engaged in misconduct and that the misconduct warrants an interruption of the lawyer's authority to practice law during the suspension period, which is a fixed period of time identified in the Supreme Court's order and until the lawyer complies with condition(s) imposed by the Court. The lawyer is not authorized to practice law during the period of the suspension."

***

Below this Avvo information is a simple "cover-up" offered by Pippenger:

"Phillip's comment: 'Error//There was no IARDC discipline pending against this attorney as of the update date.'"

This is sleight of hand, or word, if you will. Avvo never said there was discipline pending or anything close. Pippenger's comment: "Error// etc., , makes it appear as if there was some kind of computer error and that he was not really suspended. The whole thing was a misunderstanding.

***

On the site, it shows that Pippenger's address is 304 Black Oak Ln, Seymour, TN, 37865, Accompanied by a small map showing the location in Seymour, Tennessee.

"Thanks for sharing, Pappy, but one of these days I'll have to leave and go back to Illinois where I'm a 'Pappy,' too!"

Whoops. It's his father who lives in Seymour, Tennessee and has the connection to Black Oak Ln.

Pippenger Jr. lists himself as, "Founder and Chair" of the "North Shore Metallurgists Society," of which no records seem available.

There was another listing for Phillip M. Pippenger with an Avvo.com site.

I opened the site and there was young Pippenger's photograph, goatee, mustache, and all.

The Avvo rating on the site gave him a 6.5 out of 10, which is a bit more respectable.

It gave his location as Chicago, IL.

Whoops. It says he's been licensed since 1969. That was the year Junior was born! The old switcheroo.

Whoops again! He must have gotten a little mixed up as he changed his father's information. He gives his address as 304 Black Oak Ln, *Chicago, IL, 37865*. The zip code is Tennessee, and there is no Black Oak Lane in Chicago.

The site also shows the same map for the location as was shown for Tennessee on his own site, or rather, his other self.

Pippenger always claimed to have gone to law school at Cornell. Yet this site shows him to be a 1969 graduate of Michigan law school. The question for me was, "How did he graduate from law school the year he was born?"

And under Professional Misconduct: "We have not found any instances of professional misconduct for this lawyer."

What? The site had young Pippenger's Chicago phone number along with his photo. I thought he'd been suspended. How did this happen?

When notified of this situation, neither the ARDC nor the USPTO responded with a concern. I was left to draw my own conclusions: "Falsifying your identity as a lawyer wouldn't be a concern of ours," said the ARDC, and subsequently, "We ditto the motion and make it unanimous," said the USPTO.

53
Direct Expressions

Things continued in this vein for a couple of months without further incident. The indignation still exists, at least from my side, but nothing is done on either side of the fence.

I don't think Pippenger feels hate. He simply does what he does. It's innate. No feeling.

His kids still pretend not to see me when I pass them on the street. Hilleory and I see each other periodically at the store, around town, or when she's unloading stuff from her car.

Pippenger still revs up his motorcycle, loudly, before taking off for work most mornings. He has started using one of the social media websites to try to promote himself and repair his image.

He also has a social media entry which I certainly question. It is: phillippippenger.wordpress.com - referring to his experience as a paraglider, insinuating that he's flown with the eagles, which for some who do the sport might be at 18,000 feet. What a man's man. A real machismo with his "steed" and what I think is his imaginary-high-flyin'-non-existin'-paraglidin'. While the whole article about paragliding insinuates that Pippenger does the sport, he is careful enough to never directly say that as a fact.

Did the author of the paragliding article write Pippenger's thesis for his master's in electrical engineering?

"A contender... I could've been somebody. And now? Let's face it, Charlie, I'm a bum with four kids, lost in Palookaville. Who's been minding my life?"

The only problem with his paragliding article is, he's probably never done it. At one point in the article that he ostensibly wrote, he said that, when you're done for the day, you can simply throw your gear in the trunk of your car. He forgot to change some wording. He doesn't have a car with a trunk. They own two vans. No trunks on vans. He doesn't spend his free time going anywhere, except to his garage to work on his "steed."

It's not exactly the same as taking on his father's identity, but still, I believe it's more of the same lies, only with a new high-flyin', draft-ridin' twist. "A lot of hot air," you might say.

***

During this down time, I found he had applied to the USPTO for reinstatement. I wrote a letter to them explaining that he had taken me to court after filing false police reports, had perjured himself in court by claiming to be currently working as a patent attorney, and had otherwise lied throughout his testimony while under oath and was deemed "not credible" by the judge.

I did not want him to be reinstated, ever.

The patent office reinstated him. As far as they were concerned, these were civil matters.

On Saturday, March 14, 2015, a neighbor had a dinner, and I was invited. It was one of the first things I had done socially for some time, as my preoccupation with Pippenger had dulled my desire for social contact. During the dinner, something was mentioned, or possibly asked of me, and I gave a one minute spiel about Pippenger and what he'd done and how my life was now somewhat twisted. I left it at that.

A friend at the dinner suggested I just let it go. The whole thing. It was over. Done. Go on with your life.

"I wish I could." I said. "The problem is, I don't know what he's going to do next. If I knew it were over, I could let it go, but as things stand now, I can't."

My friend is a retired psychotherapist, and I listen when he speaks. He knows a great deal about the mind and its' inner workings.

The following day, Sunday, I decided to try to exercise outdoors on the bike path that runs along Lake Michigan from south Evanston to Northwestern University. I tried periodically to do more than a walk. While I can no longer actually run, I can kind of trot for twenty or thirty yards before my replaced hips, start protesting the effort. After the running yardage, I'd walk for forty or fifty yards and then try the trot again. It feels strange to be in this position; I used to run regularly and ran ten marathons back in my thirties and forties.

When I got home, having gone three miles wearing a jacket and sweats, I was ready for a shower. First, I thought, I'll take the recycling to the alley. It's something that I usually do on Sunday and then again on Wednesday, the day before the pickup.

So with my small recycling bin in hand, I headed to the alley to dump the contents--papers, cans, and plastic bottles--into the large bin. In our neighborhood, each home has its own recycling bin.

In the alley, I saw Pippenger's youngest son on a small two-wheel bicycle, a little north of where my back gate is. My recycle bin is about six feet north of my gate. I went there, raised the lid, and started dumping when I saw, peripherally, someone approaching. I turned my head to look.

It was Pippenger, all 260 to 270 pounds of him, walking toward me, glaring. He's got broad shoulders, and beneath all the fat, he's a strong guy. He was fifty feet away and closing in, and his son was across the alley, ten feet beyond me. Pippenger was clomping his feet hard and from his hunkered down posture it seemed to me there were gonna be some punches thrown.

I stayed at my bin, with my small container in my left hand, and I got ready to counter as best I could with what I hoped would be a good right. It was like Bluto and Popeye. I wanted to hit him where there was an opening, maybe around his eye, bust his glasses, cut his face.

His shoulders were hunched forward and he was moving pretty fast. We kept our eyes locked.

He couldn't see my fist. I had to stay cocked and let him swing first. Nothing's happened till then.

And then, when he was about two feet from me, he abruptly cut at a ninety degree angle and headed across the alley to where his son was standing, apparently unable to get started by himself.

I finished my dumping and looked over at him. He was next to his son. I needed to know where he was before turning my back to him to head back through my gate.

When I looked over at him, he said, "I think that's against the law."

I figured he was saying I'm not allowed to look at him when he's standing across the alley with his youngster.

"Recycling is not against the law," I said.

"No, but staring at my children is," he said.

"Call the police!" I said.

He then yelled down the alley to another of his sons, Elias, who was riding his bicycle, "Hey! Elias! Look at this!"

I didn't like how he was setting things up, and I exited through my gate. I could imagine us later in court, and Elias saying, "Yes, I saw him standing in the alley staring at my little brother."

"Jesus Christ!" I said to myself, as I headed to my deck door to get in the house and take my shower, "What's with this pedophile shit?"

These were the first words we had spoken to each other since the spring of 2012. He apparently had stored up a bit of anger.

He'd been out of town for a few days and had just returned on that Sunday. I knew that. I try to stay alert to his whereabouts, and I look over my shoulder regularly to see what might be going on or where the next attack might come from.

Earlier in the day, I had been at Peter's house. As I was walking home, a van appeared when I was about two blocks away. It was going slowly enough to catch my attention, and I looked over and saw that it was Pippenger with two of his kids. They were all wide-eyed and staring as they passed.

I thought at the time, "Ah, he's home and loaded for bear."

Sure enough, he was. In his own way, of course. Maybe he'd been to Disneyland or some other fantasy park and he couldn't quite let go of the world of make-believe. When I got out of my shower, and before I'd finished dressing, there was a loud knocking, almost a pounding, on my front door.

"Just a minute!" I yelled.

When I opened the door, still barefoot, there were two policemen standing there.

They interviewed me about the "incident with my neighbor in the alley," and I told them what had happened, that we had previously been to court over his false police reports, and that the judge had concluded he was "not credible." I told them how he had also been suspended from his law practice for what he had done to me and that now he seems obsessed with retaliation.

I asked them if they wanted to come in, but they didn't. So I stood on my front porch and apologized, awkwardly, for wearing no shoes.

271

It occurred to me that they probably didn't want to come in because they were probably cautioned by Pippenger that I had a Glock 9mm pistol.

The three of us talked for a couple of minutes, and one officer wrote some things down as we spoke.

I didn't think much of the incident that afternoon, but when evening set in, I couldn't get it out of my mind. It stayed with me all night till I went to bed.

In the morning, it was still with me, and I was tired of it all. I got in my car and went to the Skokie Courthouse and filed a Stalking/No contact order against Pippenger. They assigned me to a courtroom, and I went there. It happened to be, once again, Judge Callie Lynn Baird.

I told Judge Baird the circumstances of the day before and said that I was asking for some protection from the court. I explained that I didn't think he was entitled to continue to disrupt my life at will. She remembered the Pippengers.

Judge Baird listened and then explained that I needed three incidents to get a hearing for a Stalking/No contact order put into effect by the Cook County Circuit Court. She also said, as I asked for help with Pippenger, that she did not have the authority to order any mental health assistance for him.

Three incidents. I need two more. I wondered how long that would take.

54

Bullseye

Since Pippenger had filed the four false police reports back in 2014, I had been periodically checking, using the FOIA, to see if new reports had been filed. I was familiar with what to do and did so after he filed the complaint on March 15, 2015.

To my surprise, when I filed an FOIA for that date and saw the police report, it was rife with errors. This was information from a lawyer who has sworn to be honest and uphold the laws of society? How could that happen? Oh, well. A little lying and cheating here and there never really hurts anybody. Right?

I sent the police a letter requesting changes to the report, or at least to please file my letter with it, so that in the future, truth might at least have a chance.

As given by Pippenger, the police report said:

"We met with Phillip Pippenger who said that his neighbor, Wendell Thomas, was "leering" at his children from his back yard as they played in the alley behind 543 Judson. He described Thomas as leaning into the alley and staring at two of his children for a prolonged period of time. I made contact with Thomas who stated that he was taking out his recycling and looked over towards where Pippenger and his children were riding bicycles. It should be noted that both Pippenger and Thomas both stated that they have had ongoing disputes over many different topics going back to 2009. Both parties were advised to avoid contact with one another for the remainder of the day, and complied. Nothing further."

***

When I received the police report on March 25, 2015, I wrote the following corrections and had the information placed in the police officer's box:

1. "I was not "leering" at Pippenger's children. Pippenger is lying. I was not looking at Pippenger's children.

2. "I was not "leaning into the alley and staring at Pippenger's children for a prolonged period of time." Pippenger is lying. I was not leaning into the alley and staring at all! I took out my recycling and Pippenger made trouble!

3. "Pippenger's children were not "playing in the alley behind 543 Judson." Pippenger's youngest son was two houses north of the 543 address when I took my recycling out. After getting the police report, I measured the distance and it was over 100' north from the 543 address.

4. "Pippenger and I do not have disputes:
   A. He has been suspended from his law practice by the ARDC for what he did to me in the past.
   B. He is currently suspended by the United States Patent and Trademark Office for what he has done to me in the past. He has been suspended since July 14, 2014.
   C. He was denied a "Stalking – No Contact Order" in court on January 8, 2015 that he tried to have placed against me. The four police reports used at that hearing that Pippenger had filed with the EPD were all

false. (The judge called Pippenger, "not credible.)

D. I have no idea where a reference of 2009 comes from. There were no "disputes" between Pippenger and myself until 2012 when I discovered what he had been doing to me for more than a year and he was subsequently prosecuted by the ARDC and the USPTO.

E. For his own sick reason, Pippenger continues to try to make my life as miserable as he can."

I hoped my corrections would be taken to heart.

Things went along smoothly for the next few months. I continued to look over my shoulder and be wary. Nothing seemed to be happening. I continued to file FOIA's at the Evanston Civic Center, and no additional police reports were filed against me.

Then things changed on August 2, 2015, as I was riding my bicycle home from having been at the AT&T Store in downtown Evanston. I came into my alley and was heading south toward my back gate, which is in the middle of the block. When I was about two thirds of the way there, I saw in my handlebar mirror that a motorcycle had come into the alley behind me.

It had to be Pippenger, I thought. I immediately took the precaution of riding on the far right side of the alley. I also realized that if I was not dismounted by the time I reached my gate, I'd better just come to a stop and lean against my fence rather than swing my leg over the seat. I did not want to provide him the opportunity to run into my swinging leg and claim I had hit him. Also, having him run into my airborne leg would certainly cause me to go down. I didn't want to find out the toll that injury might take.

I stayed far, far to the right.

Pippenger neared and I continued to concentrate on staying to the right, ready to stop and cling to a fence.

It grew quiet for a few seconds and then, right next to me, there was a loud explosion of the fully accelerating motorcycle. Pippenger had put his motorcycle in neutral and was coasting until he got a couple of feet behind me. Then he opened the throttle of his engine full blast.

I wobbled, as the concussion and noise upset my balance, and quickly grabbed onto of my fence.

Pippenger coasted on to his garage quietly. I looked at him as he was in my line of sight, and he never batted an eye. He never looked back as he pulled forward into his garage, and I clung to the fence, my knuckles white. It was disconcerting.

I used to have a motorcycle, and I know how to ride one. I know how to be courteous and decent.

I've ridden a bicycle across this country from Evanston to Seattle, and I know how to ride a bicycle. I know when someone is aiming for me.

This was unacceptable. I went to the police station that evening and filed another report. The information I gave ended up not to be an incident report but was classified as "Disorderly Conduct" on Pippenger's part.

I thought about this motorcycle incident, and also about the "leering" claims Pippenger had made in March. Then I realized there was another situation I could use: December 2014, when Pippenger would stand outside my window taking photos of me while I read. I had sent an email to Bill Luby describing this weird and aggressive behavior.

Here were my three incidents.

On August 4, 2015, I went back to the Skokie Courthouse and filed another request for a Stalking/No contact order against Pippenger. Once again, I was given a courtroom number, and once again, I got Judge Baird. This time, with this dangerous act by Pippenger, along with the two other incidents of which there were records, Judge Baird gave me a hearing date of August 26, 2015.

I felt now that he'd trapped himself with his ongoing misconduct. I would get a judgment against him. He was gonna leave me alone. I'm gonna have some peace. It's been a long time coming. I actually exhaled with relief.

55
What?

About ten days before the hearing, I was walking up my front walkway in the morning, and I saw what I thought was a baby opossum lying on the bricks. When I got closer, I saw that it wasn't a baby opossum; it was a rat, a full-grown rat, with one side of its head crushed in a smooth line, as though it had been killed in a powerful trap.

I had an idea how this had come about, and so did some other people.

The woman I spoke with at Animal Control told me they didn't want anything to do with it. "Yes," she said, "it would be highly unlikely for a rat to fall off the roof of your house onto its head. Or to walk down your sidewalk and suddenly jump into the air and land on its head and kill itself," and she laughed. "I think maybe somebody doesn't...," and she stopped mid-sentence, before adding, "Hey, what's gonna be the name of your movie?"

I got a shovel from the garage and a plastic bag, and I scooped it up and put it in the garbage.

I ran into a cop I know and told him about the upcoming hearing and the dead rat. "Not too hard to figure that one out," he said, and we both laughed.

It was probably done the night before, when I was asleep. It would be as fruitless to pursue the culprit in the "Rat Case" as it would be to find out what happened to my missing letter from the ARDC.

The day arrived for the hearing, and I had hired a lawyer. Pippenger was acting, *pro se*, without counsel.

Before the hearing, he tried to cut a deal with my lawyer to see if we could agree to leave each other alone without a hearing. "I don't want anything to do with that," I told my guy. "I've never done anything in the first place."

When we got before Judge Baird, the first thing Pippenger did was ask, "with all due respect," for a different judge to hear the case.

We waited around for about half an hour, and then Judge Marguerite Quinn was available to do the hearing.

The hearing began with Pippenger acting like he didn't know what he was doing. The Judge said, "You are a lawyer?"

Pippenger said, "I do patent law. I write patents."

At least he hadn't perjured himself yet, as the USPTO had reinstated him in May.

Judge Quinn said, "You know how it works."

We took our respective oaths and the hearing began. Pippenger seemed not to remember much of what he might have wanted to say and devoted quite a bit of effort to twisting words and meanings and blowing smoke.

With regard to the motorcycle incident, he asserted, erroneously, that there are garbage cans in the alley that take up at least six feet of the fifteen-foot-wide space. (The alley is, in fact, nineteen feet wide, and the garbage containers take up a maximum of three feet.) He said his motorcycle is four feet wide. My bicycle is two feet wide. That would leave a scant three feet of space, meaning that two cars could never pass each other, which they often do.

When Pippenger asked me about the letter I had sent to Bill Luby concerning his photographing me, he said, "I don't understand, yes or no, were you scared?"

I answered, "I was wary."

Pippenger claimed not to know what the word "wary," meant. He said he didn't understand.

Judge Quinn said, "Look it up in the Oxford Dictionary. Go ahead, next question."

He grew more confused when he brought up the March 15, 2015, incident that took place when I went out to do my recycling.

Pippenger said, "On March 15, of 2015, I filed a police complaint against you for approaching my six-year-old child—five-year-old child, is that correct?"

I responded, "That is not what the complaint said. But okay, you filed a police report."

Pippenger then betrayed just how twisted things had become in his own mind: "On March 15 of 2015, did you file a police complaint against me?"

I responded, "No. You filed a complaint, a police complaint, against me."

I acknowledged that I sent a letter to the Evanston Police Department, and I said that I corrected some things on their report. "First, I corrected that I was not 'leering' at your children. Second, I was not leaning against my fence staring at them for a prolonged period of time. Third, we have not had ongoing disputes since 2009."

Then Pippenger wanted to know--in court, in front of a judge, why--"you [meaning me] told the Police Department you were not leering at my five-year-old son."

I replied, "Yes. I was not leering at your five-year-old son."

Pippenger said, "Why did you tell the police that if it was not an allegation in the report?"

The judge intervened, once again, to inform Pippenger that it *was* in the police report and that it was an allegation that *he* had made and that *he* was now corroborating what was in the report.

I'm sure Pippenger was not intentionally bumbling. But continue he did to make up, rather than leaving out, information

280

from the police report. The judge corrected him again and gave a short dissertation regarding police reports and that if Pippenger had said what he claimed to have told them, they would not have left that information out of the report.

Pippenger then became the witness and was the one being questioned by my attorney.

In his responses, he talked about how rough I had been on him, reporting him to the ARDC and the USPTO more than once.

He said how hard it had all been on his family. They just wanted peace and quiet. I just would not leave him alone.

Then he looked out in the courtroom and saw that his wife had left. The only one left of his support group was Priscilla MacDougall, their mainstay. And she was still awake!

He said, as he began to cry there in the witness box, "Now my wife isn't here. We are probably going to have to move, because we can't get him to stop. Out of sight, out of mind, maybe. All we want is peace."

"So we are dragged down here today on these allegations of leering and riding a motorcycle in the alley. I am not trying to denigrate him. But it is nonsense. "I done [sic] no harm to him. I do no harm to him."

My lawyer resumed his questioning of Pippenger.

Asked about the "fictitious judge in the judge's chambers," Pippenger said he didn't remember that. He didn't remember why he was disciplined. "I have a strong recollection of signing a consent agreement to 60 days. I served the 60 days, I took the class."

At what appeared to be near the close of the hearing, when Pippenger stepped down from the witness box, I wanted to correct a number of his false representations, if given the chance.

Judge Quinn asked, "Any case in rebuttal?"

I nodded to my attorney, indicating that I wanted to talk.

Judge Quinn said, "Really? Do you want him to come up again?"—while her tone said, "Don't you dare!"

So I then shook my head "No" to my attorney.

He said to the Judge, "I don't think anything new is going to come out."

Judge Quinn said, "Right. I don't think so either."

The "Arguments" were then presented by my attorney and by Pippenger.

The Judge made her statement, and here is what Judge Marguerite Quinn said:

"This is a very sad case. It is a very sad case mostly because Mr. Pippenger's children have been adversely affected by this. I think it is   terrible. I think it is just terrible.

"I have to say, Mr. Thomas, I think that you have a right to file all these complaints. I don't know if it is the smartest thing in the world to continue to file these complaints.

"It certainly has caused a great deal of animosity between you and your neighbor.

"Mr. Pippenger, I find it next to impossible that you don't recall what was in the ARDC agreement. I think it is next to impossible that you forget an allegation that is wildly, wildly inappropriate.

I mean the idea that a Judge, the allegation   against you whether it is true or false-"

Pippenger interrupted with, "Well –"

Judge Quinn responded and continued:

"Wait a second, this isn't a conversation. This is my ruling.

"The idea that an allegation that a fictitious Judge was involved in a lawsuit that you were handling. My God, in all my years of being a lawyer and a Judge,   I never heard of such a thing. I never heard of such a thing.

"The fact that you don't remember that something like that had to do with your ARDC beef that was filed against you, I find that absolutely incredible, absolutely incredible.

"By the way, there is nothing in the report that you made to the police about Wendell Thomas's stepping within two or three feet. Nothing about him walking towards the child. Nothing about that. Just that he was leaning into the alley.

"Once again, police officers miss things, they don't always write everything down. They are summaries. But those are two, you know, those are two things that make me wonder about this.

"The other thing that I am concerned about is that if I enter a stalking no contact order, it absolutely has an effect on your law license. There is no question it could jeopardize your law license. I can't imagine why anyone would jeopardize his law license.

"I can't even imagine it. So now I am stuck trying to decide whether it is – whether to enter this order and jeopardize your entire livelihood and jeopardize your four children.

"So this is what I am going to do. I am going to enter and continue this case. I want the ability to look at some case law, to review my notes. I am going to enter and continue this for a very long time. I am going to see if there are any other complaints.

"If there is anything, anything, that will not bode well for your, for this case. Am I making myself clear?"

Pippenger said, "Yes."

Judge Quinn then addressed me and said she was not entering the Stalking/No Contact Order. She told Pippenger to behave, and he said he understood. She ended with, "Think about your law license, sir. Think about your kids."

After missing much of the hearing and coming back in time for the closing statement, Mrs. Pippenger piped up from one of the benches for the public viewing, as she sat with her dear friend, the lawyer and neighbor Priscilla. In the official court report she was listed as "Unidentified Speaker."

Judge Quinn responded: "Are you really, really going to make an audible comment about this now?"

Hilleory Pippenger said, "I didn't realize it was audible."

Judge Quinn said, "It certainly is. There are four people in this courtroom. I can hear everything. The acoustics-"

Hilleory Pippenger said, "I didn't mean to. I am sorry."

Judge Quinn said:

"I can't believe–really, maybe this is ridiculous I am giving – I am giving Mr. Pippenger a chance. I think – maybe it is ridiculous because you are all going to walk out of here and talk about how horrible Mr. Thomas is. It is just the opposite. It is just the opposite.

The only reason why I am not entering anything today is because I am concerned about his children. That is the only reason. So if you want to prolong this Hatfield and McCoy behavior, go right ahead. And there will be consequences.

"So I am entering and continuing this hearing. I am going to bring it back December 10. You are going to room 104 at 1:30.

"Now, Mr. Thomas, let's put it this way, if you achieve the peace that you have expressed you want here, then you don't have to show up on December 10.

"Okay, if you wish to come back, you can come back."

Thus ended the hearing that I had hoped was going to afford me some protection.

I've never figured out why it mattered whether or not he was a lawyer if he had done what I claimed he had done. My case was proved in her court smack-dab in front of her.

I did not once mention his children in my testimony that day or in my request, earlier in the month, for the hearing.

Judge Quinn took it upon herself to decide that this hearing was really about Pippenger having four children. She decided that this hearing was really about protecting his law license. If Judge Quinn had allowed me to speak, I would have said, "Your Honor, Phillip Pippenger knew when he did all the things he has done to me that he had four children and he also knew he has a law license."

The hearing was not, therefore, about the court affording me any protection from the intimidation, physical threats, and bullying from this man, which was the reason I requested it in the first place.

But let's give some credit where credit is due. I think that while I am not a lawyer and was only a guest on Judge Quinn's playground, she did do a sincerely good and effective job to get just what she wanted despite the twist of reality it took to do it.

If you want to know the truth, just ask Phillip Pippenger,

56
Starting to Get It

A welcome break for me, I'd say. No continuation of my court hearing until December. Of course, Judge Quinn made it clear that I needn't show up. In the meantime, Pippenger will behave. He has to believe that Judge Quinn will act if he doesn't.

In one sense, my situation with a malicious neighbor is abhorrent. Beyond abhorrent.

Here I am, elderly by definition; retired, by fact; lucid, by belief; and still alive, by luck.

For these past four years, I've been fighting (1) for my mental stability and (2) for my life, literally. It has not been fun. It's one thing to read about what it's like to inadvertently get mixed up with someone like Pippenger, but here's hoping you can avoid the reality of it.

I was unwilling to let this neighbor walk all over me for some inexplicable, perverse pleasure. He is who he is. I can't say if he experienced some childhood trauma, or if he was just born this way. Some people come into the world without what the rest of us know as "conscience." It's not his fault, but at the same time, it does not exempt him from full responsibility for his actions.

In the past, he lied in court with the assumption that the judge did not have most of the information that concerned what he was lying about. He doesn't present evidence to back his assertions. "I've got it in writing," he bluffs, and delivers nothing.

His blundering can be like a TV sitcom, at once comical, absurd, and pathetic.

286

In the hearing at which Callie Lynne Baird was the Judge, he accused the Evanston Police Department of doing a "cut and paste" on one of the police incident reports that he had filed. Actually, "cut and paste" is more his specialty. It's what he did when he "altered" the USPTO Electronic Acknowledgement receipt.

He was almost joyful with his imaginative scenerio in describing me coming into his backyard at night to "approach his children," with his arms flailing in different directions, showing the various routes his children took to avoid me.

Two minutes later, the charade had given him dry-mouth. He held his hand up and pointed his index finger toward his mouth, trying to make Judge Baird understand that he needed water, while she sat impassively. He rolled his head around a bit and looked up at the ceiling. He moved the sides of his big cheeks over the sides of his teeth, while he tried to get some saliva going. He worked it out after about thirty seconds and then continued with his lies, including being unable to catch a 74-year-old man who was fifteen feet from him, whose hips have each been replaced and who can't run. "I chased him," he claimed.

Somebody put super glue in his tire valves—oh, yeah. He reported that to the police five days later… after, of course, he had "fixed" the tires himself.

Regarding this particular report, a policeman told me that he'd heard, "This guy was really from outer space."

Peter sat in the second row during the hearing and observed. The first row is set aside for lawyers and police personnel. One man in the first row, directly in front of Peter, turned to his companion during Pippenger's testimony and said quietly, "This guy is *so* full of shit." He then got up and left the courtroom.

Judge Baird may have felt the same way but she was required to stay.

287

In the hearing eight months later when Marguerite Quinn was the Judge, he said repeatedly that he was not leering at me, mixing up which one of us was on defense and for what. "Leering," was the accusation he had made in the police report against me. I never said anything about him leering at me.

He asked, before an incredulous Judge Quinn, about the police report I had filed, when he was the one who had filed the police report.

He stammers that the alley is not wide enough for a bicycle and motorcycle to pass without jeopardy. He envisions garbage containers where they never were, reduces the width of the alley to accommodate his reenactment, and then says, "It's mathematically proved." To which Judge Quinn responds, "Nothing is proved."

She maintained her judicial decorum, (i.e., refrained from laughing), as the alley, by his account, got narrower and narrower. Judge Quinn seemed to acknowledge that Pippenger was a liar and at the very same time she validated his behavior. She let him off the hook.

I was finding out that not everybody cared. I cared a lot because I wanted to get him in the position to be accountable. He tried to destroy me. What's more important is, I have wanted to, have been willing to, and have worked at surviving this guy.

I wanted to derail his runaway train.

Judge Quinn had decided that the hearing was not about me getting the protection from the court that I sought. She decided that the hearing was really about her concern for Pippenger's four children. I had never mentioned his children.

It would have been good if she had cared about me, actually.

I sought protection against Pippenger, the man who had done a great many things against me for no fathomable reason; the man who had done things to hurt me for his own pleasure; the man who actually wanted to see me end up a felon, with the threat of jail hanging over my head; the man who seemed to be near the point of physical violence toward me; the man who had evolved into bullying in his behavior toward me.

I wanted protection.

Judge Quinn, who herself is a lawyer, did not want to hurt Pippenger's law career. Forget my dilemma. Her concern was that his career would be damaged. Her other major concern was in some way tied in to his children.

Among other things, Judge Quinn said to Pippenger when she gave her ruling: "The other thing I am concerned about is that if I enter a stalking no contact order, it absolutely has an effect on your law license. There is no question it could jeopardize your law license."

Wow! Judge Quinn's reasoning on my protection blew my mind.

But the long and short of it is, I'm just the public. I ain't in the club.

"Hold on for a minute; don't be so sour. I've got some really good news for you:" An article on the Internet entitled, "Disbarred – but Not Barred from Work." This article was posted on June 5, 2007, by Hope Viner Samborn. The crux of what was important is quoted:

"Disbarred or suspended attorneys sometimes choose to work as paralegals or law clerks. But while they are allowed to do that type of work in some states, in others they could end up in even deeper trouble if they attempt to do so.

In fact, states vary as to whether they permit disbarred or suspended attorneys to work in any capacity in a law firm. ' Massachusetts, for example, defines law firms broadly to include private practices and legal departments in corporate or legal services organizations, says Constance V. Vecchione of the Office of the Bar Counsel of the Supreme Judicial Court of Massachusetts.'

'They can't be employed as a janitor' in any of those places, Vecchione says. Ditto for Illinois, which asks disciplined attorneys to 'remove themselves completely from the law firm environment,' according to James J. Grogan, chief counsel of the Illinois Attorney Registration and Disciplinary Commission."

The good news for me was that James J. Grogan was still the chief counsel of the ARDC. I happened to have discovered that Pippenger worked as a lawyer throughout his suspension from the practice of law. I knew he couldn't be going to work every day and just ordering paper and pencils for the law firm. He would be doing legal work because rules didn't apply to him.

I looked up some information on the Internet which is available to the public and found that Pippenger had signed on to be the back-up counsel to Michael R. Hull, his partner, the lead counsel in a case before the USPTO, from approximately January 2, 2014, through July 15, 2014. The IPR (Inter Partes Review) Case Number was given as: IPR2014-00151. This situation seemed to fit to a tee because Pippenger's suspension from the practice of law was from April 4, 2014 until June 3, 2014.

When a complaint is filed with the ARDC, they generally respond within two weeks. I filed a complaint with the ARDC against Pippenger, once again, and gave all of the evidence of the trial number and dates and other pertinent information given by the USPTO regarding the case.

I also complained that he had failed to place my monies, previously, in an IOLTA (Interest on Lawyer Trust Account) which is in violation of ARDC rules.

So Pippenger had worked as a lawyer during his suspension. I submitted evidence that he had. And I had the backup of James J. Grogan saying that the suspended lawyer should not even be in the law firm environment.

After not hearing back from the ARDC for about three weeks, I went to their offices in Chicago on Friday, October 9, 2015.

Unannounced, I asked at the reception desk if I might speak with someone about a complaint that I filed. After a few minutes, a paralegal, Susan Scorzo, who was very pleasant, came out to speak with me.

The conversation that ensued was so mind-boggling that later that same evening, I became preoccupied about it and wrote down what had happened. This is my information from the ARDC, the group that is in existence to protect the public from lawyers who engage in "illegal, unethical or dishonest conduct":

1. I met Susan Scorzo (ARDC paralegal) this morning and we discussed the state of affairs with the complaints I had filed against Pippenger on both September 22, 2015 (for not putting my money in an IOLTA account) and September 30, 2015 (for working as a lawyer while suspended). IOLTA is the acronym for: Interest on Lawyer Trust Accounts.

2. Susan said that she did not think there would be any prosecution as a result of the complaints and the information that was tendered.

3. I was dumfounded!

4. I said that he had $6000 dollars of mine sitting in his personal account for work he had committed to do and then did not do. "What if he died 6 months after he took the money? I would then have to sue his estate to get my money back.' I said that I thought that rule 1.15 existed to protect clients from being in this hazardous position.

5. She asked me if I had something against Mr. Pippenger.

6. I explained some of things that he has done to me over the years and she said, "Oh well."

291

7. She said that, no doubt, he will be turned in by someone else that he does such things to in the future, and that it always works that way. "He will do it to others," she said.

8. I explained that, in my opinion I am his target and that all of his other clients are accounts like "Caterpillar" or "Microsoft" and that he isn't doing anything to anyone else.

9. She said that lawyers often continued to work as lawyers during their suspension by the ARDC.

10. I said that the ARDC could look at his computer records during the time of his suspension and they would probably find that he worked pretty continually as a lawyer.

11. She said she was taking time from her work to talk with me and wondered why I had come to the office?

12. I told her that I had not heard from the ARDC for more than two weeks and that I did not want to wait through the weekend with no response. I also mentioned that I previously had missed mail that was sent to me by the ARDC and that I didn't want that to happen again.

13. I mentioned that regarding one of my current complaints, I didn't see how it could really be too complicated because I had submitted the court documents that showed that he worked a trial case while suspended. I said, "He either violated his suspension or he did not." Of course, with the obviousness of my proof, I know that he did violate his suspension.

14. At this point she indicated that she really had to get back to work.

15. She said that if I do not like the ARDC decision that will be forthcoming, I could file a complaint (or a

suit?) at a Federal or District Court. (I am obviously confused as to what court she said I should go to and what it is that I should file. Does she want me to sue the ARDC?)

16. In the meantime, I continue to live my surreal life. What a Daliesque landscape this has become at age 75!

What Susan forecasted turned out to be true. The ARDC did not prosecute Pippenger for working as an attorney during his suspension. Even though he was working as a trial attorney in front of the USPTO (and you must be a lawyer to do so), the ARDC said that did not count.

They said that even though he was working out of his Chicago office in the State of Illinois as a trial lawyer, he wasn't really working in Illinois, and he wasn't really working as a lawyer.

The ARDC has some discretion, if you don't mind.

The ARDC protects the public from unscrupulous lawyers, of which Pippenger is not. He is a fine, upstanding lawyer and recognized by the ARDC as such. It has become much clearer to me as time has passed.

I am currently in the luxurious position of weighing the advantages and disadvantages of purchasing the Brooklyn Bridge from the ARDC. They've made a nice offer.

December 10, 2015, rolled around, and the hearing, once again with Judge Quinn, took place, if you'd like to stretch your imagination and call it that.

A hearing would be something that happens in court where you think you might have the opportunity to have your voice heard. That was not the case at this hearing, as Judge Quinn did not want me to say what I wanted to say and said so.

Well, la-di-da. So it's your ball and your playground. Club members only.

Of course, club member Pippenger-the-lawyer spoke with Judge Quinn, and here is some of what was said as taken by the court reporter:

"Judge Quinn: Mr. Pippenger, has there been any hardship to you not to have any contact with Mr. Thomas?

Pippenger: None at all. I've been videotaping my face every day for the past four months for all me [sic] comings and goings.

Judge Quinn: What? You've been videotaping yourself? Why?

Pippenger: Just because if you see me and I'm not videotaping myself, you could say I'm leering at you all you want, and what would I say? I'm not? So I've got four terabytes of my face. I used to tape myself even sleeping, but –

Judge Quinn: Wait. I don't understand this at all. What do you mean by you're videotaping yourself?

Pippenger: I have a GoPro. And so on my motorcycle I put it when I'm driving and in my car anywhere in the neighborhood. I stop it once I get a few miles away. And then on my car I put it when I'm driving and then when I walk to and from my garage.

Judge Quinn: Yeah. But why do you feel like you have to do that? The whole idea was just to–

Pippenger: Because anybody could say anything about me if I can't say, 'Look, here's me.' And I date it with my phone.

Judge Quinn: Right. I know. But, Mr. Pippenger, you know what you're kind of missing here is that I really wasn't entirely sure of your credibility in your testimony. Okay?

Pippenger: I understand.

Judge Quinn: So the idea that you're telling me that what you've had to do is videotape yourself all the time sounds, you know, bizarre at best. And things have been difficult for you.

Pippenger: Right

Judge Quinn: And I don't want to make it more difficult by entering an order like this against you. And the reason why I'm doing this is because you do have four children. This could endanger your law license. That's why I'm doing this. All right. I am not going to enter the no-contact, no-stalking order."

***

In other words, this is the kind of guy we want to keep in business, whatever his business might be. We want to set his train back on the tracks.

I quickly thought, *"And you, Mr. Thomas, your bus will arrive shortly. Forget about anything you're concerned about and just get on with your terminal life.* You don't have cause in this court to object about the behavior of a man who is bizarre, at best. A man who is hardly able to speak through his tears. A man with children. A man who swears an oath as a lawyer. *A man of great misunderstanding, who is greatly misunderstood. A man whose blatant lies are wonderful!"*

And that was that, the protection that I got from the court, and the help I got from the other sources of support lent to the public.

I dream to be a part of the public, wherever thou art.

Quite a ride. An interesting series of events to take place at the tail end, or what is referred to as, "The waning years of life." For me, the serious fact that I'm still here and able and willing to defend myself against the various onslaughts is what makes me realize that I'm actually still alive.

57
Trial

I remain out on the limb. I have had no monies returned to me and will not. The statute of limitations for malpractice became effective two months after the hearing that was held at the Attorney Registration and Disciplinary Commission offices. As a lay person, was I negligent in not knowing this? My focus was on the hearing and it took twenty-two months for that to take place from the time the original complaint was filed.

I wait quietly for the next transgression and am fairly certain that at some point and at some place something will happen. It has continued unabated since my first discovery and has moved closer and closer toward physical violence. The detective from the Evanston Police Department who handled the original complaint and had all of the evidence concerning what I thought were, by definition criminal acts, has told me that this file is closed. Well, he's in charge. He said that he considers this to be, "A neighborhood dispute."

I have always been under the impression that a dispute involved a disagreement between two parties. There has not been a dispute. There have been acts done by one party against another. There has been no dispute. There has been no argument or disagreement about anything.

The same reasoning that the detective utilized leads me to ask, "Does that then mean that Charles Manson and Sharon Tate had a dispute?"

What is lacking for individuals in the structure of our society is the ability to act reasonably within the confines of what we call, "The Law," and have results, pro or con that reflect our laws and are just and fair. Reasonableness does not, by any stretch of the imagination produce fair, equitable or just results in Cook County, Illinois.

The experiences that I've had for the last five years with the individual(s) that I've been dealing with have brought about one, and only one, fair and just conclusion. The irony of saying that, is that in that one instance, I was found to be not guilty to any of the myriad of false accusations and slanders made in court by an officer of the court (a lawyer) and his spouse while both had sworn on their honor that they would tell the truth. I have taken the liberty in this description to use the words, "not guilty," which is actually the terminology used in a criminal case rather than "denied," which is used in a civil case.

Perjury is lying while under oath. Lying is done with intent. It is a crime to commit perjury.

Once a person swears an oath and testifies in court they are protected by our legal system for all of what they say, unless they are lying. This is done to allow testimony offered in court to be done freely, without fear of retribution through lawsuits or to be used in other ways against witnesses. Most of us abide by the sanctity in and out of court when we swear to tell the truth or promise that we are doing so.

Somewhere, way back when, it was thought that someone who swore to tell the truth actually would. The thing that makes this a more difficult situation in our society today is that the courts are overloaded with cases. There are backlogs for months or sometimes years and the system is currently unable to deal with those who perjure themselves and who have the foreknowledge that they will not be prosecuted.

Today, in Cook County, Illinois, swearing to tell the truth in court and then not doing so generally results in nothing. It used to be a felony that might ostracize the perjurer socially and sometimes cause a jail sentence. Perjury in Cook County has now become something that is assumed and accepted although not encouraged. It has been my experience that it is not even verbally addressed to the perpetrator by the authorities who are aware of the perjury.

Unless it is a high profile case, on the news at night and in the papers during the day, perjury will go unnoticed. The State's Attorney's Office is undermanned and understaffed to such a degree that it does not address a crime as petty as perjury. They have bigger fish to fry.

What can be done?

What if we had courts that specifically handled "White Collar Crimes?" What if perjury were a crime that would be prosecuted. What if the "White Collar" criminal knew that his crimes, if discovered, would quickly take him to court? The investment that we would make in our society to have this function would pay dividends in much more than the prosecution of a few high profile felons. It would act as a deterrent to many and would abruptly reduce "White Collar" crime overall.

Citizens could go without so much as a hesitation from a civil court to a "White Collar Court" with evidence of perjury in hand, and have it prosecuted expeditiously without having to make the attempt, which would surely fail, of going thru the State's Attorney's Office.

Perpetrators in Evanston, Illinois and other parts of Cook County, Illinois could actually be prosecuted for filing false police reports which is criminal.

With the availability of a "White Collar Court" would it be possible to prosecute someone for causing, or encouraging, a third party to commit perjury even if it were a spouse?

Deterrents could exist.

We could have courts that would handle, with expediency, a "White Collar Crime."

Sure, it would cost money up front. In the long term it would save much more than it would cost. And, without a doubt, it would reduce crime.

What if the Attorney Registration and Disciplinary Commission actually stood by their own by-laws or credos and actually did not tolerate violations of their rules, standards and ethics? What if they sincerely prosecuted lawyers who violated the rules that lawyers swear to uphold? What if they were not able to choose "discretion" as a way of avoiding the prosecution of a dues paying member?

Active lawyers of high moral character could serve in the capacity as an oversight of the ARDC on a voluntary basis. They could work in teams and oversee each other. The ARDC could easily and effectively be monitored.

The ARDC could and should be prohibited from allowing former employees to be the representative counsel for accused and investigated lawyers. A number of lawyers who represent other lawyers before the ARDC in hearings are former employees of the ARDC in Chicago. The business of the ARDC is actually to act in behalf of the public and investigate and prosecute errant, immoral and unethical lawyers. That could be made to happen.

I have had the pleasure of knowing dozens of lawyers in my life and have known only one who was dishonest. Lawyers have a life that is considerably different than mine. They are able to think in patterns and ways that are deep and incisive and are able to use words that lend precise descriptions to the subject at hand. That doesn't make them bad. That allows them to be good at what they do.

In Shakespeare's play, *King Henry VI* an anarchist, Dick the Butcher said, "The first thing we do, let's kill all the lawyers." This quote is often misinterpreted and misquoted by lay-people as, "first let's kill the lawyers," to show their dislike and disdain for the profession. In the play, Dick the Butcher's wish and intent was that without the lawyers, all hell could break loose and society could be in complete upheaval as it unraveled. Ahh, what a great time for an anarchist!

***

The experiences that I've had for the past five years have been astounding and painful. They have put me through emotional turmoil, travails, jeopardies and threats. I've been blind-sided and deceived. I've been lied to, defrauded, swindled, slandered and cheated. And... much, much more.

It need not be this way. There are ways and means that can be taken to help our society function in a more honest, equitable and just way. Certainly I would not be the one who could begin to make the changes or effect things. My impact is evidenced by: What has been done to me in various scenarios repeatedly: What I have done in response: What our various agencies have tendered in support of my pursuits of Justice.

This is not a cry from me for help. I am saying that something can be done. Something could be changed for the better. As a society, we could experience Justice.

A little more than one hundred years after Kafka wrote *The Trial*, lives and segments of lives on this side of the Atlantic are still as fragmented as they were in Europe in his novel. Maybe Kafka was writing about the senselessness or absurdity of life. Maybe he was simply the prelude to some of the tenets of Albert Camus. Yet, while Kafka wrote his story as a novel, his ideas did originate somewhere. The "somewhere" is the fact that these nightmares occur in real life as well as in fiction and my experience of that has been the memoir, *Trial*.

"Somewhere," might actually be anywhere in the United States because what has happened in this memoir is not unique to Illinois, to Cook County or to Chicago; although, it might

300

certainly be more prevalent here than in other parts of the country. As various situations from this memoir have unfolded and been related to people, they have listened and then have tossed the episodes out of mind; "It's the way things work,"; "Too bad for you,"; "Bad break," and so on and so forth. Our lives are too congested to take the time and energy required to delve into situations that don't have a direct effect on us.

We might ask ourselves: How far has our society actually moved forward in the past one hundred years and how much have we changed? The answer might be that today there are simply more of us, and while we seem to move forward faster, truly, we have stayed on the same beaten path and have gone nowhere. Our hamster wheel is just more crowded.

As citizens, if we are able to move forward and find a way at some point, to allow ourselves as individuals within the context of our society, to be acknowledged and responsible for what we do, we will have Justice.